Every thing in the world holds yang and caries yin. Yin and yang interact with each other to achieve harmony.

— Laozi (老子)

Discovery Publisher

©2014, Discovery Publisher
All rights reserved

No part of this book may be reproduced in any form or by any electronic or mechanical means including information storage and retrieval systems, without permission in writing from the publisher.

Author : Dejun Xue (薛德钧)
Editor in Chief : Adriano Lucca

Chinese Ink Artwork:
Huang Pingping, Zhuhai, China (黄萍萍，中国广东省珠海市)
Chinese Calligraphy:
Zhang Chuanxu, Dali, China (张川旭，中国云南省大理市古城)

616 Corporate Way, Suite 4888
Valley Cottage, New York, 10989
www.discoverypublisher.com
edition@discoverypublisher.com
facebook.com/discoverypublisher
twitter.com/discoverypb

New York • Paris • Dublin • Tokyo • Hong Kong

Preface

"Yi"—or "Yi Jing"—is the Chinese spelling of the two Chinese characters: 易经(Yì Jīng), which literally means "change". Around 6,500 years ago, when there was no written language, the Chinese philosophy of Yi was created. Completely abstract, its core is "yin and yang", eight trigrams and sixty-four hexagrams, which are fully elucidated in this book.

This book is composed of two parts:
- PART I introduces Yi
- PART II explains the texts associated with the 64 hexagrams

Those who wish to consult Yi right away, may spend less than an hour reading the first chapter (on love, about 13 pages) or the second chapter (on business, 10 pages), follow the example on selecting a hexagram, and then find the advice from the associated text in Part II, "Commentary on Yi Text."

Those who wish to know the Yi way of thinking, or the Chinese culture, may just read Part I. Readers who have a strong interest in Yi, wanting to appreciate the depth of insight of Yi or research it, may read through the entire book.

Origin and interpretations of Yi

Yi was created around 6,500 years ago. As stated in *Zhou Li* (~1100 BC), there are three versions of Yi: *Gui Cang Yi* (归藏易/歸藏易), *Lian Shan Yi* (连山易/連山易) and *Zhou Yi* (周易). All three address eight trigrams and sixty-four hexagrams.

Around 500 BC, Confucius and his disciples compiled ten commentaries (十翼) on Zhou Yi. These commentaries emphasize Confucianism, and provide instruction on how to handle fifty yarrow sticks for divine reading. Later on, around 200 AD, Zhou Yi and the commentaries were combined, into what is known today as Yi.

Based on fifty years' experience in science and research on Chinese classics, the author of *The Power of Yi* reveals the true nature of Yi and how to use it to live in harmony with others and benefit yourself.

TABLE OF CONTENTS

PREFACE — i

ORIGIN AND INTERPRETATIONS OF YI — ii

PART ONE: INTRODUCTION TO YI — 12

CHAPTER 1: ENJOY SUCCESSFUL MARRIAGE — 14

  1. Eight Images — 14

    0—EARTH — 15
    1—MOUNTAIN — 16
    2—WATER — 17
    3—WIND — 17
    4—THUNDER — 18
    5—FIRE — 18
    6—LAKE — 19
    7—HEAVEN — 19

  2. Subject and Object — 20
  3. Yi Text — 20
  4. Follow The Example — 23

CHAPTER 2: YI IN BUSINESS — 24

CHAPTER 3: YIN AND YANG — 32

  1. Instances of Yin and Yang — 32
  2. Yin and Yang are Natural Complements — 33
  3. Definition of Yin and Yang — 34
  4. The nature of Yin and Yang — 35
  5. The Rule of Harmony — 36
  6. Becoming a Peacemaker — 37

CHAPTER 4: TRIGRAMS — 39

   1. A Primitive Sundial — 39

   2. Image of Trigrams — 39

      1—THUNDER — 39

      2—FIRE — 40

      3—LAKE — 40

      4—HEAVEN — 40

      5—WIND — 41

      6—WATER — 41

      7—MOUNTAIN — 41

      8—EARTH — 41

   3. Value of Trigrams — 42

   4. Seasonal Cycle — 45

   5. The Seasonal Change in Reality — 46

   6. Selecting Trigram — 49

CHAPTER 5: SIGNIFICANCE OF THE "THREE LINES" IN TRIGRAM — 51

   1. Bottom Line: Action — 51

   2. Middle Line: Essence — 52

   3. Top Line: Attitude — 54

   4. The Personal Trigrams in Reality — 57

CHAPTER 6: HEXAGRAM — 59

   1. Subject Trigram and Object Trigram — 59

   2. Titles of Hexagrams — 62

   3. Importance of ID number of Hexagram — 63

   4. Conversion from ID numbers to serial number in Zhou Yi — 64

CHAPTER 7: ANALYSIS OF STRUCTURE OF HEXAGRAMS — 66

   1. Special Hexagrams — 67

      1 HEXAGRAMS 5:2 AND 2:5 — 67

      2 HEXAGRAMS 7:Ø AND Ø:7 — 68

      3 HEXAGRAMS 1:6 AND 6:1 — 68

      4 HEXAGRAMS 4:3 AND 3:4 — 69

   2. Complementary Lines — 69

3. Correctness of Positions 70
  4. The Central Lines Correct and Complementary 71
  5. Supporting or Suppressing 71
  6. Analysis of hexagrams for Relationship 72

CHAPTER 8: CHANGES 76

  1. Favorable Change 77
  2. Manageable Change 78
  3. Natural Change 80
  4. Making the Right Strategy 82

CHAPTER 9: YI TEXT 85

  1. Title 85
  2. General Text 86
  3. Texts of Lines 87
  4. Seeing the Possible Changes 89
  5. Verbatim Translation 90

END OF PART I: MOVING FORWARD 92

PART II: COMMENTARY ON YI TEXT 94

COMMENTARY ON YI TEXT 95

CHAPTER 10: WHEN EARTH (☷) IS THE SUBJECT 97

  1. Hexagram Ø:Ø Earth (In Zhou Yi, hexagram 2) 97
  2. Hexagram Ø:1 Deprivation (In Zhou Yi, hexagram 23) 101
  3. Hexagram Ø:2 Closeness (In Zhou Yi, hexagram 8) 104
  4. Hexagram Ø:3 Watching (In Zhou Yi, hexagram 20) 108
  5. Hexagram Ø:4 Delight (In Zhou Yi, hexagram 16) 111
  6. Hexagram Ø:5 Promotion (In Zhou Yi, hexagram 35) 114
  7. Hexagram Ø:6 Gathering (In Zhou Yi, hexagram 45) 117
  8. Hexagram Ø:7 Denial (In Zhou Yi, hexagram 12) 121

CHAPTER 11: WHEN MOUNTAIN (☶) IS THE SUBJECT 125

  1. Hexagram 1:Ø Modest (In Zhou Yi, hexagram 15) 125
  2. Hexagram 1:1 Stop (In Zhou Yi, hexagram 52) 128

3. Hexagram 1:2 Lame (In Zhou Yi, hexagram 39)	131
4. Hexagram 1:3 Gradual (In Zhou Yi, hexagram 53)	133
5. Hexagram 1:4 Tolerance (In Zhou Yi, hexagram 62)	137
6. Hexagram 1:5 Travel (In Zhou Yi, hexagram 56)	141
7. Hexagram 1:6 Enjoyable (In Zhou Yi, hexagram 31)	144
8. Hexagram 1:7 Flee (In Zhou Yi, hexagram 33)	147
CHAPTER 12: WHEN WATER ( ) IS THE SUBJECT	**151**
1. Hexagram 2:Ø Army (In Zhou Yi, hexagram 7)	151
2. Hexagram 2:1 Ignorance (In Zhou Yi, hexagram 4)	154
3. Hexagram 2:2 Pitfall (In Zhou Yi, hexagram 29)	158
4. Hexagram 2:3 Flood (In Zhou Yi, hexagram 59)	161
5. Hexagram 2:4 Solution (In Zhou Yi, hexagram 40)	164
6. Hexagram 2:5 Imperfect (In Zhou Yi, hexagram 64)	168
7. Hexagram 2:6 Adversity (In Zhou Yi, hexagram 47)	171
8. Hexagram 2:7 Sue (In Zhou Yi, hexagram 6)	174
CHAPTER 13: WHEN WIND ( ) IS THE SUBJECT	**179**
1. Hexagram 3:Ø Rising (In Zhou Yi, hexagram 46)	179
2. Hexagram 3:1 Bugs (In Zhou Yi, hexagram 18)	182
3. Hexagram 3:2 Well (In Zhou Yi, hexagram 48)	184
4. Hexagram 3:3 Yield (In Zhou Yi, hexagram 57)	188
5. Hexagram 3:4 Persistence (In Zhou Yi, hexagram 32)	191
6. Hexagram 3:5 Cauldron (In Zhou Yi, hexagram 50)	194
7. Hexagram 3:6 Overburden (In Zhou Yi, hexagram 28)	198
8. Hexagram 3:7 Encounter (In Zhou Yi, hexagram 44)	201
CHAPTER 14: WHEN THUNDER ( ) IS THE SUBJECT	**205**
1. Hexagram 4:Ø Return (In Zhou Yi, hexagram 24)	205
2. Hexagram 4:1 Care (In Zhou Yi, hexagram 27)	208
3. Hexagram 4:2 Prospect (In Zhou Yi, hexagram 3)	211
4. Hexagram 4:3 Gain (In Zhou Yi, hexagram 42)	214
5. Hexagram 4:4 Shock (In Zhou Yi, hexagram 51)	217
6. Hexagram 4:5 Bite (In Zhou Yi, hexagram 21)	220
7. Hexagram 4:6 Follow (In Zhou Yi, hexagram 17)	223

8. Hexagram 4:7 Innocence (In Zhou Yi, hexagram 25) — 226

CHAPTER 15: WHEN FIRE (☲) IS THE SUBJECT — 230

1. Hexagram 5:Ø Hurt (In Zhou Yi, hexagram 36) — 230
2. Hexagram 5:1 Ornament (In Zhou Yi, hexagram 22) — 233
3. Hexagram 5:2 Perfect (In Zhou Yi, hexagram 63) — 236
4. Hexagram 5:3 Matriarch (In Zhou Yi, hexagram 37) — 239
5. Hexagram 5:4 Totality (In Zhou Yi, hexagram 55) — 243
6. Hexagram 5:5 Brightness (In Zhou Yi, hexagram 30) — 246
7. Hexagram 5:6 Change (In Zhou Yi, hexagram 49) — 249
8. Hexagram 5:7 Coalition (In Zhou Yi, hexagram 13) — 252

CHAPTER 16: WHEN LAKE (☱) IS THE SUBJECT — 256

1. Hexagram 6:Ø Approach (In Zhou Yi, hexagram 19) — 256
2. Hexagram 6:1 Loss (In Zhou Yi, hexagram 41) — 258
3. Hexagram 6:2 Limitation (In Zhou Yi, hexagram 60) — 262
4. Hexagram 6:3 Sincerity (In Zhou Yi, hexagram 61) — 265
5. Hexagram 6:4 Marry (In Zhou Yi, hexagram 54) — 267
6. Hexagram 6:5 Stare (In Zhou Yi, hexagram 38) — 270
7. Hexagram 6:6 Pleasure (In Zhou Yi, hexagram 58) — 274
8. Hexagram 6:7 Treading (In Zhou Yi, hexagram 10) — 276

CHAPTER 17: WHEN HEAVEN (☰) IS THE SUBJECT — 280

1. Hexagram 7:Ø Peace (In Zhou Yi, hexagram 11) — 280
2. Hexagram 7:1 Build Up (In Zhou Yi, hexagram 26) — 283
3. Hexagram 7:2 Expectation (In Zhou Yi, hexagram 5) — 286
4. Hexagram 7:3 Accumulation (In Zhou Yi, hexagram 9) — 290
5. Hexagram 7:4 Reckless (In Zhou Yi, hexagram 34) — 293
6. Hexagram 7:5 Acquisition (In Zhou Yi, hexagram 14) — 296
7. Hexagram 7:6 Menace (In Zhou Yi, hexagram 43) — 300
8. Hexagram 7:7 Heaven (In Zhou Yi, hexagram 1) — 303

APPENDIX 1: VERBATIM TRANSLATION OF YI TEXT — 307

Hexagram Ø:Ø • Earth — 307
Hexagram Ø:1 • Deprivation — 307

Hexagram Ø:2 • Closeness	308
Hexagram Ø:3 • Watching	308
Hexagram Ø:4 • Delight	308
Hexagram Ø:5 • Promotion	309
Hexagram Ø:6 • Gathering	309
Hexagram Ø:7 • Denial	310
Hexagram 1:Ø • Modest	310
Hexagram 1:1 • Stop	311
Hexagram 1:2 • Lame	311
Hexagram 1:3 • Gradual	311
Hexagram 1:4 • Tolerance	312
Hexagram 1:5 • Travel	312
Hexagram 1:6 • Enjoyable	313
Hexagram 1:7 • Flee	313
Hexagram 2:Ø • Army	313
Hexagram 2:1 • Ignorance	314
Hexagram 2:2 • Pitfall	314
Hexagram 2:3 • Flood	315
Hexagram 2:4 • Solution	315
Hexagram 2:5 • Imperfect	315
Hexagram 2:6 • Stranded	316
Hexagram 2:7 • Sue	316
Hexagram 3:Ø • Rising	317
Hexagram 3:1 • Bugs	317
Hexagram 3:2 • Well	318
Hexagram 3:3 • Yield	318
Hexagram 3:4 • Persistence	319
Hexagram 3:5 • Cauldron	319
Hexagram 3:6 • Overburden	319
Hexagram 3:7 • Encounter	320
Hexagram 4:Ø • Return	320
Hexagram 4:1 • Care	321
Hexagram 4:2 • Prospect	321
Hexagram 4:3 • Gain	322

Hexagram 4:4 • Shock	322
Hexagram 4:5 • Bite	323
Hexagram 4:6 • Follow	323
Hexagram 4:7 • Innocence	323
Hexagram 5:Ø • Hurt	324
Hexagram 5:1 • Ornament	324
Hexagram 5:2 • Perfect	325
Hexagram 5:3 • Matriarch	325
Hexagram 5:4 • Totality	325
Hexagram 5:5 • Brightness	326
Hexagram 5:6 • Change	326
Hexagram 5:7 • Coalition	327
Hexagram 6:Ø • Approach	327
Hexagram 6:1 • Loss	327
Hexagram 6:2 • Limitation	328
Hexagram 6:3 • Sincerity	328
Hexagram 6:4 • Marry	329
Hexagram 6:5 • Stare	329
Hexagram 6:6 • Pleasure	330
Hexagram 6:7 • Treading	330
Hexagram 7:Ø • Peace	330
Hexagram 7:1 • Build Up	331
Hexagram 7:2 • Expectation	331
Hexagram 7:3 • Accumulation	332
Hexagram 7:4 • Reckless	332
Hexagram 7:5 • Acquisition	332
Hexagram 7:6 • Menace	333
Hexagram 7:7 • Heaven	333

APPENDIX 2: UNDERSTANDING BINARY NUMBERS   335

INDEX   337

PART ONE
Introduction to Yi

Happiness in Love

CHAPTER 1
Enjoy Successful Marriage

YOU PROBABLY KNOW AT LEAST one couple like Karen and Ronald, who, after eight years of marriage, is beginning to drift apart.

Karen is a musician who likes reading novels in her spare time. Ronald is a physician whose work is very demanding. In the first few years of marriage, they frequently went out for dinner, dancing, a movie, or a concert. Gradually Ronald changed that pattern, saying he was tired and preferred to relax at home, reading medical journals and writing academic articles. He asked Karen to resign from her job, to take care of their children and provide home-cooked meals.

At first she went along with the change, but her resentment over her loss of freedom and independence grew. She saw her future as an endless round of cooking and cleaning, and nothing to discuss at dinner-time but the children's sports and her husband's work.

Now Karen is unsure about her options. Since they no longer go out together, she feels that she has little in common with Ronald. She understands that he has very little free time and is absorbed in his professional life, but she thinks it's unfair of him to want her to give up her own interests and pleasures.

In the following months, she struggles to be the kind of wife her husband seems to expect, but she can't help feeling neglected and restless.

Her manner unsettles Ronald. He feels that he works very hard all day and deserves tranquility and pleasantness at home. He can't understand what has disturbed their happiness. He begins to spend less and less time with Karen, retreating into his study as soon as possible after dinner so he doesn't have to think about what might be bothering his wife.

To find a way out, Karen is seeking help from Yi.

1 Eight Images

As she washes dishes alone in the kitchen, Karen wonders why she has so little to show for all the sacrifices she has made. She feels like water that has been constrained in a bottle.

Water is one of the eight images associated with the Eight Trigrams.

A trigram is a set of three lines, one above the other, each of which could be solid (━) or broken (━ ━). You can see that the eight trigrams, shown in the diagram below, represent all of the ways the various combinations of three solid and/or broken lines could occur. There could never be any more trigrams because there are no other possible ways to construct a set of three lines with only two types of lines. Historically, in China, the eight trigrams associate the images of: Thunder, Fire, Lake, Heaven, Wind, Water, Mountain and Earth as shown in the diagram.

There are two sides to most things which the Chinese call yin and yang. In our trigrams the broken line is called a yin line and the solid line is called a yang line. You will see the importance of this in later chapters.

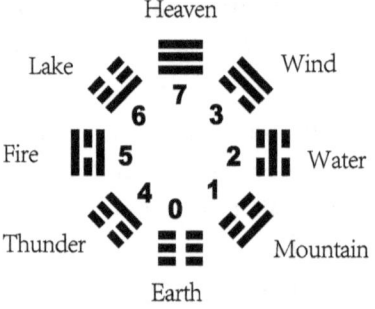

Figure 1.1: Eight Trigrams

In the previous diagram, each trigram is drawn with its image. This circle of trigrams is very familiar to every Chinese person, and to you, too, if you have spent time in China or Chinese shops in other cities. The bottom line of the trigram is the line closest to the center of the circle and the top line is the one on the outside. So each trigram has a bottom line, a middle line and a top line. In addition to their images, in this diagram each trigram has been assigned an ID number from 0, 1, 2, 3, 4, 5, 6 and 7. Consider trigram 4, thunder. Its bottom line is a solid line or a yang line and the middle and top lines are both broken or yin lines.

Now, let's look at the eight images one by one.

0—Earth

Earth is still. It receives energy from heaven, as well as light, heat, and rain. Living things on the earth adapt to the changes imposed by the heavens. Earth is nurturing, sustaining all living things, like a mother caring for her children. Earth is in a lower position. If we consider Heaven as being above, we think of

Earth as below.

A person would be assigned the Earth trigram if he were:

- like students or others with unrealized potential
- jobless, with nothing to do, not moving (still), receiving benefits (nurturing) from society
- divorced — free, leaving the constraints of marriage
- caught by police — yielding, subordinate
- a senior, advanced in years — still, receiving care from outside, with few demands
- in an unknown place, unknown market, unknown country, unknown group
- trying to be calm and waiting for a chance
- relaxed, enjoying peace
- involved in a business that has closed
- ending a relationship

Among the eight images, water is the only one that can represent Karen's situation. She selected trigram 2 for herself.

Next, she turns to analyzing Ronald's situation and has to acknowledge that he hasn't made an active effort to improve their relationship. He is like the rocky mountain, standing still without caring about her situation and making it difficult for her to enjoy their marriage. The Mountain image fits best with his situation. She selected Trigram 1 for her husband.

1—Mountain

Mountains are tall, and they stop everything that approaches. Mountains are stable, never changing position. Mountainous areas often have beautiful scenery, but are tiring to climb. Mountains look huge, but normally do not exhibit great power to damage or threaten human life, except in the instance of volcanoes, rock slides or collapsing ledges.

A person would be assigned the image of "Mountain" if he:

- were retired, finished working
- insisted on a position, or refused to negotiate
- refused to communicate with others
- split up a relationship

- were a dictator
- defended a stronghold resolutely
- isolated himself
- were stubborn
- became bankrupt, or could not pay his debts
- tried to stop a present action

2—Water

Water exists all over the world, and inside every living thing. Water moves downward only; it never flows upward by itself. It can be contained in a lake, constricted by the banks of a river, held back by a dam, or even kept in a bottle or a cup.

A person would be assigned the image of Water if:

- he were close to retirement age; his effective work energy were limited
- he were suffering loss in business and could find no way to improve it
- he were sick
- he were having difficulty making a correct decision
- he were facing a dangerous situation
- he were bound by a contract or agreement, limiting his freedom
- he were in a battle situation and unable to extricate himself
- he were unable to decide upon a course of action
- he were losing money, his business were in recess, or facing a bad market
- he were in conflict with others in a relationship

3—Wind

Wind blows everywhere. It can go through anything that is open to it, even a tiny hole. If something blocks its way, it detours around, over or under the obstacle. Wind acts with real power, bestowing a cool, chilly feeling, and may even cause serious damage.

A person would be assigned the image of "Wind" if he were:

- middle aged, after thirties
- following, supporting, or inflating the ego of others for his own benefit

regardless if the others were right or wrong
- not successful in business, but trying to use discounts, financing, advertising, etc. to keep afloat
- holding power, but trying to cover wrongdoing with fraudulent evidence, lying
- very tired after hard work
- resigned from a position and trying to do something else.
- cleaning up after a party as the guests are leaving
- trying to do what is easy and feasible; taking the easy path.

4—Thunder

Thunder usually comes abruptly and loudly. It is frightening. It sounds like a huge explosion, shocking and vibrating and often preceding a torrential rain. Even low, rumbling thunder — in remote skies on a clear summer day — shatters tranquility, and threatens rain. Thunder impacts life, but, in itself, causes very little damage and does not directly result in immediate serious consequences.

A person would be assigned the Thunder image if he were:
- a newborn baby
- a new employee
- dating for the first time in a new relationship
- a challenger
- a creator
- starting a new business
- embarking on an adventure
- launching a new offensive action
- angry

5—Fire

Fire is bright and hot. Its airless center is cooler and dim. It always flames upward, but clings to flammable material and consumes oxygen.

A person would be assigned the Fire image if he were:
- a teenager

- a recently promoted employee
- an inventor
- on the offence, and making progress
- a smart person
- beautiful, handsome, fashionable, or sexy
- running a good business with high sales
- boastful
- falling in love, trying to get to know his partner

6—Lake

The symbol refers to a geographical area that abounds in rivers and lakes. These areas are rich in fish and grains. The scenery is beautiful and enjoyable.

A person would be assigned the Lake image if he were:

- an adult in his twenties
- happy and pleasant
- rich
- successful
- emotionally mature
- gaining high profits in business
- healthy
- enjoying happiness or peace of mind
- in a sweet relationship

7—Heaven

Heaven is a donor. It donates energy, light, heat and rain to the earth. Its power is mighty and uncontrollable. Heaven is above it all, at the top position, unreachable and untouchable.

A person would be assigned the Heaven image if he were:

- a mature adult, in his thirties
- powerful
- domineering

- a leader, officer, CEO, manager, supervisor, police
- controlling a monopoly, dominating, or having great success
- running a business with the best product
- a champion
- trying to control, to manipulate, or to use others
- a teacher
- marrying, (at the highest position of the cycle of love)

2 Subject and Object

She puts Trigram 1 on top of Trigram 2, resulting in Hexagram 2:1.

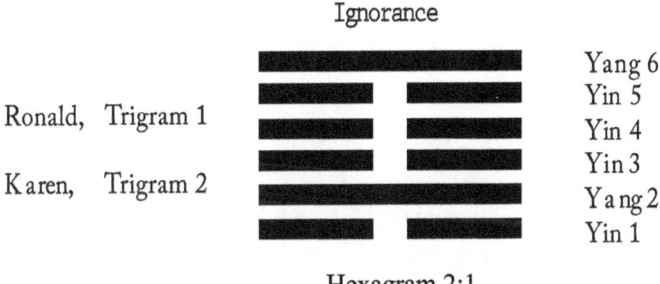

Figure 1.2: Hexagram 2:1, Ignorance

2:1 is the ID number of the hexagram Karen made and indicates that the trigram representing Karen is Trigram 2 and the one representing Ronald is Trigram 1. Because the assessment is from Karen's view, Karen is the subject and Ronald is the object. The trigram referring to the subject is a subject trigram and the one referring to the object is an object trigram. In a hexagram, the subject trigram is on the bottom, and the object trigram is on the top.

The lines in a hexagram are counted from bottom to top. The names of the lines are derived by adding the nature, Yin or Yang, and the line number.

3 Yi Text

In Part II of this book, there are texts of 64 hexagrams. For each hexagram, the text is in three parts:

1. Title
2. General text, explaining the relationship, in general

3. Texts of lines, referring to each line

According to Part II of this book, the title of Hexagram 2:1 is Ignorance, which immediately gives Karen some idea that she and Ronald have a lot to learn about harmonious relationships. She reads the general text for Hexagram 2:1.

> *Things are going smoothly.*
> *The teacher says,*
> *"It is not I seeking pupils,*
> *but the pupils beg me.*
> *The question will be answered the first time.*
> *The repeated questions,*
> *which show impertinence,*
> *will not be answered."*
> *It is beneficial to stay on the current course.*

This text suggests to Karen that staying with her husband is beneficial, but she should not be too obedient to his ignorant demands: "The question will be answered the first time. The repeated questions, which show impertinence, will not be answered."

Then she goes on to read the texts for each line of the hexagram Ignorance.

Yin 1

> *The teacher shows the ignorant the model,*
> *who feels the freedom gained from learning,*
> *like getting rid of fetters and handcuffs.*
> *It is mean to ask pupils to do too much.*

The text suggests that Karen should make an effort for her husband, even if it's very limited — like a teacher exposing an ignorant student to the "model, who feels the freedom gained from learning, like getting rid of fetters and handcuffs." Then it is up to her husband to learn from this example; Karen should not push her husband too forcefully: "It is mean to ask pupils to do too much."

Yang 2

> *Taking care of an ignorant person is favorable*
> *To marry a woman is favorable.*
> *The woman might give birth to a son,*
> *who will grow up and become a householder.*

The text suggests Karen do something for her husband: "Taking care of an ignorant person is favorable." Despite the fact that her husband is stubborn and uncooperative, this care could turn out to be valuable: If you marry an ignorant woman, she may not be smart, but her child might prove capable of being a householder.

Yin 3

*Do not marry a woman
who seeks a wealthy man,
and loses possession of herself.
It is not beneficial.*

The text suggests that Karen should not be too humble and agreeable, if her husband pursues his own goal, only. "Do not marry a woman, who seeks a wealthy man, and loses possession of herself." If Karen behaves too humbly and agreeably, "it is not beneficial."

Yin 4

*Dealing with weary ignorance
is mean.*

The text tells Karen that her husband is like a tired, ignorant student who just wants to sleep or leave the class. Karen needs to compromise. If Karen tries to overcome this sluggishness she seems mean.

Yin 5

*Teaching youthful ignorance
is favorable.*

The text tells Karen that her husband is in a weak position, like anyone who displays "youthful ignorance." He needs help from Karen. While Karen helps her husband, Karen also gains. That is favorable for Karen.

Yang 6

*Teach violent ignorance
that it is beneficial not to be a robber,
but to be a defender against robbers.*

The text suggests that her husband is in the grip of "violent ignorance." Karen should help her husband change this rough attitude, and bring out the best in her husband, teaching that "it is beneficial not to be a robber, but to be a defender against robbers."

From the texts above, first, Karen learned that she needs to talk with her husband like a teacher, tutor, and a student. After Karen talked with Ronald, he understood that staying home every night is making her feel restless and bored. Second, she learned that she needs to take care of her husband like "an ignorant person". She engaged in a discussion with her husband and decided to hire a babysitter and go out the following weekend.

Karen and Ronald look forward to enjoying many more years of a successful marriage, following the change that they were fortunate enough to rediscover.

4 Follow The Example

You may want to follow the example above, selecting two images for you and for the others, making a hexagram, and looking at the attached texts in Part II of this book.

You must first take the time to become familiar with the eight trigrams presented above, in order to begin to understand the process used to evaluate relationships and decision making. Once this familiarity has become second nature, it is a simple matter to consider a person or a situation in terms of one of the trigrams. But you don't have to be an expert to make use of this information. This book provides the expertise for you and eventually, you will discover that you need not refer to it as often. Later on in this book, the fundamental qualities of each trigram will be discussed in more detail.

If you wish to use Yi immediately, with no further interest in knowing the insight of Yi, you may skip the next chapters. If you prefer to know more about Yi, continue reading.

To enjoy a successful marriage, remember: if there are any problems, do the following three steps:

- Select two images: one for you, and one for your spouse.
- Make a hexagram, your trigram on bottom, your spouse's trigram on top.
- Look at the corresponding texts of the hexagram.

CHAPTER 2
Yi in Business

VICKI AND CAROL ARE HAVING dinner at Friendly's. Vicki asks Carol, "What are you going to do this weekend?"

"Drive to Macy's," Carol said.

"I will be going to Kohl's," replied Vicki. "The clothes there are cheaper."

"I used to shop at Kohl's," said Carol. "But I switched to Macy's. We customers are like the wind, blowing to and fro. We like to go where the quality of merchandise, or the service, or the price is better."

"I agree," said Vicki. "Customers are like the wind."

"That is trigram 3," replied Carol.

"What?"

"Trigram 3 of Yi. It's associated with the wind image."

A trigram is a symbol with three lines. The lines may be solid or broken; the solid line symbolizes yang, and the broken line denotes yin. Yang and yin are the concepts in Chinese philosophy. In general, yang closely resembles the nature of heaven, while yin closely resembles the nature of earth.

There are eight possible combinations of three lines with two types; therefore, three lines with the two types, yang or yin, make eight trigrams. The eight trigrams associated with eight images are as shown below:

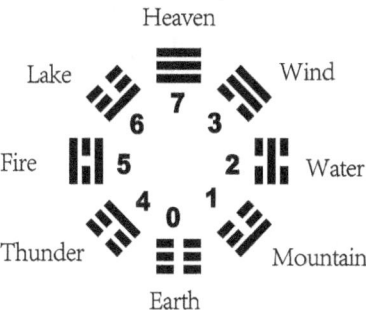

Figure 2.1: Eight Trigrams

The three lines of the trigram associated with wind are yin, yang and yang. If we replace yang line with 1, and yin line with 0, this trigram becomes 011, a three digit number of the binary number system. The value of binary number 011 is 3. "3" is the numeric value of this trigram, unique in eight trigrams and serves as its ID number. That is why Carol said the nature of customers can be expressed with trigram 3.

"Which trigram is for Macy's?" Vicki asks.

"Macy's is successful in business," Carol replied.

"How can a business succeed?" Vicki asks.

"It must perform as trigram 4, like thunder," Carol said.

"Why?"

To make the best strategy for business, the company has to adapt well to its market. If we have a trigram representing its customers, we need to choose a trigram to represent the company. From the view of the company, the company is the subject, while the customer is the object. The trigram representing the subject is a subject trigram, and the trigram representing the object is an object trigram. Two trigrams, with the subject trigram under the object trigram, form a hexagram. The ID of the combined hexagram is the combination of the two component trigrams with ":" between, such as 4:3 (Be aware, it is just an ID, not a ratio). Each hexagram has a unique title.

Since there are eight trigrams, when the object trigram is trigram 3, there are eight options for selecting an object trigram to form a hexagram.

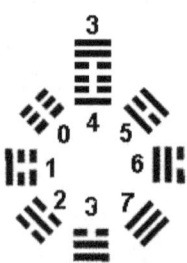

Figure 2.2: Options of subject trigrams

The IDs and titles of the resultant hexagrams are:

        0:3   Watching

        1:3   Gradual

        2:3   Flood

        3:3   Yield

        4:3   Gain

5:3	Matriarch
6:3	Sincerity
7:3	Accumulation

From the eight titles shown above, we know that hexagram 4:3 is the best choice. Its title is Gain, meaning the company will gain from the relationship with customers. The three lines of trigram 4 representing the company are yang, yin and yin, while the three lines of trigram 3, representing customers, are yin, yang and yang. The corresponding lines on both of them are yang with yin, or yin with yang. That is to say, all of the lines in this hexagram are complementary, in the best status of harmony. In the world, everything naturally tends to be in harmony. Harmony is favorable, while discord is unfavorable. Like the sounds of music, the sounds in harmony are enjoyable and help us feel good, while the sounds in discord create the opposite effect.

You may be aware, that the sum of the IDs of the two component trigrams of hexagram 4:3 is 7. If the sum of the IDs of the two component trigrams of a hexagram is 7, the component trigrams are complementary. In general, if the two IDs of component trigrams in a hexagram is 7, the hexagram might be favorable to the subject; although, it is not the only criteria for favorability of a hexagram, as can be noted in latter parts of this book. Therefore, if the object trigram is known, you might select a complementary trigram as a subject trigram, and make a strategy, behaving as the image associated with the subject trigram.

In Yi, a hexagram associates with a text (Yi text) that comments on the hexagram. Below is the Yi text for hexagram 4:3.

General Text: (Comment on the whole hexagram)

It is beneficial to go further.
It is beneficial to cross a big river.

Texts of Lines: (Comment on each line of the hexagram. Yang 1 and Yin 2, etc. denote the name of the line, yang and yin denote the nature of the line, and 1 and 2, etc. denote the location of the line, counting from bottom to top)

Yang 1

This situation is promising for great work,
It is very favorable and blameless.

Yin 2

It is impossible to refuse the contribution of

A tortoise worth ten pairs of seashells.
It is favorable to stay on this course forever.
The king performs a ritual
Praying to his ancestors for favor.
It is favorable.

Yin 3

Receiving help at a bad time
Is blameless.
Holding a jade tablet and
Speaking gingerly,
Like walking in the middle of a road,
One advises the lord.

Yin 4

Like walking in the middle of a road,
One speaks with the lord gingerly.
The lord accepts one's advice.
Based on that,
The capital is relocated.

Yang 5

Sincerity makes people feel better.
Certainly it is very favorable.
Sincerity makes me want to be more virtuous.

Yang 6

Do not help
But beat.
Not persistently being virtuous
Is unfavorable.

The text describes how the situation is favorable to the company. The text for line 3 and 4 advises the company to provide the best service to the customers, like a servant holding a jade tablet, which was used by the servants of the emperor as a symbol of their sincerity and trustworthiness. The servants choose words and actions deliberately, like walking carefully in the middle of a road. The customers are like a "lord" following the advice of a servant and relocating the capital of the country.

The text of line 5 stresses sincerity in the service of the company.

The text of line 6 advises how the company has to deal with the customer, who is not sincere, but rude and bossy.

"Does Macy's act like thunder?" asks Vicki.

"Yes. Macy's often gives a big impact, like the loud exploding sounds of thunder," responds Carol.

"What?"

"I receive coupons from Macy's almost every month," said Carol. "Some coupons offer 20% off, some offer $20 off with a purchase of $50 or more. I bought two shirts for $45, then I added one pair of slacks for $5.25. I was charged only $30.25 plus tax, for two shirts and one pair of slacks. I receive advertisements from Macy's every other week and find interesting items in them. Recently, I bought a beaver fur coat."

"A beaver fur coat must be very warm," claims Vicki.

"I believe so. I saw beavers while touring Denali. To nest, the lively animals built their lodges on the surface of lakes. As they live in such a cold area, their fur must be very warm. They swim and dive through water in order to enter their lodges, so their skin and fur must be strong. I think beaver fur is good fur, so I wanted to have a beaver fur coat."

"Well, why don't you buy a beaver fur coat from Alaska?"

"I tried. I found a web site www.denalifur.com displaying many pictures of beaver fur coats. But when I clicked on the item that interested me, I was instructed to call for pricing. I don't know why they don't like to post their price. Then I sent them an email, telling them I wanted a woman's 44" long, beaver fur coat with hat, size PL, and asked for their price. When I did not receive any response that day, I called the company the next night, and a lady confirmed that they did receive my email. She asked me, 'How much do you want to spend?' You know, I hate questions like that."

"Me too," interjected Vicki. "Why should we expose our privacy to them?"

"I asked," Carol continued, "'How much do you want?' She told me, 'Seven to eight thousand dollars.' I said, 'Okay, please send me some pictures showing the options for the coat I want.' She promised to do so but a week passed before I received the pictures.

"That is not nice," Vicki said.

"That afternoon I received a phone call from them stating they would like to custom make a long beaver fur coat with hat for me for $3,800 dollars, with free shipping."

"They dropped the price!"

"Yes," Carol replied, "The price was good. But the call came too late. I had already bought a coat. Do you understand what this company is like?"

"Their performance is not like thunder."

"Correct," replied Carol. "They are like a mountain. When we, the wind, blow to them, they stand still, not moving, even blocking us."

"Did you get your coat from Macy's."

"Not Macy's in Smith Haven Mall, but the one in Manhattan."

"How did you know Macy's in Manhattan had the beaver coat you wanted?"

"When I drove to Macy's in Smith Haven Mall, I was very disappointed. All the fur coats there were made of mink. But the attitude of the saleslady was so great. She comforted me and made several calls for me. Finally, she found Macy's in Manhattan, their biggest store, had beaver fur coats. She said she could order one for me, and have it shipped free to my home. However, I preferred to go to Macy's in Manhattan, and try on the coat before buying it. So I drove to Macy's in Manhattan and do you know what?"

"What?"

"I found a beaver fur coat that fit me just right. The length is below my knees, and shoulder, chest and sleeves fit me very well. The hat, a hood, lies on my shoulder like a shawl collar. Most interesting is, it's my favorite color."

"Well. Good for you."

"The price was very good, as well. With 50% off the original price, which was $5,995 and another 20% off from my coupon, plus tax, I paid only $2,608.65."

"That's even cheaper than the offer from the Alaskan fur company."

"So many exciting events come from Macy's. Macy's performs just like thunder. And that is what I believe: to run a successful business, the company must behave like thunder."

"It makes sense," agreed Vicki. "Apple Computer is also a success. Mac, Iphone, Ipad, etc. are so many loud explosions of thunder emitted from Apple."

"There are so many computer makers in the world; all of them make black boxes of laptops, but only Apple made the exception," exclaims Carol. "Their Mac is so delicate, even its power socket is magnetic, helping users to easily connect their laptops to AC."

"My son is a business man," said Vicki. "I will tell him that the best strategy to run a business, is to behave like thunder."

"Thunder is not the only option, as there are eight options. The other options are certainly not very bad, but they do require some improvements," explained Carol. "For example, hexagram 6:3 is another option. Its title is Sincerity. That implies the company needs to be more sincere when dealing with customers. Even if the company behaves like a mountain, the corresponding hexagram is 1:3, titled Gradual, and the situation is not too bad for the company. The general text of hexagram 1:3 says:

> *The marriage is favorable to the lady.*
> *Staying on the current course is beneficial.*

In the text, the 'lady' refers to the company. The business might still benefit the company, but the progress might be very slow, the company needs to be 'staying on the current course' "

"So," said Vicki, "acting like thunder is the best option for the company, serving customers with more explorations, more discoveries, and more creations."

"Yes," said Carol. "It is true. However there is a predefined condition that the customers must be like the wind."

"How do we achieve that?"

"Marketing. Investigate what the people want, and make sure people will come to buy like a strong wind during a thunderstorm, not a weak wind."

"That makes sense," said Vicki. "But I have a question. When trigram 3 is used for customers and trigram 4 is used for company, they can make two hexagrams. If we locate trigram 3 under trigram 4, we get hexagram 3:4. What is that?"

Carol: "It is the situation from the customer's point of view. In this case, customers are the subject, while the company is the object. The hexagram shows how the customers should deal with the company."

"Interesting."

"The title of hexagram 3:4 is Persistence. That means if the company is like thunder, always exciting us with good products or nice service, we should do business with it persistently."

To use Yi as a tool for making life strategies, remember to do the following three steps:

Find a trigram associated with an image which best fits with the situation of the others.

- *Select a complementary trigram for yourself.*
- *Pile the two trigrams up with your trigram beneath the trigram for others. Follow the instructions of its title and text.*

CHAPTER 3
Yin and Yang

WHEN MY FRIEND CARL SHOUTED angrily at his wife, Linda, she remained quiet and calm. Once his storm was over, he said to his wife, "I'm sorry I lost my temper. I love you."

Linda waited until then to ask Carl, "Why did you do that?"

Even though she never learned about Yi, Linda naturally used the rule of harmony of yin and yang to keep her marriage stable. When her husband was verbally abusing her, she remained quiet. She used yin to deal with yang. When Carl apologized to her, he was in retreat and defensive; so, she took a yang action, asking him why he had been so angry, to shed light on their situation.

1 Instances of Yin and Yang

Understanding yin and yang is the gateway to understanding and using Yi. If you understand yin and yang, you will find that our complicated and perplexing world is, at its heart, quite simple.

No exact English translation exists for yin or for yang. The words should be directly imported from Chinese; otherwise, we risk losing the sense of their abstract, universal nature.

The Chinese people have no difficulty in comprehending and using the concepts of yin and yang in daily life. In Chinese, the sunny side of the mountain is called "shan yang," and the shady side is called "shan yin." The solar calendar is called "yang li," and the lunar calendar is called "yin li." An introvert might be described as "very yin"; an extrovert is "yang."

But the concept of yin and yang is confusing to Western people. Yin and yang were translated as darkness and brightness, yielding and firm, softness and hardness, female and male, evil and good. This is insufficient. Darkness, softness, femininity, and evil are particular instances of yin but not expressions of its entire meaning. Brightness, hardness, masculinity, and goodness can be aspects of yang, but are not synonyms for it.

Often people try to explain yin and yang in terms of paired opposites: night and day, winter and summer, cold and hot, female and male, defensive and offensive, software and hardware, conservative and creative, lower and upper, evil and good, closed and open, inner and outer, negative and positive, back and forth, off and on, no and yes, minus and plus, etc. These pairs are instances of yin and yang, but their mutual exclusivity can be misleading. Opposite implies that the two qualities are in conflict with each other, and yin and yang are complementary to each other.

In a family, for instance, a husband is yang, and the wife is yin. If they are opposites, always in conflict, how can they live happily together?

2 Yin and Yang are Natural Complements

Yin may be used to represent the background of a sheet of paper while yang represents the black characters on that sheet, together they make the display of a text possible. When you take a shower, the hot water is yang, and the cold water is yin. You adjust the two taps to ensure that the water is a comfortable temperature for you. In a classroom, the teacher is yang, and the students are yin: a complementary give-and-take between teacher and students makes learning possible.

You may have heard that yang is positive, and yin is negative, but this is an oversimplification. Modesty, kindness, grace, and flexibility are positive traits, and they are instances of yin. And we think of arrogance, roughness, brutality, and stubbornness as negative characteristics, but they are representations of yang.

Most people reveal themselves as combinations of yin and yang personality traits that can be positive or negative. If you are hiring a new employee, you have to choose among the applicants. Let's say the first has little experience but is modest and willing to learn. The inexperience is a negative value and can be represented by yin; the modesty is a positive virtue and can also be considered yin. The second candidate is well-qualified but arrogant — the excellence in job performance, a positive quality, is yang, while the arrogance, a negative, is also yang. In this case, the better choice-yin or yang-depends upon the particulars of that job.

A very common misunderstanding is the assumption that yin is female and yang is male. This is only partially correct. A woman may be associated with yin when she gives birth and nurtures a child; but when a male drunk driver is caught by a female police officer, you cannot say that the male driver is yang and the female officer yin. In that scenario, the reverse is true: The female officer is yang because she is in a position of power, and the male drunk driver is yin because he has to yield to the commands of the female officer.

3 Definition of Yin and Yang

Of all the philosophies we humans have devised to grasp our existence, only Yi uses yin and yang by expressing them with trigrams. The Bible begins with heaven and earth, demonstrating that the ancient Western people also recognized these as two fundamental elements of their changing world.

Later Western thinkers, from Plato to Hegel, spoke in terms of opposites and developed dialectics to describe the states of "being" and "nonbeing." They also mentioned "becoming" — the middle state between "being" and "nonbeing" — but very vaguely. Yi and only Yi elaborates and describes this middle plane of existence where most of us conduct our life.

The ancients noticed that between summer and winter, between night and day, interesting and important stages, such as autumn or sunrise, occurred. Looking for ways to combine the symbols for yin and yang that would also describe these vital in-between stages, they devised the trigrams and hexagrams of Yi.

The broken line (━ ━) is a symbol of yin. The solid line (━━) is a symbol of yang.

Yin is defined by Trigram Ø (☷), which defines yin as the nature of earth. (Ø means there is no yang line in this trigram.) This trigram is a symbol of pure yin, consisting of three yin lines. The name of this trigram is Earth, or "Kun" in Chinese. We can understand that yin is a general abstract concept, representing the nature of earth. Since a mother nurses a baby, just as the earth nurtures all living things, the female nature is yin.

Hexagram Ø:Ø (☷☷) — built by combining two Trigram Øs — is also titled "Kun." The Yi text for this hexagram says: "It is better to stay on the current course like a docile mare." This image of the gentle mare is useful to keep in mind while envisioning the nature of pure yin: like the earth nurturing living things, like a mother kindly and gently caring for a child.

Yang is defined by Trigram 7 (☰), consisting of three yang lines. (Seven means the highest possible amount of yang.) The name of this trigram is "Heaven" — in Chinese, "Qian" — which is also the name of Hexagram 7:7 (☰☰), built by combining two trigrams of pure yang.

The character "Qian" appears in the Yi text twice for Hexagram 7:7, where it says, "The gentleman is qian qian all day," suggesting that the gentlemen struggles all day, in the way heaven moves around the earth, ceaselessly and persistently. The text also repeatedly uses the image of a dragon to describe the nature of yang, beginning with "a hiding dragon" and "a dragon appearing in a field," then "a dragon jumping out of an abyss," and finally "a dragon flying in the sky." When you think of pure yang as the nature of heaven, envision a dragon expressing power, strength and mobility.

4 The nature of Yin and Yang

You probably realize now that the complementary concepts of yin and yang represent a natural balance — what the ancients saw as the eternal interaction between heaven and earth. This vital force, sometimes creating and sometimes destroying, was so crucial to their survival, that they used yang and yin to describe the elements necessary to achieve harmony, resolution, and peace. Even today the clearest way to experience the true nature of yin and yang is to regard them in terms of earth and heaven.

The ancient people of China sought explanations for the way their world changed. With sundials they observed the shortening and lengthening of days, and they noticed cycles in months and years. By studying this constant interplay between heaven and earth, they concluded that yang symbolized the characteristics of heaven, and yin symbolized aspects of earth. Heaven, they decided, is the donor of energy and strength, moving and active. Earth is the receptor of energy, nurturing living things, gentle, passive, and still.

These concepts of yin and yang may apply to all things, from nature to the human condition. For example, the day is yang because heaven is bright, and the night is yin because the earth does not generate light. Wealth is yang and poverty is yin because heaven is rich in energy and earth can get energy only from heaven. Arrogance is yang, and humility is yin because from the ancient people's perspective, heaven was in the top position and earth was below.

Heaven was important to these people for obvious reasons: it gave sunlight, water, and air. Earth was equally important, as the source of nourishment. Heaven and earth were the two supreme conditions of their survival. Through observation and experience, the ancients found parallels between the cycles of heaven and earth and the changes in their own life.

Watching the rising and setting of sun and stars, they saw heaven as moving around the earth. Based on this relationship, they concluded that heaven is dynamic and earth is static. Because heaven gives sunlight and earth receives it, yang gives and yin takes. Yang is active, and yin is passive.

Can you see this contrast between active yang and passive yin in everyday life? Of course. Trying to initiate or improve a friendship is yang; trying to withdraw from a relationship or alienate a friend is yin. Active communication is yang; isolation is yin. A creative attitude is yang, and a conservative attitude is yin.

Adventure is yang, caution is yin; revolution is yang, preservation is yin. Asking, inquiring, and researching are yang; answering, waiting, and pondering are yin.

Another defining difference between yin and yang has to do with position. Looking at heaven, a human being will suppose that heaven is higher than earth. So in society, a high position is yang, and a lower rank is yin. The boss is yang; a subordinate is yin. A high value or number is yang; a low one is yin. Arrogance is yang; humility is yin. Strength and domination are yang; flexibility and yielding are yin. The head is yang; the feet are yin.

One more basic difference between heaven and earth will help you categorize elements in your life as yin or yang. The heavens were a mystery to prehistoric people. Sunlight, clouds, vast spaces, the Sun, the Moon, and the stars were all so far away, no one could touch or measure them. Earth was more tangible to them. Mountains, lakes, fields, rivers, woods, animals, and all earthly things could be directly felt and measured. As a result, yang describes abstract aspects of life, and yin applies to the concrete. Emotions, thoughts, and dreams are yang; sensations, conversations, and experiences are yin. Watching a bird fly across the sky is yang; having a bird perch on your finger is yin.

5 The Rule of Harmony

So far you have learned how to define the concepts of yin and yang. But how do you recognize these forces at work in real-life situations? This is the key to everything you will learn in the rest of this book. Once you know how to conceptualize situations in terms of yin and yang, you will be able to use Yi to achieve harmony. Here are some examples:

When bananas were on sale, Bob bought three pounds. Now that bananas cost 68 cents per pound, he only buys a half a pound. Decreasing prices are yin, and increasing prices are yang. Bob benefited by purchasing more (yang) when prices were low, and buying less (yin) when the price of bananas rose. He answered yin with yang, and then yang with yin, harmonizing with the changes in his situation.

When the audience was sitting quietly (yin), Phyllis made a speech to explain her opinion. When someone raised his hand (yang), she stopped talking and listened carefully to the question. This balancing of yin with yang achieved harmony between the speaker and the audience.

Yin and yang have long been considered so powerful and mysterious, incorrectly depicted in legend as two epic polar forces or spirits, or two primal cosmic principles that determine destinies or fate. Yin and yang certainly play their part in great myths, but are also at work daily in the smallest details of life. Their power comes from the tendency always to arrive at harmony, the balance of yin and yang. Harmony brings happiness; discord leads to disaster.

In Daodejing, Laozi says, "Nothing in the world is softer and weaker than water, but, for attacking the hard and strong, there is nothing like it! For nothing can take its place. That the weak overcomes the strong, the soft overcomes the hard, this is something known by all, but practised by none."

Consciously or unconsciously, we apply (or fail to apply) this rule of harmony to all aspects of our existence. When a teacher is strict in assigning homework (yang), the student is wise to listen carefully and obey (yin). After being laid off, an employee who immediately hunts for a new job is using yang action to defeat yin unemployment.

In The Art of War, Sunzi (400-320 B.C.) suggested, "When the enemy advances, I retreat; and when the enemy retreats, I advance." This theory regards war as a particular relationship between two sides, "I" and "the enemy," and suggests the use of yin (retreating) to deal with yang (advancing), and vice versa.

The concept of yin and yang and the rule of harmony apply to all relationships, from war to love, from the office to the home. It is necessary to understanding a relationship fully from both sides and to keep yin and yang in harmony. This is the role of the peacemaker, and Yi is the peacemaker's essential guide.

6 Becoming a Peacemaker

Even when the forces of yin and yang coexist in harmony, you are not living in a perfect world. Harmonizing these forces successfully does mean that your life can flow toward a peaceful resolution, whereas discord dictates that trouble lies ahead and any problem you have is bound to get worse. This rule of change is the foundation of the Yi text, which tells you how to become a peacemaker, not a troublemaker, in complex situations.

You know that any family or team functions best when all its members are in harmony, with a balance of yin and yang. In real life, however, to heal the problems in a relationship, you are usually a member of the family or team rather than standing outside the system. As a peacemaker, you have to apply the rule of harmony from within the relationship, dealing yang for yin, and yin for yang.

Of the two sides involved in a relationship, one or both might be the peacemakers and create or restore harmony. In a situation where both sides cannot win, the rule of harmony favors the peacemaker. Linda was a peacemaker. Her husband realized his wrongdoing and apologized to her.

Carl's situation is less clear. He might or might not be better off with the harmony that Linda was able to restore to their marriage. What if his objective in picking a fight with Linda was to give himself an excuse for having an extramarital affair? Then he was actually a troublemaker who failed to achieve his desired goal.

When caught in the middle of a storm, not everyone can be a natural peacemaker like Linda. In the next chapter, you will learn how to understand change in terms of the universal Yi symbols. This will help you achieve the perspective of an outside observer, a peacemaker, even when you are in the eye of a storm.

Remember, be a peacemaker:

- *Deal yang for yin, and yin for yang.*

CHAPTER 4
Trigrams

WHEN WE FIRST MET HARRY, he was jobless, having been laid off when his technology company went out of business. Then he found a job at AFR, a software company. He was successful in his career and promoted. However, after ten years, he resigned from AFR and became jobless again. This cycle is a regular change which can be represented by The Eight Trigrams.

1 A Primitive Sundial

In Chinese, the word for trigram, 卦 [guà], is a symbol for a primitive sundial, made from a stick stuck into the ground. The left part symbolizes a pile of soil, 圭 [guī], made up of two characters meaning dirt, 土 [tǔ], one piled on top of another. The right part symbolizes the stick with a shadow, 卜 [bǔ].

At the time of Fuxi (~4500 B.C), ancient people used these simple sundials to track changes in the stick's shadow as the sun moved across the heavens. These observations allowed them to measure how the length of a day changes during the course of a year. They recognized a predictable, cyclical pattern of the days being shortest in winter and longest during summer. They created the Eight Trigrams to reflect this basic truth:

2 Image of Trigrams

Chapter 1 introduced how to select a trigram by pondering the visual images; i.e., Thunder, Fire, Lake, etc., associated with them. Each has its own characteristics. They are, in sequence:

1—Thunder

A typical characteristic of thunder is movement. It does not refer to specific kinds of movement, such as running, flying, or throwing, but rather to the impulse of movement itself: starting, initiating, or setting out to accomplish something. The image of thunder stresses the vibrating, shocking impact of this force on others, and also implies an associated weakness, such as that of a newborn, a newly emerging force.

Thunder usually comes abruptly and loudly. It is frightening. It sounds like a huge explosion, shocking and vibrating and often preceding a torrential rain. Even low, rumbling thunder — in remote skies on a clear, summer day — shatters tranquility, and threatens rain. Thunder impacts life, but, in itself, causes very little damage and does not directly result in immediate serious consequences.

2—Fire

The typical characteristics of fire are brightness and a tendency to cling. Positive attributes include cleverness, talent, and an ability to shine or succeed; negative qualities can be rage, recklessness or roughness.

Fire is bright and hot. Ancient people used fire to cook food, to light their dark cave homes, to illuminate a rocky path at night, to warm themselves in cold seasons, to chase away dangerous animals, to defend themselves, and to communicate with each other. Sometimes, wild fires burned woods, injuring or killing people. Fire is bright on the surface, but its airless center is cooler and dim. It clings to flammable material and consumes oxygen. Its yang action always flames upward.

3—Lake

The typical characteristic of lake is pleasure. This not only describes a general feeling, but also the joy that flows from an exhilarating adventure, a successful mission, and an optimistic prospect, as well as a graceful, flexible and modest manner.

The symbol refers to a geographical area that abounds in rivers and lakes. We can imagine the pleasure of the ancient people as they came down a steep, rocky mountain path to a flat meadow by the lake, where they might find small animals, easily hunt for food, and encounter fresh water to drink. The lake attracts people and gives them a feeling of pleasure.

4—Heaven

The typical characteristic of heaven is strength — not only physical power, but also creativity, aggressiveness, offensive action, and also recklessness, a rough attitude, and arrogance.

Heaven is a donor. It donates energy, light, heat and rain to the earth. Its power is mighty and uncontrollable. Heaven is above it all, at the top position, unreachable and untouchable.

5—Wind

The typical characteristic of wind is flexibility. This can mean adaptability or a willingness to yield, but also a threatening blow and a great power.

Wind blows everywhere. It can go through anything that is open to it, even a tiny hole. If something blocks its way, it detours around, over or under the obstacle. Wind acts with real power, bestowing a cool, chilly feeling, and may even cause serious damage.

6—Water

The typical characteristics of water are danger and difficulty. This can be danger and difficulty that one faces or that one imposes on others.

Water exists all over the world, and inside every living thing. In ancient times, rivers were huge obstacles in overland travel. Floods bring disaster, and someone who falls into water can drown. Water moves downward only; it never flows upward by itself. It can be contained in a lake, constricted by the banks of river, held back by a dam, or even kept in a bottle or a cup.

7—Mountain

The typical characteristic of mountain is to stop or block.

Mountains are tall, and they stop everything that approaches. Mountains are stable, never changing position. Mountainous areas often have beautiful scenery, but are tiring to climb. Mountains look huge, but normally do not exhibit great power to damage or threaten human life, except in the instance of volcanoes, rock slides or collapsing ledges.

8—Earth

The typical characteristic of earth is adaptability. This means responding to others without resistance, strength, or roughness; gently, docilely, and peacefully.

The earth is still. Ancient people believed that the earth does not move. The earth is a receiver. It receives energy from heaven, as well as light, heat, and rain. Living things on the earth adapt to the changes imposed by the heavens. The earth is nurturing, sustaining all living things like a mother caring for her children. The earth is in a lower position. If we consider heaven as being above, we think of earth as below.

A thorough comprehension of the characteristics of the Eight Images will help you select the trigram that best fits a real situation. It will also help you understand and interpret the meaning of the trigram you have selected. Use these images to verify whether a trigram you have selected or built line by line accurately reflects reality.

3 Value of Trigrams

Confucius and his disciples described how the Yi was developed: "The Yi has Taiji. The Taiji produces two forms. The two forms produce four images. The four images produce the eight trigrams."

Based on this description, the famous scholar Shao Yong (1011—1077 A.C) drew this formation:

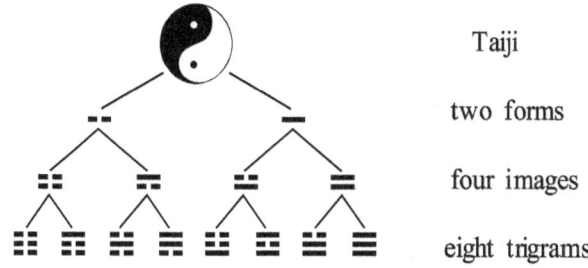

Figure 4.1: From Taiji to Eight Trigrams

Before yin and yang were shown as broken and solid lines, the trigrams were expressed by ancient numbers — even for yin, odd for yang. If we use Ø for yin and 1 for yang, we can see that the Eight Trigrams are eight numbers.

A number expressed with only the two digits, Ø and 1, is called a binary number. Binary numbers are very frequently used in science and technology; for instance, a light turned off or on can be indicated with Ø or 1.

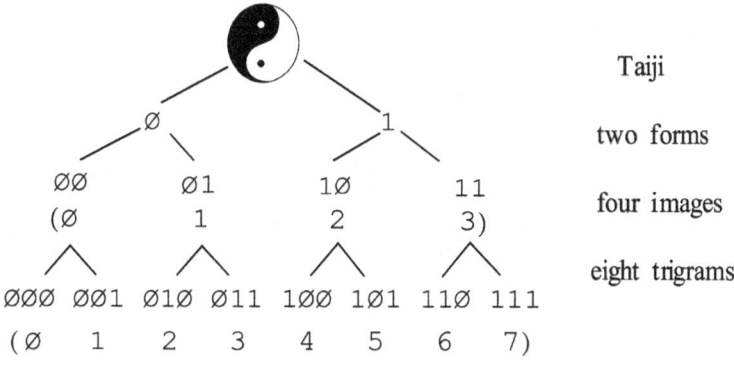

Figure 4.2: Taiji divides into eight binary numbers

So in the first step, one yin and one yang, Taiji divides into two forms: Ø and 1. The binary numbers branch out from there:

After reading this chapter, you will be able to look at a trigram and know its number immediately.

In an earlier section, you looked at the Eight Trigrams arranged in a circle. If you put them into a straight line instead, with pure yin at one end and pure yang at the other, the sequence looks like this:

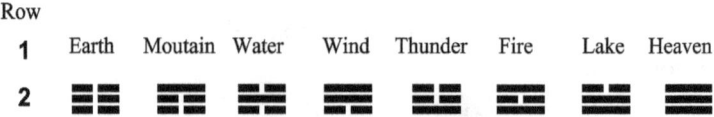

Figure 4.3: The sequence of eight trigrams in one row

You can see that moving in from either end, the trigrams go from pure yin or yang toward a center point of reversed images. (Compare Earth to Heaven, Mountain to Lake, Water to Fire, and Wind to Thunder.) In this movement to the center, the top lines alternate between yin and yang; the middle lines seem to alternate in pairs — two yin, two yang, or two yang, two yin; and the bottom lines remain the same, yin or yang:

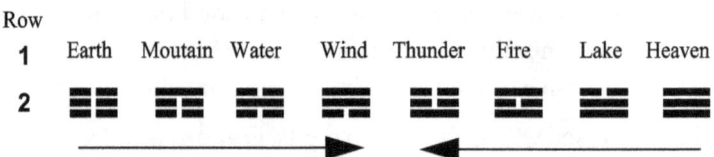

Figure 4.4: Change of Yin and Yang in Eight Trigram Row

Now turn each of the trigrams in a clockwise direction and position them as a third row of symbols:

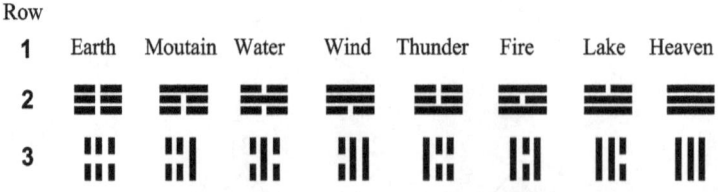

Figure 4.5: Turning trigrams to vertical

Substituting zero (Ø) for yin and one (1) for yang, you obtain the series of binary numbers:

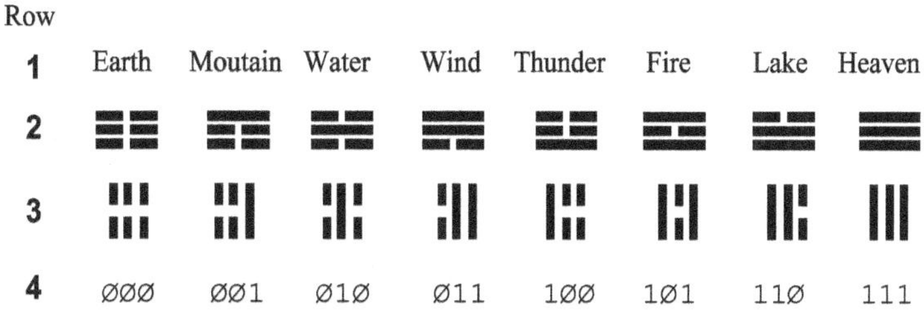

Row
1 Earth Moutain Water Wind Thunder Fire Lake Heaven
2
3
4 ØØØ ØØ1 Ø1Ø Ø11 1ØØ 1Ø1 11Ø 111

Figure 4.6: Yin line comes up with 0, yang line with 1

If counting by zeros and ones seems confusing to you, don't worry: you can convert these binary numbers into the Arabic numerals we normally use, as shown in the fifth row, starting from Ø and increasing by 1 from left to right:

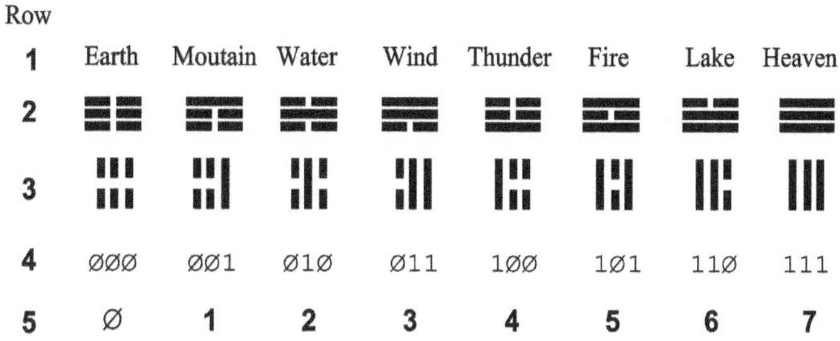

Row
1 Earth Moutain Water Wind Thunder Fire Lake Heaven
2
3
4 ØØØ ØØ1 Ø1Ø Ø11 1ØØ 1Ø1 11Ø 111
5 Ø 1 2 3 4 5 6 7

Figure 4.7: Values of trigrams

These numbers, zero through seven, uniquely identify each trigram and can be used as their ID numbers. Below are the ID number and binary number for each trigram.

Ø 1 2 3 4 5 6 7
ØØØ ØØ1 Ø1Ø Ø11 1ØØ 1Ø1 11Ø 111
Earth Moutain Water Wind Thunder Fire Lake Heaven

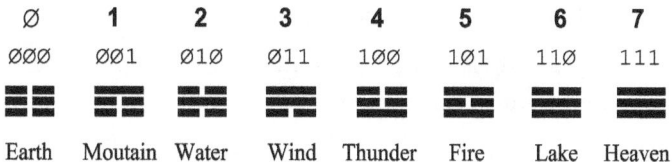

Figure 4.8: ID numbers are the values of trigrams

Can you figure out the shape of a trigram from its ID number? To find the symbol for Trigram 4, its binary number is 1, Ø, Ø or one, zero, zero. Since 1 is yang and Ø is yin, the structure of Trigram 4 always building from the bottom line up — is yang, yin, yin, or ☳. You can use this same procedure for any of the eight trigrams.

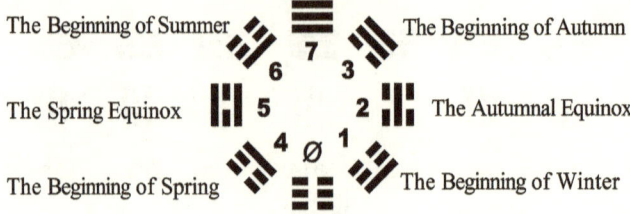

Figure 4.9: Eight Trigrams with Seasons

Look at the Eight Trigrams with Seasons. Trigram 7 (☰), at the top of the calendar wheel, is pure yang, with three yang lines. It serves as the symbol for summer, when days are longest. Trigram Ø (☷) is pure yin, with three yin lines to symbolize winter, when days are shortest. The three trigrams on the left, 4 (☳), 5 (☵) and 6 (☱), represent the increasing length of days from winter to summer. And the three on the right, trigrams 3 (☴), 2 (☲) and 1 (☶), signify the shortening of each day from summer to winter.

4 Seasonal Cycle

After observing the movements of the sun, the moon, and the stars and passing down the information from generation to generation for thousands of years, the ancient people were ready by the time of the Yellow Emperor (~2500 B.C.) to devise a calendar. They designated twenty-four solar periods in one year, corresponding roughly to the term from a new moon to a full moon and another term from the full moon back to a new moon.

Below is a list of these divisions in the Chinese calendar. The Chinese New Year starts around the end of January. Then:

The Beginning of Spring	February 3rd - February 5th
Rain Water, February	18th - February 20th
The Waking of Insects	March 5th - March 7th
The Spring Equinox	March 20th - March 21th
Pure Brightness	April 4 - April 6th
Grain Rain	April 19 - April 21th
The Beginning of Summer	May 5th - May 7th
Grain Full	May 20th - May 22th
Grain in Ear	June 5th - June 7th
The Summer Solstice	June 21th - June 22th

Slight Heat	July 6th - July 8th
Great Heat	July 22th - July 24th
The Beginning of Autumn	August 7th - August 9th
The Limit of Heat	August 22th - August 24th
White Dew	September 7th - September 9th
The Autumn Equinox	September 22th - September 24th
Cold Dew	October 8th - October 9th
Frost's Descent	October 23th - October 24th
The Beginning of Winter	November 7th - November 8th
Slight Snow	November 22th - November 23th
Great Snow	December 6th - December 8th
The Winter Solstice	December 21th - December 23th
Slight Cold	January 5th - January 7th
Great Cold	January 20th - January 21th

Yi reveals four phases common in nature based on the observation of changing days and seasons. You see these same four stages in all forms of nature — in the germination, growth, bloom, and going to seed of annual plants; the birth, growth, maturity, and death of animals; the beginning, developing, climax, and decline of all things. In this manner all change normally occurs along a spiral track.

So the Trigrams represents one cycle in the spiral track, starting from Trigram 4 (☷), through Trigram 5 (☶), 6 (☵), 7 (☴), 3 (☳), 2 (☲), 1 (☱), and ending with Trigram Ø (☷). Each trigram marks a stage of three solar terms in this cycle.

There are two key points: one is between Trigram 0 and Trigram 4, when the value jumps from Trigram Ø (☷) to Trigram 4 (☷), it indicates a newborn thing. And the other is between trigram 7 (☴) and Trigram 3 (☳), when the value drops 3, indicating a thing is declining after reaching its peak position.

5 The Seasonal Change in Reality

To understand better how this seasonal sequence can correspond to the natural stages in our life, let's look at Harry and the changes in his career.

When Harry has been laid off from work, life resembles the Winter Solstice, when the days are shortest and the future seems depressingly limited. Trigram Ø (☷), Earth, applies to this period of three solar terms:

Slight Snow	November 22th - November 23th
Great Snow	December 6th - December 8th
The Winter Solstice	December 21th - December 23th

After a successful interview, Harry starts a new job at AFR, a software company, and this begins a new cycle for him. His status can now be represented by Trigram 4 (☳), Thunder, because his new beginning is comparable to the change from winter to spring, like the first of the twenty-four terms:

Slight Cold	January 5th - January 7th
Great Cold	January 20th - January 21th
The Beginning of Spring	February 3rd - February 5th

After the first few weeks at his new job, Harry begins to feel comfortable with his environment, like a plant getting rain in the early spring. He is intrigued and excited, like a butterfly emerging from a cocoon in the time of "The Waking of Insects."

As Harry learns what is expected of him at AFR and starts to cooperate with his coworkers, his boss and colleagues recognize his knowledge, talent, and capability. This period is like new, bright green leaves sprouting over a vast field in the Spring Equinox. His status can now be represented by the next stage of the Pre-heaven Eight Trigrams, Trigram 5 (☲), Fire:

Rain Water	February 18th - February 20th
The Waking of Insects	March 5th - March 7th
The Spring Equinox	March 20th - March 21th

The good performance he is able to display after becoming familiar with his job corresponds to "Pure Brightness," and Harry is convinced that AFR is the right place for him. With the appreciation he receives and the sought-after assignments, he begins to feel like a growing and thriving plant being showered with "Grain Rain."

After a few years, Harry earns a gratifying promotion and supervises a team of software engineers. With this he proceeds to the "Beginning of Summer," when it is hot but still comfortable. His status can be represented by Trigram 6 (☱), Lake:

Pure Brightness	April 4 - April 6th
Grain Rain	April 19 - April 21th
The Beginning of Summer	May 5th - May 7th

With Harry as its leader, the team produces a record amount of good work, like wheat coming into "Full Grain." Word of his achievements spreads throughout the company, and Harry acquires strength and power, like grain showing sharp ears.

Harry is made the head of his department, replacing the boss who had hired and encouraged him. This success feels to him like the "Summer Solstice," when the days are longest and most full, as represented by Trigram 7 (☰), Heaven:

Grain Full	May 20th - May 22th
Grain in Ear	June 5th - June 7th
The Summer Solstice	June 21th - June 22th

With company-wide expectations focused on him, Harry begins to feel uncomfortable, as in a time of "Slight Heat." He discovers that he's not a natural leader who enjoys taking risks but a competent engineer who prefers what is easy and safe. As Harry's department labors under increased performance goals, his situation resembles the time of the "Great Heat," when people look for a shelter for protection against the sun's harmful rays. Harry learns that when mistakes are discovered, he takes the blame solely because department heads occupy such a high-profile position. He keeps a lower profile and puts less effort into his work. This period of cynicism corresponds to the "Beginning of Autumn," when the temperature starts dropping and plants stop producing new leaves. This time when growth slows or stops is represented by Trigram 3 (☴), Wind:

Slight Heat	July 6th - July 8th
Great Heat	July 22th - July 24th
The Beginning of Autumn	August 7th - August 9th

Now comes the "Limit of Heat," when Harry's work seems repetitive and boring. Dissatisfaction sets in. His long commute to the office from home wears him down, and the benefits offered by AFR are less attractive than those offered by other companies. This is like the time of the "White Dew," when moisture appears on the grass in morning and one's footing may slip. Although Harry keeps working, he also considers leaving AFR.

Harry's realization that his work no longer excites or fulfills him comes like the "Autumn Equinox," when days and nights are equally long. His cooling attitude can then be represented by Trigram 2 (☵), Water:

The Limit of Heat	August 22th - August 24th
White Dew	September 7th - September 9th
The Autumn Equinox	September 22th - September 24th

After this stage, he works with less enthusiasm, like grass covered with the "Cold Dew." By the time he turns in his resignation, he is feeling the "Frost's Descent," when the smooth sailing is behind him and icy patches cover the road ahead.

When the process of negotiating his resignation starts, everyone at AFR hears that Harry will be leaving. Many coworkers give him a wide berth. This is like the "Beginning of Winter," when the world gets cold, represented by Trigram 1 (☶), Mountain:

Cold Dew	October 8th - October 9th
Frost's Descent	October 23th - October 24th
The Beginning of Winter	November 7th - November 8th

Harry's last days at AFR are like the time of the "Slight Snow," when all the doors and windows must be closed. Once he leaves the company, he enters the "Great Snow," when the road is covered with high drifts, vision is obscured, and driving becomes difficult. As Harry stays home without a job, he is once again plunged into the "Winter Solstice," when days are short and nights are long. His status can once more be represented by Trigram Ø (☷), Earth:

Slight Snow	November 22th - November 23th
Great Snow	December 6th - December 8th
The Winter Solstice	December 21th - December 23th

Although Harry might feel as if his world has come to a screeching halt, he is simply going through a natural process that will continue to evolve with or without his intervention.

6 Selecting Trigram

Choosing a trigram to match a specific human situation is the fastest way to consult Yi and is best suited to circumstances where the subject and object are in stages that can be recognized as part of the natural order. An example might be the beginning of a love affair, Trigram 4 (☳), Thunder; or the cooling of a friendship, Trigram 2 (☵), Water.

Regarding a particular situation, such as Harry's job at AFR, only one trigram represents each particular stage of the changing process. To determine which single trigram is most applicable, you must consider the entire process of development and then determine the trigram that best describes the stage of development at any given moment.

You might practise this method by comparing your own career to Harry's. Which trigram best applies to the point you have now reached in your own work? Does it feel like the beginning of spring, when you are embarking on a new venture or assignment? Or are you feeling the chill that sets in after you realize that you've been passed over for a promotion too many times? The first situation would best be characterized by Trigram 4 (☳), Thunder; and the second corresponds to Trigram 1 (☶), Mountain.

For example, Harry has been working at one job for a long time, so his performance is adequate because of his experience. He is not very interested in making changes. Which of the trigrams best describes this situation? Since he is doing the work very well because of his experience, but only doing what is required, following and yielding but not actively seeking change, the trigram that best captures his reality is the one for Wind (☴).

This is Trigram 3, which also corresponds to the "Beginning of Autumn" — so you can see that one method of selecting a trigram can be used to verify a selection arrived at by the other method.

How is the position of your career? Rising or declining? What is the prospect? Remember, to evaluate your current situation, you may use these two easy methods:

- *Compare the characteristic with the eight visual images.*
- *Determine the phase in a seasonal cycle.*

CHAPTER 5
Significance of the "Three Lines" in Trigram

Cathy wants to know what she should do about George, a married man who is interested in her. She is young, just out of college, and starting her career at a company where George is a senior executive. To answer her question, first, she needs to construct one trigram to define her situation within the relationship, and then construct another for George.

In the profound systematic language of Yi, every line of each trigram has a special significance that refers to a specific aspect of your life and links it to the cycle of change in the world. You will find that the process of learning to construct trigrams to define your own situation within relationships will help you understand your role in regard to others.

1 Bottom Line: Action

Let's consider the meaning of each line in a single trigram, which corresponds to a specific point in the cycle of seasonal change. If we turn the figure of the Eight Trigrams a half-space counterclockwise, bend the straight lines into arches, then make the yang lines black and the yin lines gray, we get the following figure:

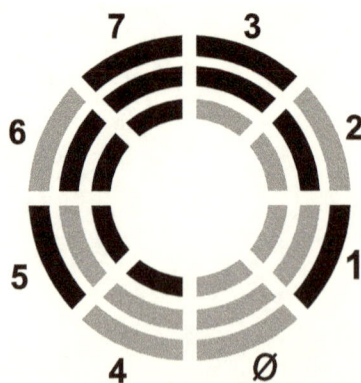

Figure 5.1: Lines in The Eight Trigrams

In this way of viewing the sequence, the inner ring represents the bottom lines of the trigrams. Let's concentrate just on that innermost ring for the moment. On the left side you see all yang lines (━); on the right side are yin lines (╍).

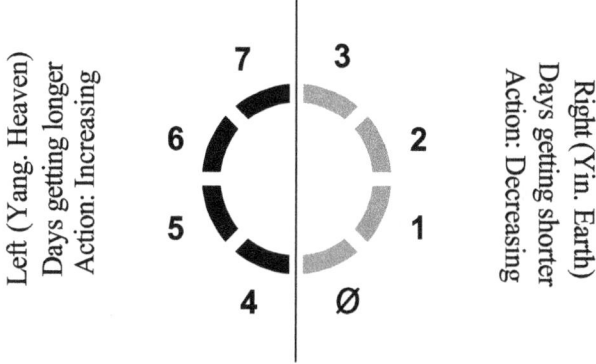

Trigram Bottom Lines

Figure 5.2: Significance of Bottom Lines

In a neat reflection of the simple sundial that the ancient Chinese created, the yang lines on the left represent the days getting longer, and yin lines on the right show days getting shorter. These bottom lines do not literally identify the exact length of the day but symbolize an action — the increase or decrease in the length of the day.

A yang line in the bottom position represents the action of heaven. Because heaven gives energy to the earth and, as perceived by the ancients, orbits the earth, the characteristics of a yang action may be active, offensive, aggressive, advancing, expanding, vigorous, or energetic. Since the earth receives energy from heaven and was believed to be standing still, a yin action, represented by a yin line at the bottom, may be passive, defensive, receding, contracting, stopping, or at rest.

Within the context of a relationship, yang action may refer to initiating, developing, or improving the bond. A yin action may refer to defending, waiting, hesitating, withdrawing from or ending the liaison. When we spoke of Harry's career in Chapter 4, his action was yang when he started a new job and improved in his work. When he lost interest in it, then resigned and left AFR, his action was yin.

2 Middle Line: Essence

Now concentrate only on the middle lines, which comprise the center ring of the eight trigrams.

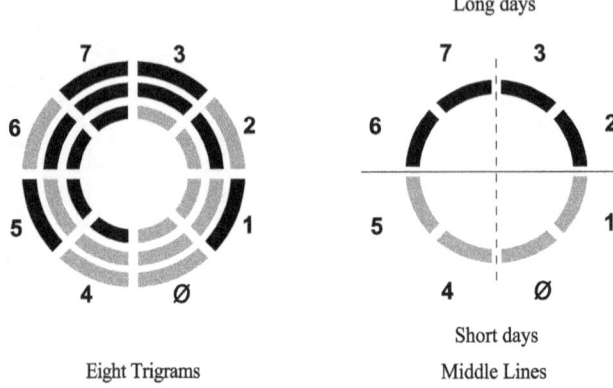

Figure 5.3: Mirror Image of Middle Lines

The lines to the left of the vertical axis are a mirror image of the lines on the right, but those on either side of the horizontal axis are in opposition. In trigrams 6 (☵), 7 (☶), 3 (☳), and 2 (☲), all the middle lines are yang lines (—), representing the time of year when the days are long. In trigrams 1 (☴), Ø (☷), 4 (☵), and 5 (☶), all the middle lines are yin lines (- -) representing the time of year when the days are short. A yang line in the middle position of a trigram denotes a long day, and a yin line indicates a short day.

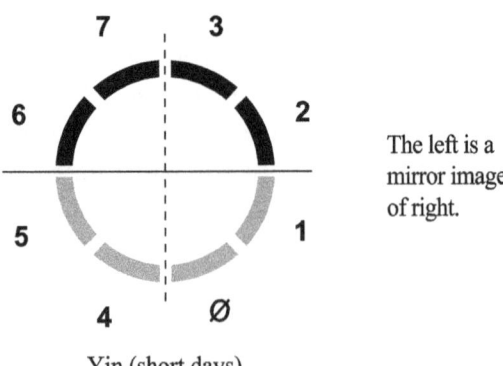

Figure 5.4: Significance of Middle Lines

The middle line of a trigram represents the essential nature, or essence, of a thing or person. A yang essence represents the traits of heaven. Since heaven has great power and strength, a yang essence indicates power and strength. Compared to heaven, the earth has less power and strength, but it is a wellspring for living things whose environment converts heaven's energy into nurturing food. A yin essence represents the traits of the earth, which are not as powerful or strong as heaven's, but are adaptable to the environment and have the potential for supporting and nurturing others.

In regard to a relationship, a yang essence suggests good character, good health, wealth, education, financial strength, sufficient information, and so on. A yin essence refers to undeveloped potential ability: a weak body, insufficient finances, a lack of information, etc.

Note that this essence must be considered in reference to a particular relationship, not to a person, in general. Good personal character, robust health, or wealth may be a yang essence vital in one relationship but may not be significant in another situation. In a relationship, a yang essence usually indicates the person who is in the stronger position, and a yin essence indicates the weaker status. In this way, a confident, well-off athlete who is pining away for a woman who doesn't care for him would have a yin essence in their relationship, regardless of his hardy personal qualities.

Consider Harry's situations during his career at AFR. In the stages represented by trigrams 6 (☱), 7 (☰), 3 (☳), and 2 (☷), he was competent in his work and dedicated to his job; he was respected and promoted. In these instances his essence was yang. In the stages represented by trigrams 1 (☵), Ø (☷), 4 (☶), and 5 (☲), he was either out of work, inexperienced at his new job, or tired of his old job. Through these stages he was still Harry — smart, well educated, and competent — but these characteristics were in a potential form, not apparent in his situation. At these stages his essence was yin.

3 Top Line: Attitude

Finally we come to the outer ring of the eight trigrams, which consists of the top lines of the eight trigrams.

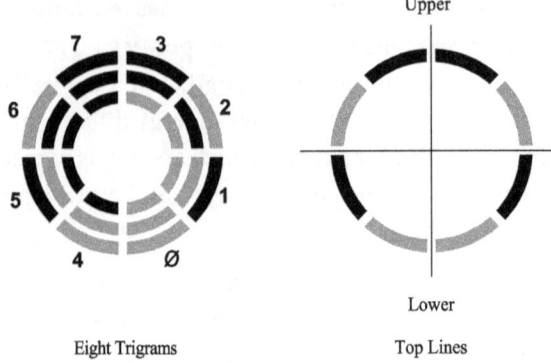

Figure 5.5: Mirror Image of the Top Lines

You see that the arrangement of the top lines on the left of the vertical axis is a mirror image of the top lines on the right; on either side of the horizontal axis, they oppose each other. That arrangement is similar to the configuration of the middle lines, but here the top lines alternate between yin and yang in every quarter of the circle.

Where the middle line of a trigram dictates whether the day is long or short, the top line augments this information by telling us whether the day is the longest, the shortest, or in between, as shown below.

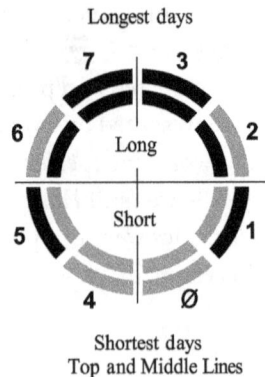

Figure 5.6: Significance of Top Lines

When the day is long, as determined by a yang middle line, a yang line on top identifies it as the longest day; a yin line on the top indicates the day is long, but not the longest. When the day is short, signified by a yin middle line, a second yin line on top tells you it is the shortest. A yang top line indicates the day is short but not the shortest.

The top line of a trigram represents a feature that is not essential; it further defines a unique nature by providing nuance. When a trigram represents a person in a relationship, this nature refers to his or her attitude.

A yang attitude represents the supplementary quality of heaven — hot, bright, remote, unpredictable, and mysterious. A yin attitude represents the supplementary characteristics of earth — stable, gentle, graceful, tangible, kind, and subordinate.

In terms of a relationship, a yang attitude can be tough, vacillating, arrogant, reckless, demanding, bossy, firm, and so on. A yin attitude might be agreeable, humble, stable, graceful, gentle, introverted, quiet, kind, open, respectful, or flexible.

Again, keep in mind that the attitude must be viewed in reference to a particular relationship. A person may be dominant in one relationship but humble in another situation. You may be naturally very aggressive, but in circumstances where you are less sure of yourself, your attitude can be yin.

We have seen the different stages of Harry's work at AFR. In the figure below, notice on the left the arrangement of the top lines, and on the right the Eight Trigrams rotated a half-space counterclockwise for comparison. The top lines of trigrams 5, 7, 3, and 1 are yang lines (▬).

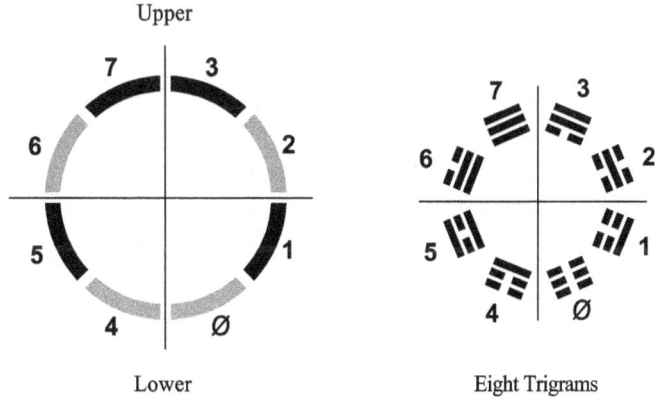

Figure 5.7: Top Lines & Eight Trigrams

In the Spring Equinox season represented by Trigram 5 (☲), Fire, Harry was displaying his talent and education. At Trigram 7 (☰), Heaven, he was bossy because of his higher position and at Trigram 3 (☴), Wind, he was not actively seeking change because he was arrogant, assessing his own job performance as superior, or complacent about his success. At Trigram 1 (☶), Mountain, he was bold in his decision to resign from AFR. In these four very different stages, his attitude was yang.

Now look at the other points of Harry's time with AFR: The top lines of trigram 4, 6, 2, and Ø are all yin (- -). At Trigram 4 (☳), Thunder, he was just beginning the job and uncertain about how well he would do; at Trigram 6 (☱), Lake, he received an important promotion and was modestly trying his best. At Trigram 2 (☵), Water, he was unenthusiastic about his work, and with the return of Trigram Ø (☷), he once more became humble and flexible in hunting for a new job. In these four stages, his attitude was yin.

4 The Personal Trigrams in Reality

When a trigram represents a person, its three lines represent his or her three aspects: action, essence, and attitude. A trigram representing a person is constructed from the bottom up, by identifying the yin or yang nature of each of the three aspects.

Remember that each of these three aspects is determined in reference to the relationship about which you are consulting the Yi. Action refers to what the person is doing for the relationship. Essence describes what kind of person he or she is within the boundaries of this relationship. Attitude is the way he or she is dealing with others in the relationship.

When constructing a trigram, you must evaluate each of the three aspects according to the facts. Once you have accurately evaluated the circumstances, the three lines are identified as yin or yang, and the trigram is built.

Aware that George has noticed her, Cathy hopes that he can help her get ahead at the company, and she approaches him to ask for his help with a presentation on which she's working. This action is yang, so the bottom line of Cathy's trigram is yang.

Because she is immature and inexperienced, Cathy is socially awkward in contrast to George's smooth confidence, and she has little power in the workplace where his status is secure. So her essence is yin, as represented by a yin middle line in her trigram.

When Cathy approaches George, she is careful to come across as polite and respectful. She knows that George can help her, but he might misunderstand or take advantage of her boldness in coming forward. So her attitude is tentative and cautious, represented by a yin top line.

So the trigram representing Cathy's situation is Trigram 4 (☳), Thunder.

Now let us consider the other side of the relationship; i.e., George's role. Since he is attracted to Cathy and made the first move to show his interest, his action is yang. He is a leader in the organization where Cathy works and derives power from his position, so his essence is yang. When Cathy approaches him, she finds that he is demanding and arrogant, with an attitude that is decidedly yang. This evaluation results in the trigram representing George's situation, which is Trigram 7 (☰), Heaven.

In Chapter 8, "Changes," we will discover whether or not a relationship with George would be advantageous for Cathy. For now, remember that in building these trigrams we are evaluating Cathy and George in relationship to each other and within the context of their workplace. If they met elsewhere — at the beach, for instance, where Cathy wears a bathing suit with confidence and George is an out-of-shape older man sitting on a blanket with his wife and children — the dynamics of their relationship would be very different, and other aspects of their personalities might dominate the situation. For the beach scenario, we would evaluate their actions, essences, and attitudes accordingly, and very different trigrams would result.

The key to building trigrams lies in the ability to make a correct assessment of the parties involved, without exaggeration or wishful thinking. Remember, a trigram is only as accurate as the honesty of your input.

Keep in mind the role of the three lines in relationship:

- *Bottom line represents action*
- *Middle line represents essence*
- *Top line represents attitude*

CHAPTER 6
Hexagram

NANCY IS VERY INTERESTED IN a work colleague named John. Nancy is an intelligent, well-educated woman who has a graceful way with others. Working with her is a pleasure for her colleagues. Her situation can be best expressed by Trigram 6 (☱), Lake.

John is a strong man with a good job, modest in his dealings with people, but timid about becoming involved with Nancy, as if a relationship with her might involve danger and difficulty. His situation can be expressed by Trigram 2 (☵), Water.

These two trigrams can form two hexagrams: Hexagram 6:2 (䷼) and Hexagram 2:6 (䷻). What is the difference in their significances?

1 Subject Trigram and Object Trigram

Gaining guidance in a relationship involves your creating two trigrams: one for the person or subject posing the question, and the other one for the person known as the object. The hexagram that describes this relationship represents the current situation from the point of view of the subject. Once constructed, these two trigrams are stacked to create a hexagram.

The subject trigram represents the one who asks for help from the Yi and to whom the judgments refer; so your hexagram consists of a subject trigram in the lower position and an object trigram on top, just like in the sentence, "I love you", where the subject "I" is ahead of the object "you". The ID number of the hexagram is the combination of the ID numbers of the two component trigrams. For example, if the subject trigram is 3 and the object trigram is 2, the ID number of the hexagram is 3:2, as illustrated below:

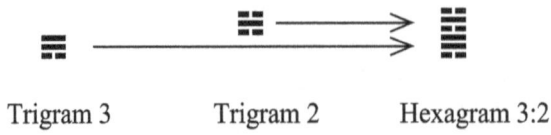

Trigram 3   Trigram 2   Hexagram 3:2

Figure 6.1: Formation of hexagram 3:2

The subject trigram must be in the lower position of the hexagram and the object trigram is on top.

The hexagram representing the relationship between Nancy and John from Nancy's point of view is Hexagram 6:2 (䷇). When we read the text associated with the Hexagram 6:2, we must remember that a favorable judgment means that this relationship or situation is favorable only to the subject, Nancy, and may or may not be favorable to the object, John.

When Nancy builds a trigram to describe John's side of the relationship, she is using the facts apparent to her to evaluate his action, essence, and attitude: when she asked him to a party, he turned her down, and when they happened to be walking in the same direction, he avoided falling into step with her. So she decides that his action line is yin.

She gives him a yang middle line for his essence, because he is a tall, strong man with a good job as manager of a large store. He never boasts about himself and listens patiently and carefully to others, so for his attitude line she decides on yin. So the hexagram representing the relationship from Nancy's point of view is based on the facts as she sees them.

This subjective viewpoint is all-important in putting together the hexagram. Do you remember the story in Chapter 5 of Cathy, the young career woman, and George, the older married executive? In that example, Cathy wanted to know how to deal with this powerful man at work who was interested in her. In the hexagram Cathy built, she was the subject, and George was the object. After evaluating her own action, essence, and attitude, and then evaluating the same aspects for George, Cathy arrived at Hexagram 4:7, as shown below, representing their current relationship from her point of view:

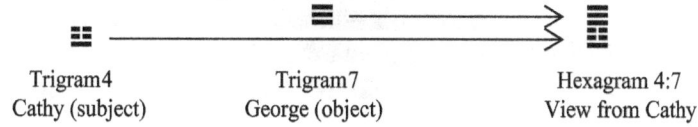

Trigram 4　　　　Trigram 7　　　　Hexagram 4:7
Cathy (subject)　George (object)　View from Cathy

Figure 6.2: Formation of Hexagram 4:7

But what if George were the one building the hexagram because he wanted to know how to deal with this beautiful young female employee? Then he would be the subject, and Cathy the object. Assuming that his evaluation of their situation is the same that Cathy came up with, his hexagram would be a reversal of hers, Hexagram 7:4, as shown below.

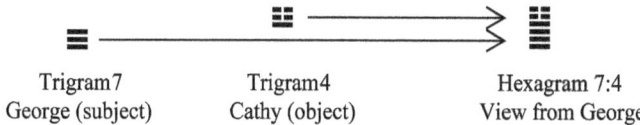

Trigram 7　　　　Trigram 4　　　　Hexagram 7:4
George (subject)　Cathy (object)　View from George

Figure 6.3: Formation of Hexagram 7:4

Actually, since two people rarely view their mutual situation in the same light, it would be very unusual for both individuals to select the same two trigrams. But this example serves to illustrate the importance of position in subject and object trigrams.

The structure and meaning for Hexagram 4:7, Innocence — Cathy's situation with George — are shown below:

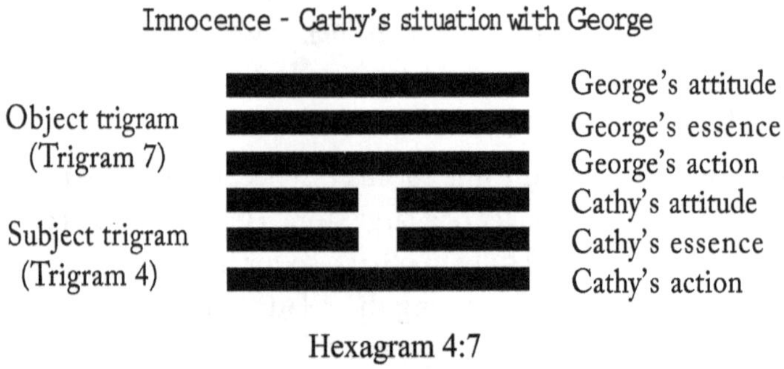

Innocence - Cathy's situation with George

Object trigram (Trigram 7) — George's attitude / George's essence / George's action

Subject trigram (Trigram 4) — Cathy's attitude / Cathy's essence / Cathy's action

Hexagram 4:7

Figure 6.4: Hexagram, from Cathy's view

And here are the structure and meaning for Hexagram 7:4, Reckless, describing George's situation with Cathy:

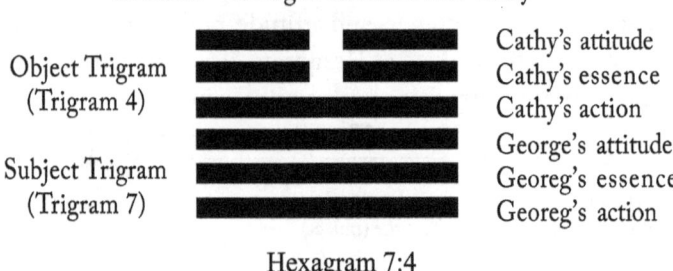

Reckless - George's situation with Cathy

Object Trigram (Trigram 4) — Cathy's attitude / Cathy's essence / Cathy's action

Subject Trigram (Trigram 7) — George's attitude / Georeg's essence / Georeg's action

Hexagram 7:4

Figure 6.5: Hexagram from George's view

The title of the hexagram provides a quick profile of the current situation and its prospects, and you can see at once from the titles "Innocence" and "Reckless" that the same situation can be dramatically different from each person's perspective. In Cathy's case, the word innocence implies mistakes she might make because of her lack of experience. In George's case, his hexagram's title warns that he might abuse his power and do something careless that could result in great loss for either or both of them.

[2] Titles of Hexagrams

As soon as you build your hexagram, consider the meaning of its unique title. The table below lists the titles of the sixty-four hexagrams:

ID	SIGN	TITLE	ID	SIGN	TITLE
0:0	☷	Earth	0:1		Deprivation
0:2		Closeness	0:3		Watching
0:4		Delight	0:5		Promotion
0:6		Gathering	0:7		Denial
1:0		Modest	1:1		Stop
1:2		Lame	1:3		Gradual
1:4		Tolerance	1:5		Travel
1:6		Enjoyable	1:7		Flee
2:0		Army	2:1		Ignorance
2:2		Pitfall	2:3		Flood
2:4		Solution	2:5		Imperfect
2:6		Adversity	2:7		Sue
3:0		Rising	3:1		Bugs
3:2		Well	3:3		Yield
3:4		Persistence	3:5		Cauldron
3:6		Overburden	3:7		Encounter
4:0		Return	4:1		Care
4:2		Prospect	4:3		Gain
4:4		Shock	4:5		Bite
4:6		Follow	4:7		Innocence

ID	SIGN	TITLE	ID	SIGN	TITLE
5:0		Hurt	5:1		Ornament
5:2		Perfect	5:3		Matriarch
5:4		Totality	5:5		Brightness
5:6		Change	5:7		Coalition
6:0		Approach	6:1		Loss
6:2		Limitation	6:3		Sincerity
6:4		Marry	6:5		Stare
6:6		Pleasure	6:7		Treading
7:0		Peace	7:1		Build Up
7:2		Expectation	7:3		Accumulation
7:4		Reckless	7:5		Acquisition
7:6		Menace	7:7		Heaven

3 Importance of ID number of Hexagram

Why is the positioning of the two trigrams so important in leading to the correct interpretation and decision? Because, just as trigrams are numbers, hexagrams are also numbers, and Yi is a mathematical system for plotting the human condition and laws of nature. You can glimpse a bit of the pattern when you turn Hexagram 6:4 clockwise to its horizontal position, as shown below:

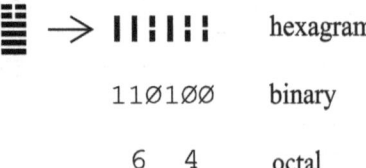

       110100 binary

       6 4   octal

Figure 6.6: Hexagram, binary number and octal number

This Yi style of ID numbers for hexagrams — using an octal, or base-eight system — is used throughout this book. To clearly indicate that a hexagram consists of two trigrams, there is a ":" between the two digits, as in Hexagram 6:4, not hexagram 64.

Hexagram

[4] Conversion from ID numbers to serial number in Zhou Yi

Nine centuries ago, Shao Yong arranged the sixty-four hexagrams in an array as shown in the following diagram. This hexagram array is attached with ID numbers of subject trigrams in the first column at right, ID numbers of object trigrams in the first row on top, and Zhou Yi (A version of Yi formatted in the time of King Wen, in the twelfth century B.C.) serial numbers in parentheses under the symbols of hexagrams.

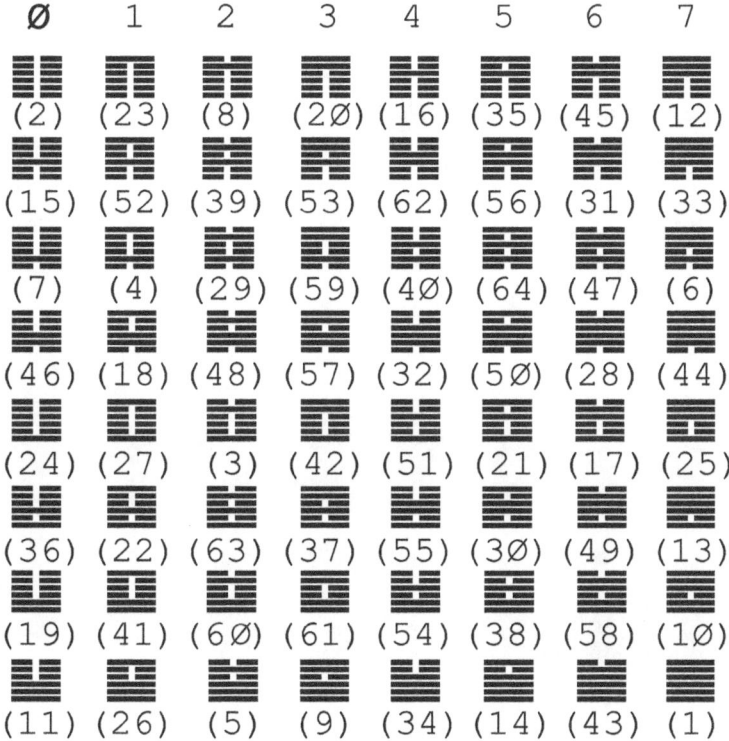

Figure 6.7: Conversion from ID number to Zhou Yi serial number

You may use the diagram above to find the shape of a hexagram and its serial number in Zhou Yi. For example, if you want to know Hexagram 6:4, the ID number of its subject trigram is 6. The ID number of its object trigram is 4. In the row 6, column 4, there is the symbol of Hexagram 6:4, ▦. It is Hexagram 54 (54 is the serial number in Zhou Yi). And for Hexagram 4:6, go to row 4, column 6: Its symbol is ▦. It is Hexagram 17 (Zhou Yi).

If you get a hexagram from other publications, it is very easy to find its ID number used in this book. For example, Hexagram 64 is the last hexagram in Zhou Yi. Its shape is ▦. The subject trigram is ▦. Its ID number is 2. The object trigram is ☵. Its ID number is 5. The two ID numbers together with a colon between become 2:5. So the ID number of Hexagram 64 is 2:5. "2:5" indicates that the hexagram consists of Trigram 2 and Trigram 5, while "64" indicates this hexagram is the last one in the Zhou Yi sequence.

Hexagram Array (of Sixty-four Hexagrams) is also used in Part II. The translation of the Yi text of hexagrams is in the order of the Hexagram Array, starting with Hexagram Ø:Ø, Earth, and ending in Hexagram 7:7, Heaven.

Now you know how to make hexagrams to represent your current situations. Remember:

- *Subject trigram is on the bottom*
- *Object trigram is on the top*

CHAPTER 7
Analysis of Structure of Hexagrams

NOW THAT YOU KNOW HOW to construct a hexagram in response to your question, you'll want to learn if your hexagram is favorable, unfavorable, or neutral in regard to the relationship.

The truth is that, like most situations in life, most of the sixty-four hexagrams are neutral, a rich mixture of good and bad. Some are notable exceptions: the four hexagrams favorable to the subject (you) are those where two complementary trigrams are in harmony; the less favorable ones consist of trigrams that are complementary but not in harmony.

In Yi, as in life, harmony is everything. For our purpose, harmony between the trigrams is contingent on three realities:

1. The two sides are complementary, meaning one side is yin and the other side is yang.
2. The two sides interact with each other.
3. The initiator of the interaction — the peacemaker described in Chapter 3 — is the subject.

Remember the example of the female police officer and the male drunk driver from Chapter 3? Looking at the situation from the point of view of the police officer — where she is the subject, and the drunk driver is the object, you can see that the situation passes these three tests for harmony:

1. She and the driver have complementary roles, with the officer as yang, having authority and power, and the driver as yin, being guilty and acquiescing.
2. They interact with each other; had they been driving on different highways, the situation would not have arisen.
3. The subject is the peacemaker by virtue of spotting and confronting the drunk driver. So the situation is in harmony and favorable to the police officer. She has fulfilled her mission.

Now consider the situation from the point of view of the drunk driver, where he becomes the subject and the female police officer is the object.

- Their roles are still complementary; he is yin and she is yang.
- The two sides interact with each other.

- The subject is not the initiator of the interaction, so the situation is not in harmony and is highly unfavorable to the drunk driver.

1 Special Hexagrams

To assist with your understanding of the rule of harmony, let's look at eight special hexagrams formed from the four diagonal pairs of the Eight Trigrams:

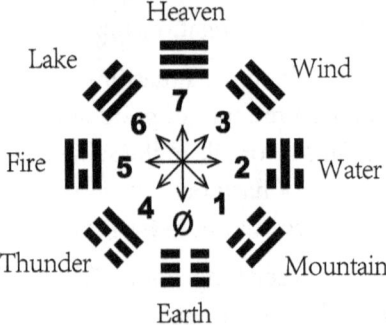

Figure 7.1: Eight special hexagrams

The ID numbers of the eight special hexagrams are 5:2 and 2:5, 6:1 and 1:6, 7:Ø and Ø:7, and 4:3 and 3:4. Notice that in every case, the sum of the two digits of the ID numbers is 7.

1 Hexagrams 5:2 and 2:5

At the left of the figure below is Hexagram 5:2, Perfect.

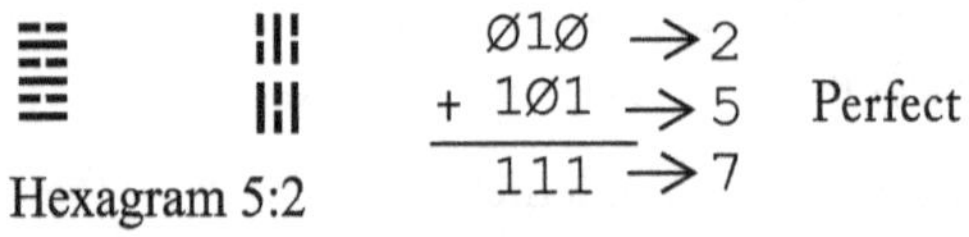

$$\begin{array}{c} \text{Hexagram 5:2} \end{array} \quad \begin{array}{r} Ø1Ø \rightarrow 2 \\ +\ 1Ø1 \rightarrow 5 \\ \hline 111 \rightarrow 7 \end{array} \quad \text{Perfect}$$

Figure 7.2: Hexagram 5:2, Perfect

Its lower part is Trigram 5 ( ), Fire, the subject; its upper part is Trigram 2 ( ), Water, the object. If you rotate the trigrams clockwise to a horizontal position, you will see that all three pairs of corresponding lines are complementary — couples matching yin to yang, or yang to yin. For example, look at the lines on the left. The top left is broken, and the bottom left is solid. The same is true for the lines on the right. The center lines are also complementary: the top is solid, the bottom broken.

Now look at the interaction between the two sides. When fire is near a container of water, the water is heated, and energy can be produced in the form of steam. Fire, the subject, is the peacemaker, by heating water, the object. So Hexagram 5:2, Perfect, is in harmony and favorable to the subject, which turns its energy into production.

Its mirror image is Hexagram 2:5, Imperfect, shown below:

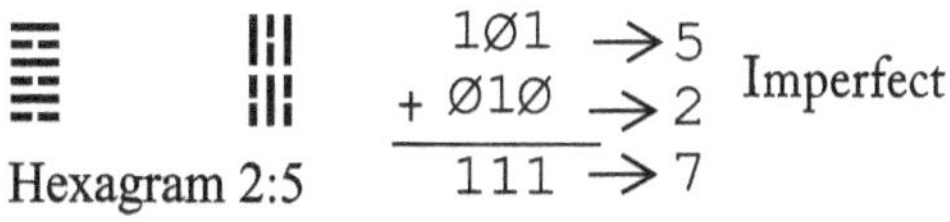

$$\begin{array}{r} 1\emptyset1 \to 5 \\ + \;\emptyset1\emptyset \to 2 \\ \hline 111 \to 7 \end{array}$$ Imperfect

Hexagram 2:5

Figure 7.3: Hexagram 2:5, Imperfect

This time, in Hexagram 2:5, water is now the subject, and it cannot initiate the interaction. If water pours onto fire, either the water itself vanishes or the fire is extinguished. So Hexagram 2:5, Imperfect, is not in harmony.

2 Hexagrams 7:Ø and Ø:7

Hexagram 7:Ø, Peace, combines Trigram 7, Heaven, and Trigram Ø, Earth:

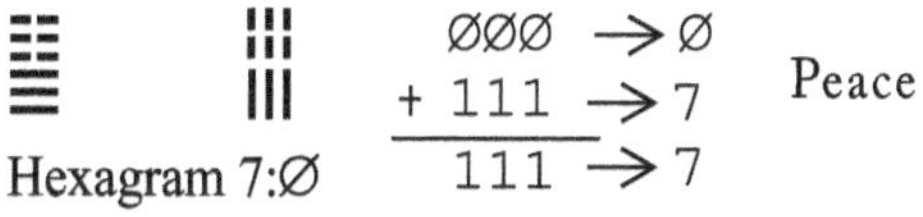

$$\begin{array}{r} \emptyset\emptyset\emptyset \to \emptyset \\ + \;111 \to 7 \\ \hline 111 \to 7 \end{array}$$ Peace

Hexagram 7:Ø

Figure 7.4: Hexagram 7:Ø, Peace

Heaven, the subject, initiates the interaction by lighting and warming the earth. So Hexagram 7:Ø, Peace, is in harmony and is favorable to the subject, which donates its energy.

Now look at the reverse situation, in Hexagram Ø:7, Denial:

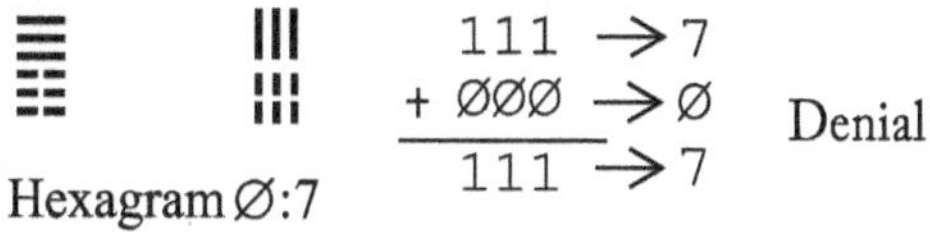

$$\begin{array}{r} 111 \to 7 \\ + \;\emptyset\emptyset\emptyset \to \emptyset \\ \hline 111 \to 7 \end{array}$$ Denial

Hexagram Ø:7

Figure 7.5: Hexagram Ø:7, Denial

Earth, which is the subject, receives energy passively and cannot initiate an interaction with heaven. This hexagram is not in harmony, even though its two component trigrams are complementary.

3 Hexagrams 1:6 and 6:1

Hexagram 1:6, Enjoyable, combines Trigram 1, Mountain, with Trigram 6, Lake:

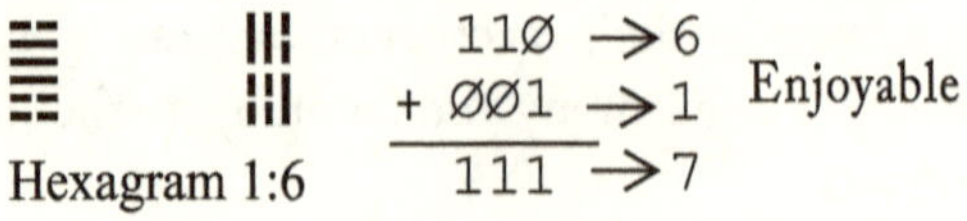

```
            ☳        11∅ → 6
Hexagram 1:6  ☶    + ∅∅1 → 1   Enjoyable
                     111 → 7
```

Figure 7.6: Hexagram 1:6, Enjoyable

The mountain is a source or barrier for water and maintains a stable level of water in the lake, so the hexagram is in harmony and favorable.

But with Hexagram 6:1, Loss, the lake cannot initiate an interaction with the mountain:

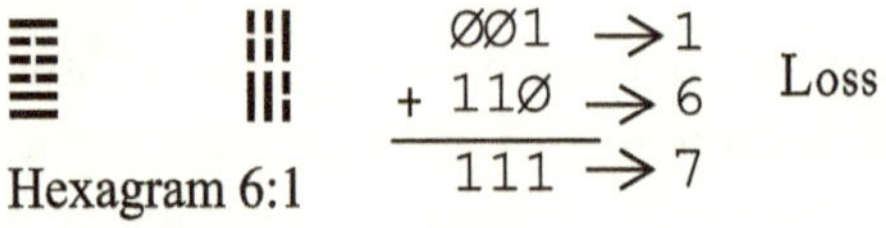

```
            ☶        ∅∅1 → 1
Hexagram 6:1  ☳    + 11∅ → 6   Loss
                     111 → 7
```

Figure 7.7: Hexagram 6:1, Loss

4 Hexagrams 4:3 and 3:4

Hexagram 4:3, Gain, combines Trigram 4, Thunder, with Trigram 3, Wind. It is favorable because, as the ancients experienced it, its harmony stems from the initiation of the subject, Thunder, heralding the beginning of the storm and causing the wind to blow.

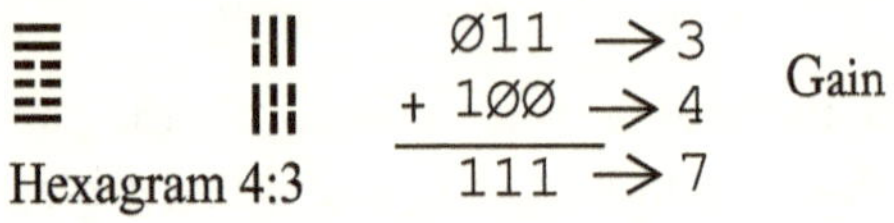

```
            ☳        ∅11 → 3
Hexagram 4:3  ☴    + 1∅∅ → 4   Gain
                     111 → 7
```

Figure 7.8: Hexagram 4:3, Gain

The last of the special hexagrams is Hexagram 3:4, Persistence, where Wind cannot have an effect on the Thunder no matter how long or hard it blows:

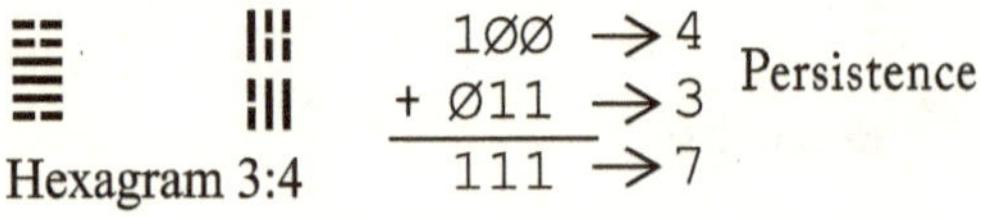

```
            ☴        1∅∅ → 4
Hexagram 3:4  ☳    + ∅11 → 3   Persistence
                     111 → 7
```

Figure 7.9: Hexagram 3:4, Persistence

Hexagram 3:4, alone among the eight special hexagrams, can be considered neutral, neither favorable nor unfavorable, as suggested by its title "Persistence." Sometimes persistence is futile and wasteful; at other times it can be admirable and wise.

2 Complementary Lines

Of the eight hexagrams discussed above, half are clearly favorable because they are in harmony. The other half are unfavorable or neutral because they are not in harmony, though their component trigrams are complementary. The neutrality of most of the sixty-four hexagrams is illustrated by their titles listed in Chapter 5.

As you work with Yi, you will come to appreciate the rich interplay between the numerical values of trigrams and hexagrams, and the symbolic relationships of the elements they represent — for instance, Fire and Mountain or Wind and Earth. While the eight special hexagrams have symbolic interactions that are easy to spot due to their obvious complementary nature, the other fifty-six hexagrams require a line-by-line analysis.

As you study the lines of a hexagram to determine its harmony, you will consider the situations of the lines in the hexagram as complementary lines

If the two corresponding lines of the two component trigrams are yin with yang, or yang with yin, they are complementary; if the corresponding lines are both yin lines or both yang lines, they are in conflict with each other. Usually, complementary lines are favorable. In the diagram below, brackets indicate the complementary lines for the eight special hexagrams discussed above.

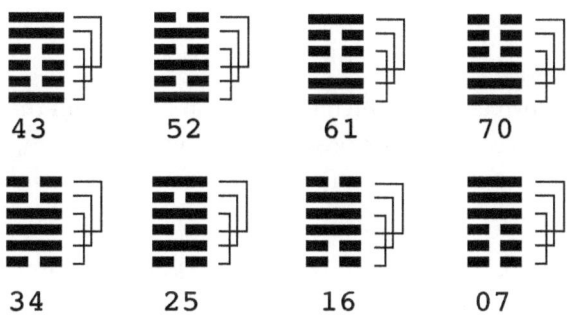

Figure 7.10: The Complementary Lines

3 Correctness of Positions

In a hexagram, the positions of lines 1, 3, and 5 are considered to be yang positions, and lines 2, 4, and 6 are the yin positions. If a yang line (▬) is in a yang position or a yin line (▬ ▬) is in a yin position, that line is correctly positioned. But if a yang line (▬) is in a yin position or a yin line (▬ ▬) is in a yang position, that line is incorrectly positioned.

Since Hexagram 5:2, shown below, demonstrates perfect harmony, it is used as a template for the correct position of lines.

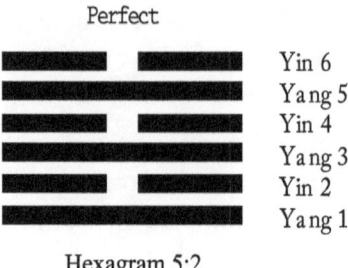

Figure 7.11: The correct position of lines

By contrast, in Hexagram 2:5 all the lines are incorrect, as shown below in gray.

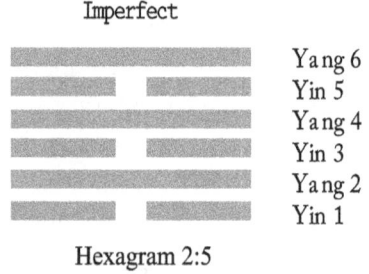

Figure 7.12: All the lines are incorrect

Normally the correct lines, which I indicate in black from this point forward for your ease of recognition, are favorable. The incorrect lines, in gray, are unfavorable.

4 The Central Lines Correct and Complementary

Lines 2 and 5 are the middle lines of each of the trigrams that make up a hexagram. When the central lines are correct and complementary, such as yin 2 (━ ━) and yang 5 (━━━) of Hexagram 5:2, ☷, it is very favorable.

5 Supporting or Suppressing

The relationship between a particular line and its adjacent lines, directly above and below, is important for you to know. In general, when a yin line and a yang line are together, the situation favors the side represented by the yang line and does not favor the side represented by the yin line.

So if a yang line (━━━) is above a yin line (━ ━), the yang line (━━━) is supported by the yin line (━ ━), as shown on the left of the following figure. This definitely favors the yang line and may or may not be good for the yin line.

supporting　　　suppressing

Figure 7.13: Adjacent lines

When a yin line (- -) is above a yang line (—), the yin line (- -) is suppressing the yang line (—). This is not especially favorable or unfavorable for the yang line, but it is definitely unfavorable for the yin line.

When looking at the relationships between yin and yang lines in a hexagram, this analogy might prove helpful: Think about the relative positions in a group of coworkers. If a manager has strong business experience and the assistant is less knowledgeable, then the manager oversees and protects the assistant. This support relationship is like a yin line under a yang line.

We easily comprehend how the support relationship benefits the manager, but its effect on the assistant depends on how the assistant behaves. If the assistant follows instructions and works hard, the reward could be a bonus or promotion. The incompetent assistant of a powerful manager could just as easily be disciplined or fired, however. So which will it be? Yi resolves this dilemma by determining whether the supporting yin line is in a correct or incorrect position: If correct, the situation is favorable for the yin line; if incorrect, the situation is unfavorable.

Anyone who has spent time in the business world has also witnessed a suppressing relationship — when the manager is less competent than the staff. Even when the staff is very capable, the manager will still fail. A suppressing relationship, when a yin line is above a yang line. This relationship is unfavorable to the yin line.

What about the yang staff being suppressed by the weak manager? These workers' position is neutral. The company may fire the manager, but the competent yang staff will survive the change. In other words, when a yang line is under a yin line, the situation is neither favorable nor unfavorable to the yang line. When yin gets in the way of yang, yang is able to persevere.

Now that you know how to analyze the positions of lines as they relate to each other within a hexagram, you are ready to resolve the questions posed by Cathy in relation to George.

6 Analysis of hexagrams for Relationship

You'll remember that the relationship between Cathy and George, from her point of view, was described by Hexagram 4:7, Innocence:

Innocence

```
7 ▬▬▬
  ▬ ▬
  ▬▬▬ ⎤
  ▬▬▬ ⎦
  ▬ ▬
4 ▬▬▬
```

Figure 7.14: From Cathy's view

When you look at the general structure of this hexagram, you'll notice two pairs of complementary lines — the top lines of each trigram and the middle line of each trigram are complementary. There are also three correct lines: yang 1 (▬), yin 2 (▬ ▬), and yang 5 (▬). The two middle lines are central, correct, and complementary. These are favorable to the subject, Cathy.

On the other hand, the two bottom lines, both yang, conflict with each other, and there are three incorrect lines, yin 3 (▬ ▬), yang 4 (▬), and yang 6 (▬). These are unfavorable to Cathy.

Can you see that this potential office flirtation is a complicated mixture of harmony and discord, a far cry from the clear-cut special hexagrams discussed at the beginning of this chapter?

Now look line by line at Hexagram 4:7. Yang 1 is a correct line, implying that when Cathy approaches George as a young employee seeking help from him, she is right to do so. But this line conflicts with George's action line, yang 4 (▬), implying if Cathy acts too aggressively, problems could result.

Yin 2 (▬ ▬) indicates Cathy's essential inexperience. It is central, in a correct position and complementary to yang 5. This suggests that George's relative power and knowledge can be helpful to her. Notice, however, that this line suppresses yang 1 (▬), implying that if she acts too aggressively, it could damage her essence.

Yin 3 (▬ ▬) is complementary to yang 6 (▬) but incorrect in position, implying that Cathy's attitude to George should be polite and respectful but not overly submissive. Already Cathy can see that she must strike a delicate balance, approaching George without too much assertiveness or too much deference.

In George's trigram, yang 4 (▬) is incorrect in position and conflicts with Cathy's yang 1 (▬). Because he is married, George noticing Cathy is not in her best interests. Yang 5 (▬) is central, correct, and complementary to yin 2 (▬ ▬), implying that George's experience and power are favorable for Cathy. Yang 6 (▬) is complementary to yin 3 (▬ ▬) but incorrect in position, which implies that George's confident attitude poses a danger for Cathy.

This line analysis of Cathy's relationship with George shows clearly that the benefit for her lies in the older man's business experience and that, as a mentor, he can prove helpful to her career. She must, however, be careful to balance this potential against the hazards of any romantic involvement, where she is clearly at a disadvantage. She would be wise to keep their friendship respectful and strictly businesslike.

Now consider Hexagram 7:4 — the exact same situation but from George's point of view.

Figure 7.15: From George's View

This relationship is also a mixed situation for George. We see two pairs of complementary lines and three correct lines, yang 1 (▬), yang 3 (▬), and yin 6 (▬ ▬). The current situation is not bad for George, but if he handles the relationship recklessly, problems could result.

Yang 1 (▬) is correct in position but conflicts with yang 4 (▬), implying that George is right to take notice of Cathy, but he should not rush into things. Yang 2 (▬) is complementary to yin 5 (▬ ▬) but is incorrect in position: George's experience and power might prove helpful to Cathy but pose a drawback for him. Yang 3 (▬) is complementary to yin 6 (▬ ▬) and in a correct position; his confidence will serve him well.

As for Cathy's place in George's life, her action line, yang 4 (▬), is incorrect in position and conflicts with yang 1 (▬); her determination to approach him is not favorable. Yin 5 (▬ ▬) is complementary to yang 2 (▬) but is incorrect in position, implying Cathy's inexperience is not helpful to him. Yin 6 (▬ ▬) is complementary with yang 3 (▬) and is in a correct position, suggesting that if Cathy behaves respectfully, their interaction will benefit both of them. Perhaps Cathy will prove an apt student and evolve into a valuable employee for their corporation. Her success could reflect well on George, who has served as her mentor.

Line analyses of both of these hexagrams shows that Cathy has something to gain from George — career advancement — while George can look forward to Cathy's respect and gratitude. But carelessness on his part or aggressiveness on hers might cause him to exploit her youth and inexperience and would be disastrous for them both.

From the example above, you see the role of harmony is important in a relationship. Remember, to know if your hexagram is favorable, unfavorable, or neutral in regard to the topic you're investigating, you must check:

- *Are the corresponding lines complementary?*

- Are the lines positioned correctly?
- Are the yang lines supported by the yin lines?

CHAPTER 8
Changes

I F YOU KNOW WHAT IS going to happen in a constantly changing world, you will be able to make an appropriate life strategy. The last chapter explained how to look at a hexagram and determine whether the current situation is favorable, neutral, or unfavorable to the subject. This chapter shows you what kinds of change are manageable and what kinds follow the natural order.

Alterations in any of a hexagram's six lines will result in a new hexagram that represents the changed situation. The lines that change are called significant lines, and the resulting hexagram is called a consequential hexagram.

For our example, we'll look again at Hexagram 4:7, Innocence, which represents the situation of Cathy's relationship with George. What if her career ambitions prompted her to seek George's help boldly, and George limited himself to the mentor's role? If Cathy's attitude were to change from yin to yang by her assertiveness, while George changed both his action and attitude from yang to yin by responding to her advances in a passive and gentle manner, the consequential hexagram is Hexagram 5:2, Perfect, shown below:

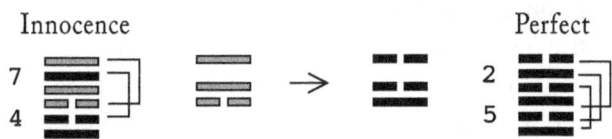

Figure 8.1: The Consequential Hexagram, Perfect

Yin 3 (**- -**) of Hexagram 4:7, which represents Cathy's attitude, changes to yang 3 (**—**) of Hexagram 5:2. Yang 4 (**—**) and yang 6 (**—**) of Hexagram 4:7, which represent George's current action and attitude, change to yin 4 (**- -**) and yin 6 (**- -**) of Hexagram 5:2.

Remember this important fact when interpreting the hexagrams of Yi: Any hexagram can change to any one of the other sixty-three hexagrams infinite times; no limitation exists to the number of changes. The subject can always choose to push the favorable changes and avoid the unfavorable, no matter what his or her past actions might have been. Yi is a guide for understanding the current situation, then working to become a peacemaker by means of favorable change. Let's look at favorable changes, manageable changes, and natural changes.

1 Favorable Change

As we discuss in Chapter 7, Hexagram 5:2 is one of the special hexagrams. It is favorable, and its opposite, Hexagram 2:5, Imperfect, is unfavorable. Obviously, moving from Hexagram 4:7 to Hexagram 5:2 would be a favorable change. Cathy and George could attain perfection in their relationship by ignoring the issue of Cathy's youthful beauty and George's feelings of desire. They could focus instead on their roles as ambitious, young employee and wise, older executive.

Perhaps, if Cathy could overcome her awe of George's higher status, her honest, straightforward way of requesting his help would not come across as flirtation, and George would be prompted to respond to her questions in a businesslike and kindly manner.

When you study a hexagram to see what favorable change might be made, look first at the lines that are incorrect in position or in conflict with other lines. For example, in Hexagram 4:7, the incorrect lines, shown in gray, are yin 3 (━ ━), yang 4 (━━) and yang 6 (━━). Changing them results in the highly favorable consequential hexagram, Hexagram 5:2. In contrast, yang 1 (━━), yin 2 (━ ━), and yang 5 (━━) are correct lines, shown in black. Changing them would result in an unfavorable consequential hexagram, Hexagram 2:5.

Often, though, simultaneously changing so many aspects in a relationship to achieve perfection may not be realistic. A better way would involve looking for what favorable outcome would result from incremental change. In Hexagram 4:7, yang 4 (━━) is incorrect in position and in conflict with yang 1 (━━). If this one line changes from yang to yin — if George shows restraint and waits to let Cathy be the one to approach him — the consequential hexagram is Hexagram 4:3, Gain, shown below:

Figure 8.2: The Consequential Hexagram, Gain

This is another of the special favorable hexagrams discussed in Chapter 9, and as its title implies, Cathy will gain from this one change.

We must all take care to avoid a change that can worsen a situation. Let's say Cathy believes that George's desire will prompt him to approach her, and she decides she should wait passively for the inevitable, becoming more yin in her actions. Were Cathy to analyze the change this would create in her trigram, then hexagram, she would know this strategy would be a mistake. In Hexagram 4:7, yang 1 (—) is conflict with yang 4 (—) but correct in position. If this line becomes a yin line (— —) because Cathy won't take the initiative in asking George for help, the consequential hexagram is Hexagram Ø:7, Denial, shown below.

Figure 8.3: The Consequential Hexagram, Denial

You can see that in the Hexagram Denial, all of the lines are complementary, but the hexagram is very unfavorable for the overly passive subject — in this case, Cathy. With her innocence and inexperience, if Cathy were to succumb to her awe of George and fail to act boldly, he would have all the power in the relationship. She would be all yin, and he would remain all yang, creating a relationship badly out of balance.

2 Manageable Change

We can understand Cathy's wanting to change her own trigram; it is often much easier to change yourself than the other person involved in the relationship. This is known as manageable change and refers to any changes made by the subject. In the example of Hexagram 4:7, Cathy can alter her situation in any way she wants. For example, if she is worried about having an affair with a married man, she can stop interacting with George. But as we just saw, this would result in the unfavorable consequential hexagram, Hexagram Ø:7, and would be a mistake.

Fortunately Cathy has options. From her current subject trigram, Trigram 4 (☷), Thunder, she can change her action, essence, or attitude to get any of the other seven trigrams: trigrams Ø, 1, 2, 3, 5, 6, and 7.

We have seen that becoming passive in her actions toward George would be a mistake for Cathy. What if she did something about her essence instead, becoming more experienced and powerful in her job before approaching George? Let's find out: in Hexagram 4:7, yin 2 (— —) is complementary to yang 5 (—) and correct in position. Were Cathy to change her essence from yin to yang by improving her work and gaining more personal knowledge, the result would be Hexagram 6:7, Treading, as shown below:

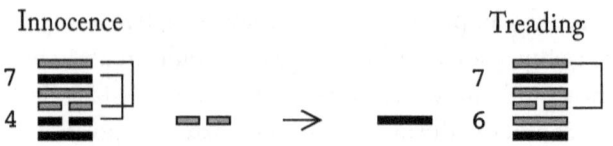

Figure 8.4: The consequential hexagram, Treading

As you can see, this change would place the two central essence lines in conflict, and Cathy's increased knowledge and status would become a challenge to George's position in the company. This change would also increase the number of incorrect lines. As suggested by the hexagram's title, Treading, this alteration could result in a stagnant situation. It is not favorable to Cathy.

Now let's consider Cathy's attitude. In Hexagram 4:7, yin 3 (--), while complementary to yang 6 (—), is in an incorrect position. When we first met Cathy and George in Chapter 6, her attitude was described as yin because she was polite and respectful toward George, as a new employee would be with a more powerful executive in the company. But what if Cathy decided that her youthful energy and enthusiasm put her on the same level as George, with his experience and power, and she responded to him confidently, as a colleague with something valuable to offer?

If Cathy could change her attitude from yin to yang, meaning that yin 3 (--) becomes yang 3 (—), this change will result in Hexagram 5:7, Coalition, as shown on the next page.

Figure 8.5: The consequential hexagram, Coalition

This hexagram is not perfect, but it is fairly favorable — all three lines of the subject trigram become correct, and the two middle lines remain complementary. The consequence of this change is favorable to Cathy because her relationship with George would become more stable and equitable — a Coalition — if her own attitude can match George's in confidence.

As we have seen throughout the story of Cathy and George, the older and more powerful man is capable of several changes beneficial to the relationship. If he stopped pursuing Cathy and allowed her to approach him, the consequence would be the highly favorable Hexagram 4:3, Gain. If both sides change to achieve the Hexagram 5:2, Perfect, Cathy would benefit from the mentoring.

But George's action, essence, and attitude do not fall within the realm of manageable change because he is the object. Cathy, as the subject, can hope for, wait for, and try to influence these changes in George, but she cannot actually manage them herself.

3 Natural Change

Often the best possible change is the kind that occurs naturally. As I mentioned in Chapter 4, Yi maintains that everything in the world moves along a spiral track, and one cycle of the track represents a circle of changes that are expected, regular, smooth, and gentle.

If allowed to flow naturally from one state to the next, the changes in both the hexagram's subject side and object side follow the sequence of the Eight Trigrams, as shown below:

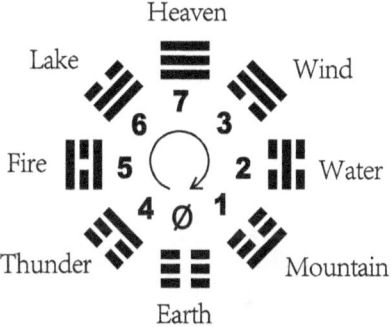

Figure 8.6: Natural change

Trigram 4 (☳), Thunder, represents Cathy's current situation. The next trigram in the sequence is Trigram 5 (☲), Fire. So her movement from Trigram 4 to Trigram 5 is a natural change — quite likely to happen, because, in time, Cathy will become less innocent and more confident in dealing with George. Her attitude will move from yin to yang. With no simultaneous change in George, the consequential hexagram will be Hexagram 5:7, Coalition.

The other two manageable changes that we decided Cathy could make on her own — becoming more passive in her actions or more experienced in her essence — are not natural or favorable. Hexagram Ø:7, Denial, appears when the subject's trigram changes from Trigram 4 (☳), Thunder, to Trigram Ø (☷), Earth, going against the sequence of regular change. Hexagram 6:7 appears when the subject trigram changes to Trigram 6 (☱), Lake, skipping Trigram 5 (☲), Fire. While occurring in the natural direction, this change is less likely to occur suddenly because it involves the conversion of Cathy's essence from yin to yang. Such a transformation is possible, but it would take time, and Cathy would have to work very hard to improve her professional skills and her relationships with colleagues and friends. At that point, George's help and support would become less important.

What if George were to go through a natural change before Cathy does? His current situation is represented by Trigram 7 (☰), Heaven, where he is on top of things in every sense of the word. For him, the next naturally occurring trigram is Trigram 3 (☴), Wind. He naturally becomes a little older and wiser and perhaps realizes the risk inherent to pursuing a beautiful young coworker. His action toward Cathy naturally becomes yin.

As we saw earlier, Hexagram 4:3, Gain, would be the desirable consequence of this natural change in George. Even if Cathy learns she cannot change anything about her own situation, she simply has to avoid making mistakes and wait patiently until George's sexual interest in her naturally cools and his action changes from yang to yin.

Yet another possibility in the natural order of change is Hexagram 5:3, Matriarch, resulting from Cathy's and George's simultaneous evolution. As Cathy gains a more confident attitude, George backs off from his pursuit of her:

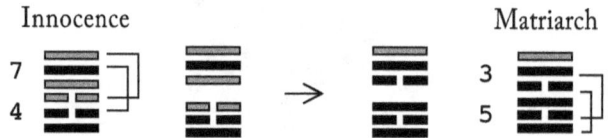

Figure 8.7: Natural change, Matriarch

In Hexagram 5:3 are five correct lines, but the two top lines are in conflict. The title of this hexagram implies that like a matriarch, Cathy will assume an important role in the relationship.

Although any of these three natural changes are possible — Cathy changes first, George changes first, or they change simultaneously — the first possibility is most likely. You might have guessed this already. Cathy's youth and inexperience make her more apt to evolve more quickly than George, who is at the top of his profession and in the prime of his life.

What you may not know is how neatly the Yi captures this logical flow from innocence to experience. In the natural cycle of change, the ascending process is more likely to occur than the descending process — that is, change occurs more easily from Trigram Ø upward, through trigrams 4, 5, and 6, to Trigram 7. Look at the picture of the Eight Trigrams sequence at the beginning of this section on natural change. Can you see the arrow showing how the cycle revolves?

So among the three possible natural consequences for Cathy and George — represented by hexagrams 5:7, 4:3, and 5:3 — the consequence represented by Hexagram 5:7, Coalition, is most likely because the change from Trigram 7 (☷) to Trigram 3 (☴) is in the descending process. What does this mean? George is less likely to give up pursuing Cathy, and Cathy is more likely to become confident around George, able to fend off his advances without being too shy or deferential.

The other consequential hexagrams that we discussed as possibilities for Cathy and George would not result from natural changes, but they still could happen. We human beings do not always go with the flow and can often act against our own best interests. We even go to extremes to reverse the natural order of decline.

As for Cathy, her current situation represented by Hexagram 4:7 is not too bad, and she doesn't have to make any drastic changes to improve things with George. In fact, many changes within her grasp could prove counterproductive. If she conducts herself prudently, avoids improper behavior with George, and patiently gains experience, her situation could naturally improve. This is what people mean when they advise letting things take their course.

4 Making the Right Strategy

Doing what comes naturally is probably the best option where Cathy is concerned, but natural consequences are not always favorable. Remember the rise and fall of Harry's career with the software company AFR, discussed in Chapter 5.

That chapter explained the natural sequence of the seasons, and we viewed Harry's changing trigrams as a reflection of his shifting situation within the company. Now that we know how to build and analyze hexagrams, we can also see his career in terms of his relationship with AFR.

Let's pretend that AFR is a startup firm, successful but not yet well-established. This company is bold and innovative but not completely sound, so we can represent it with Trigram 5 (☲), Fire. Now suppose that Harry has just peaked and is entering the "Beginning of Autumn" cycle, represented by Trigram 3 (☴), Wind. That's when he started to keep a lower profile and put less effort into his work.

Harry's current situation with AFR, from Harry's point of view, can be represented by Hexagram 3:5, Cauldron:

Cauldron

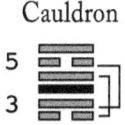

Figure 8.8: Harry's current situation with AFR

As you can see, Harry's situation is less than ideal: The only correct line is yang 3. Two pairs of complementary lines — the two bottom lines and the two middle lines — show that his passive action and experienced essence might be advantages for him at this bold, unstable company. This hexagram is neutral, neither favorable nor unfavorable.

In the sequence of Eight Trigrams, what follows Trigram 3 (☴), Wind, is Trigram 2 (☵), Water. From Hexagram 3:5, Cauldron, Harry's natural change leads to the consequential hexagram shown below:

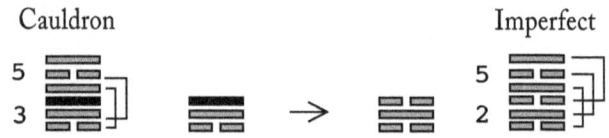

Figure 8.9: The consequential hexagram, Imperfect

As you know, Hexagram 2:5, Imperfect, is one of the few special hexagrams that is unfavorable, so Harry would not be better off if he allows his situation to change naturally. Because AFR is a young company, it is likely to change rapidly to Trigram 6 (☱), Lake, becoming less bold and more solid as a corporate entity, the consequential hexagrams will be either Hexagram 3:6, Overburden, or if Harry and AFR both change naturally, Hexagram 2:6, Adversity. Neither possibility is favorable for Harry.

If Harry wants to improve his situation with AFR, he can't afford to let nature take its course. In Eight Trigrams, Trigram 7 (☷), Heaven, comes before Trigram 3 (☴), Wind. Should Harry reverse his decline by changing his action on the job from yin to yang — applying himself with renewed vigor and achieving new heights — then the consequential hexagram would be Hexagram 7:5, Acquisition:

Figure 8.10: The consequential hexagram, Acquisition

With this alteration, the number of correct lines increases to two, while the two middle lines remain complementary; the situation will be an improvement over the current one. So for Harry, the choice is between accepting a natural decline of his relationship with the company or choosing a manageable change that will improve his career outlook.

Based on the analysis above, you may make an appropriate life strategy by:

- *Identifying which changes are favorable,*
- *Using manageable change to let the situation benefit you,*
- *Being patient, waiting for the favorable natural change.*

CHAPTER 9
Yi Text

GARY AND HIS FATHER-IN-LAW, WALTER, who suffers from Alzheimer's disease and requires Gary's help as a caregiver, are fighting with the disease. Gary has great difficulty with that role. We can represent that situation with Trigram 2, Water.

As the patient who receives help from others, Walter resembles the earth receiving energy from heaven. His situation is like Trigram Ø, Earth.

From Gary's point of view, these two trigrams represent his relationship with Walter, and the resulting hexagram is 2:Ø, Army. Gary is the commander of one soldier, Walter. Together they fight against a common enemy, Alzheimer's disease. What kind of specific strategy should Gary take to win the fight?

Although the structure of a hexagram can show whether the current situation is favorable, unfavorable, or neutral, it cannot advise you in regard to specific actions to take. The Yi text — an elegant, orderly, and lyrical unfolding of the system's meaning — will help you apply Yi to your life easily and accurately.

The Yi text for each hexagram includes three sections: a title, the general text, and a passage for each of the six lines.

1 Title

The title puts a name to the theme for all the text associated with that hexagram. The general text illustrates the basic situation. The text of each one of the six lines offers advice relating to the aspect associated with that particular line.

"Army" is the theme for all the text associated with Hexagram 2:Ø, as shown below:

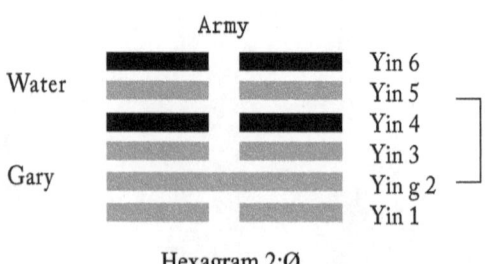

Figure 9.1: Situation of Gary

Title Army indicates that Gary is the commander of one soldier, Walter. They are together in the battle against a common enemy, Alzheimer's disease.

2 General Text

Stay on the current course.
It is favorable to an older person.
There is no blame.

The general text describes the overall circumstances of the current situation and gives general advice to the subject for handling it. In this example, the "older person" refers to Gary, the subject, not Walter, who is literally the older person.

Yi text is much more concrete and visual than the six-line symbols of the hexagrams but is still abstract and universal — more like poetry than prose. That is why in this text, the "old man" should not simply be interpreted as the one who is older than others — in this case, Walter. More interestingly, the original Chinese characters of the "old man" is zhang ren, meaning father-in-law. If we are constrained by the very narrow meaning and interpret the sentence "it is favorable for the old man" as "it is favorable to the father in-law, Walter," that would be an incorrect interpretation.

We must base our interpretation on the structure of the hexagram. The sentence, "It is favorable to an older person" should not be simply interpreted as "the current situation is favorable." Here is the structure of Hexagram 2:Ø:

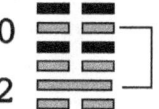

Figure 9.2: The structure of Hexagram 2:Ø

In this hexagram, only two lines, yin 4 (--) and yin 6 (--), are in correct positions. The others are in incorrect positions. The two central lines are complementary to each other, but the two bottom lines and the two top lines are in conflict. The structure of this hexagram indicates that the current situation is less favorable.

In general, older people are usually more experienced, prudent, slower paced, rational, and in control of their emotions than younger people. The text suggests that in the current circumstance, the subject (Gary), represented by the "older person," should handle the problem expertly, prudently, and rationally. If Gary is not an expert on Alzheimer's disease, then in this particular instance, he should acquire the knowledge necessary to be a qualified caregiver, the "old man" of the general text.

3 Texts of Lines

Yin 1

After departure,
The army must be highly disciplined,
Otherwise there will be tragedy.

Remember from Chapter 4 that yin 1 is the subject's action line. The text of yin 1 is a suggestion regarding Gary's action. His action is yin. He is exhausted from taking care of Walter. This line is in an incorrect position and in conflict with yin 4, indicating that Gary's yin action is unfavorable. Furthermore, the text suggests that Gary should overcome his feeling of frustration and reluctance: "The army must be highly disciplined."

Yang 2

During the expedition,
The situation is favorable.
There is no blame.
The king assigns a mission three times.

The text of yang 2 is a suggestion regarding Gary's essence. Gary's essence is yang. He has an important role and the strength for taking care of Walter. This line is central and complementary to yin 5, indicating that Gary's yang essence is favorable. The text suggests Gary uses his strength to fulfill his obligations: "The king assigns a mission three times."

Yin 3

Sometimes
When there are so many casualties,
The soldiers' bodies are removed with wagons.
It is unfavorable.

The text of yin 3 is a suggestion regarding Gary's attitude. Gary's attitude is yin. He is humble, agreeable, and kind, and he loves Walter. Normally this attitude is positive. In the current circumstance, it is not totally appropriate, however, because Walter's behavior is abnormal. What if Gary is kind and does everything for Walter, including tasks Walter could do for himself? Then his father-in-law may feel the futility of his situation. What if Gary is patient, teaching Walter to do something again and again? Then his father-in-law may feel frustrated by his inability to learn. This line is in an incorrect position and in conflict with yin 6, indicating that Gary's yin attitude is unfavorable: "Sometimes, when there are so many casualties. The soldiers' bodies are removed with wagons."

Remember that lines 4, 5, and 6 refer to the object, Walter, and apply to his action (4), essence (5), and attitude (6).

Yin 4

The army retreats.
There is no blame.

The text of yin 4 suggests that Walter's action is yin. The patient passively receives help. At times he could be agitated or aggressive, but those behaviors are symptoms of his disease, not exhibited by choice. This line is in a correct position but in conflict with yin 1, indicating that Walter's action is neutral: "The army retreats. There is no blame."

Yin 5

There is game in a field.
It is beneficial to facilitate communication.
There is no blame.
While an older son leads the armies into the battle,
A younger son removes the corpses with wagons.
Staying on this course is unfavorable.

The text of yin 5 suggests Walter's essence is yin. He is sick. This line is in an incorrect position but complementary with yang 2. Walter's yin essence is neutral; the situation depends on how Gary approaches the care-giving.

Walter has lost much of his short-term memory and his ability to reason and use language properly. Communication becomes an extremely important issue between the men. If Walter wanders, Gary might wonder if his father-in-law might be feeling bored or looking for something, such as a glass of water or the bathroom facilities. If Walter yells at a visitor, Gary might wonder if his father-in-law might feel frustrated because he cannot remember the newcomer's identity. Gary must try to understand what message underlies Walter's behavior and do something about it: "While an older son leads the army into the battle, a younger son removes the corpses with wagons." The two brothers symbolize a lack of communication. "Staying on this course is unfavorable."

Yin 6

The great leader taught,
That to create a new country, or
To build an inherited family,
Never use an unqualified person.

The text of yin 6 is a suggestion regarding Walter's attitude, which is yin. Because of the impairment in brain functions, his attitude is indifferent. This line is in a correct position but in conflict with yin 3. Walter's yin attitude is neutral. Since caring for a patient with Alzheimer's disease is a very complicated issue, Gary should seek help from professionals, as the text suggests: "Never use an unqualified person."

4 Seeing the Possible Changes

Gary cannot manipulate Walter's action, essence, or attitude. Even though these circumstances seem bleak, the text clearly suggests that Gary can improve the situation by changing some of its aspects. He does not have to change his own essence, but he can change his action and attitude, the two unfavorable aspects under his control.

If he changes his action from yin to yang, the consequence hexagram is 6:Ø, Approach, as shown below:

Figure 9.3: The consequential hexagram, Approach

This change makes the first line yang, in correct position and complementary to yin 4. The title of hexagram means that the situation is approaching a better prospect. The general text of this hexagram reads:

Things are going very smoothly.
It is beneficial to stay on the current course.
There will be an unfavorable time after eight months.

This hexagram is more favorable than Hexagram 2:Ø, although it mentions "an unfavorable time after eight months." Eventually Walter's illness will enter the last stages. For now "Things are going very smoothly;" and Gary should "stay on the current course."

Let's say that instead of changing his action, Gary changes his attitude from yin to yang. The consequential hexagram is hexagram 3:Ø, "Rising," as shown below:

Figure 9.4: The consequential hexagram, Rising

This alteration makes the third line favorable, in correct position, and complementary to yin 6. The general text of hexagram 3:Ø states:

> *Things are moving very smoothly.*
> *It is beneficial to visit a great person.*
> *Do not worry.*
> *Expedition toward the south is favorable.*

The text states, "Things are moving very smoothly" and suggests that Gary should consult with professionals to take care of Walter appropriately.

If Gary changes his action and his attitude from yin to yang, the consequential hexagram is 7:Ø, which we have discussed in the earlier chapters. This hexagram, "Peace," is very favorable, a combination of the trigrams Heaven and Earth.

All three possible changes — his action, attitude, or both — would result in favorable consequences. Gary should be able to improve his situation, regardless of how helpless he may feel. This example demonstrates the ability of the Yi text to help us look beyond our current difficulties and view the situation as a whole, with all its possibilities for positive change.

5 Verbatim Translation

If you want to verify the translation of the Yi text or wonder about your own interpretation, you will find the verbatim translation in Appendix 3. The material comes from the very concise ancient texts engraved on bones or strips of bamboo.

Let's look at the text of the fifth line of Hexagram 2:Ø, used for Gary and Walter's dilemma. The verbatim translation of the first half of the text of yin 5 is composed of eight Chinese characters: field, have, bird, benefit, execute, word, no, and blame.

In this book, you will find these characters translated as:

> *There is game in a field.*
> *It is beneficial to facilitate the communication.*

There is no blame.

Can you see how amazingly well it fits with Walter's losing the ability to express his thoughts with language and rely on his behavior for communication? Gary should carefully observe Walter's actions and strive to understand their underlying meaning. If Gary's interpretation is correct, then he and Walter will improve their situation in spite of the incurable condition. Similarly, to maximize the possibility of success, hunters in a field must carefully observe their prey's behavior.

When the Alzheimer's disease progresses to its final stage, Gary should not be blamed. Following the advice of Yi, Gary will able to be a qualified caregiver.

END OF PART I
Moving Forward

Now that you have reached the conclusion of Part 1, you can begin to use these lessons. Apply them to your own situation or the situations of your friends, family members, or business partners.

- First, create an appropriate hexagram by combining two trigrams, subject and object, or pro and con, as you have been shown.

- Study the hexagram's correct and incorrect lines, and the complementary lines or lines in conflict, to understand the general nature of the hexagram.

- Next, refer to the actual Yi texts, interpret the situation, and determine how it might be changed by altering lines that are weak.

Part II of this book provides the translation of Yi text for the sixty-four hexagrams, along with my comments. You do not have to read all of them; just pick the text for the hexagram you create.

Always remember that the statements of the Yi text refer to you, the subject, and the roles of the lines in the hexagram. Create your own interpretation of the text so it fits your particular situation. Know you are always supported by the profound wisdom of those who have studied and codified the ways of the world so many millennia ago.

PART II
Commentary on Yi Text

Commentary on Yi Text

THE CODE OF YI IS the eight trigrams and sixty-four hexagrams. They are completely abstract and universal. Yi text comments on the hexagrams, and facilitates comprehension of them. But the text was very concise archetypes and, unfortunately, misleading in its translation and interpretation for divination purpose.

This part presents a new translation of Yi text and a commentary on the translation. The commentary is based on the view that a hexagram represents the status of the two sides of a relationship and contains two trigrams. One is the subject trigram, and the other is the object trigram. The three lines symbolize three aspects: action, essence and attitude. The status of harmony between the aspects makes judgment on the current situation and produces advice for the subject who selected the hexagram.

The Yi text for a hexagram includes title, general text and texts for lines. Comments are derived from analysis of the structure of hexagram.

The order of hexagrams in this part is set by Hexagram Array. The sixty-four hexagrams are organized into eight groups. Each group has eight hexagrams with the same subject trigram. The object trigrams are in the order of the Sequence of the Eight Trigrams. The subject trigrams of each group are in the order of the Sequence of Eight Trigrams, as well.

If you get a hexagram from other publications, it is very easy to find its ID number used in this book by utilizing the diagram shown below (also shown in Chapter 6).

In this diagram, the array is attached with ID numbers of the subject trigrams in the first column at left, ID numbers of the object trigrams in the first row on top, and Zhou Yi serial numbers in parentheses under the symbols of the hexagrams.

You may use the diagram beow to find the shape of a hexagram and its serial number in Zhou Yi. For example, if you want to know hexagram 6:4, the ID number of its subject trigram is 6. The ID number of its object trigram is 4. In the row 6, column 4, there is the symbol of hexagram 6:4, ☷. It is Hexagram 54 (54 is the serial number in Zhou Yi). And for Hexagram 4:6, go to row 4, column 6: Its symbol is ☷. It is hexagram 17 (Zhou Yi).

	Ø	1	2	3	4	5	6	7
	(2)	(23)	(8)	(20)	(16)	(35)	(45)	(12)
	(15)	(52)	(39)	(53)	(62)	(56)	(31)	(33)
	(7)	(4)	(29)	(59)	(40)	(64)	(47)	(6)
	(46)	(18)	(48)	(57)	(32)	(50)	(28)	(44)
	(24)	(27)	(3)	(42)	(51)	(21)	(17)	(25)
	(36)	(22)	(63)	(37)	(55)	(30)	(49)	(13)
	(19)	(41)	(60)	(61)	(54)	(38)	(58)	(10)
	(11)	(26)	(5)	(9)	(34)	(14)	(43)	(1)

For example, hexagram 64 is the last hexagram in Zhou Yi. Its shape is ▦. The subject trigram is ▦. Its ID number is 2. The object trigram is ▦. Its ID number is 5. The two ID numbers together with a colon between them become 2:5. So the ID number of hexagram 64 is 2:5. "2:5" indicates that the hexagram consists of trigram 2 and trigram 5, while "64" indicates this hexagram is the last one in the Zhou Yi sequence.

CHAPTER 10
When Earth (⚏) is the Subject

THIS CHAPTER CONTAINS Yi text of eight hexagrams from Ø:Ø to Ø:7. Their subject trigrams are trigram Ø, Earth. The typical characteristic of earth is adaptability. This means responding to others without resistance, strength, or roughness, gently, docilely, and peacefully.

1 Hexagram Ø:Ø Earth (In Zhou Yi, hexagram 2)

The title, Earth, means that this relationship is relaxing and peaceful, like the wide, quiet earth.

In this hexagram, both components are trigram Ø (⚏), Earth (adaptability). In the relationship, both the subject and the object are adaptive, kind and gentle. The relationship is peaceful and relaxing, like the situation just after an older relationship has ended, or a new one is beginning. Feeling chilly and tentative in the relationship, as if "treading on ground covered with frost," the subject should start to interact with others, and move toward a more solid relationship.

1 General Text

Things are going very smoothly.
It is better to stay on the current course
Like a docile mare.
The wise person may move forward cautiously, possibly going astray at first
But mastering the course in the end.
It is beneficial.
Going to the southwest, the home land,
Meet with friends.
Going to the northeast, the foreign country,
Lose friends.
Calmly staying on the current course is favorable.

Since both sides of the relationship are adaptive, "things are going very smoothly." The subject and the object are very polite and responsive; they do not know each other and do not want to interfere with other's business. Since the first impression plays a very important role in the future, the subject should be very prudent, polite and gentle — "docile like a mare." A horse is a docile animal, and a mare is more docile than a stallion. The subject should adapt to the environment, and to the object, like a mare.

At the beginning of the development of a relationship, the subject knows little about the object and does not know what he or she should do, maybe "going astray at first." In the event of any missteps, the subject should be calm, relaxed, cautious, and patient. Then, as the subject gets to know the object better, he or she will "master ... the course in the end."

The subject should also be prudent before moving forward, clearly knowing which direction is right and which is wrong. When the Yi text was revised by King Wen, who ruled the country Zhou, it was southwest of the country Shang, which was hostile to King Wen. This is the inspiration for the phrases, "going to the southwest, the home land, meet with friends," and "going to the northeast, the foreign country, lose friends." This stresses the importance of one's direction in finding and keeping friends. The subject should calmly stay on the current course — being polite like a mare, getting to know the object and figuring out the right direction.

2 Structure

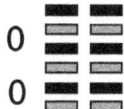

Figure 10.1: Structure of hexagram 0:0

Three lines — yin 2 (▬ ▬), yin 4 (▬ ▬) and yin 6 (▬ ▬) — are in correct positions; the other three are incorrect. There is no line complementary to other lines; all corresponding lines are in conflict with each other. Hexagram Ø:Ø is neutral, or less favorable.

3 Texts of Lines

Yin 1

While treading on ground covered with frost,
One knows that the solid ice may come soon.

Yin 1 (▬ ▬) indicates that the subject does not want to push the relationship forward. The object does not either. There is no interaction between the subject and the object; the relationship is cool and the subject feels chilly, as if treading on ground covered with frost. If the subject maintains this yin action, the relationship will become even cooler. The subject should anticipate that a difficult time is coming, as "the solid ice may come soon." The subject should change his or her action from yin to yang.

This line is in an incorrect position and in conflict with yin 4 (▬ ▬). The yin action of the subject is unfavorable.

Yin 2

The world is straight, square and large.
Gain benefit without practice.

Ancient people believed that the earth was big, flat, and square. In a relationship this relaxed, the subject and the object feel as though they are freely living on the vast earth.

Yin 2 (▬ ▬) indicates that the subject is in a weak position, having little strength. However, the yin essence does not hinder the subject from success, since there is plenty of room for him or her to move around. The environment is so relaxed and the way of gaining benefit is so easy, the subject could even gain benefit without the experience that comes from practice.

This line is in a central and correct position, but in conflict with yin 5 (▬ ▬). The yin essence of the subject is neutral, or a little favorable.

Yin 3

Covering his or her brilliance,
One may stay on the current course.
If one serves the country,
One might be not successful,
But will have a good ending.

Yin 3 (▬ ▬) indicates that the subject is very humble, covering up brilliance, and not showing off talent. "The country" refers to the object. Since the object does not know the capability of the subject, "if one serves the country," one might not be successful. But finally, through this service, the object will come to know the subject and the subject will "have a good ending."

This line is in an incorrect position and in conflict with yin 6 (▬ ▬). The yin attitude of the subject is unfavorable.

Yin 4

A sack is tied.

There is no blame,
Nor honor.

Yin 4 (- -) indicates that the object is unwilling to open up to the subject: "A sack is tied." The subject should respect the object's privacy, and does not have to try to untie the sack. The tied sack is not the business of the subject. The subject should not be blamed or praised.

This line is in a correct position, but in conflict with yin 1 (- -). The yin action of the object is neutral.

Yin 5

The situation is like wearing a yellow garment,
Which shows nobility.
It is very favorable.

In ancient China, the emperor rewards the servant with "yellow garments" as an honor and a symbol of high rank in the government. Yin 5 (- -) indicates that the object needs help from the subject. If the subject extends this help, the subject could be repaid for the offer. So the situation becomes favorable to the subject, like a reward of "yellow garments."

This line is central but in an incorrect position and in conflict with yin 2 (- -). The yin essence of the object is neutral or a little favorable.

Yin 6

The dragons were fighting on a field.
The blood of the dragons turned to black,
Mixed with yellow dirt.

"Dragons" are legendary animals, very active and with great strength. In hexagram Ø:Ø, both the subject and object are adaptive, represented by trigram Ø. So these dragons cannot be interpreted as representing the subject or the object. Instead, this is the time of a new beginning, after the battle of dragons is over and their blood has soaked into the earth.

Yin 6 (- -) indicates that the object is humble, adaptable, agreeable and flexible. The subject has the same attitude as well. Both subject and object do not care to be arrogant or rough, like a dragon interested in fighting. So the relationship is at peace, like a quiet field where the fighting between the dragons is over: "The blood of the dragons turned to black mixed with yellow dirt." The fighting is history. The subject and the object are ready to start a new stage of the relationship.

This line is in a correct position, but in conflict with yin 3 (⚋). The yin attitude of the object is neutral.

Use Yin

It is beneficial to stay on the current course forever.

The text of "Use Yin" offers general instruction on how to use the yin lines in all the hexagrams. This text applies to the general interpretation of yang lines in all of the sixty-four hexagrams, except hexagram 7:7, which contains no yang lines.

"The current course" refers to the situation where the subject is now. The text suggests that the subject remain wherever he or she is. This does not mean that things remain static, without change, but means that the subject should be patient in waiting for a favorable chance to come.

Things in the world are always changing. Even if the subject stands still at a point in the road, the subject's situation will keep changing: The aspects of the object could change and the situation of the subject also undergoes a natural change. (See Chapter 8.)

The text of "Use Yin" tells the subject that the yin line is like a red light at the intersection. Be patient, it says; wait at the stop line. The green light or green arrow will come soon, to guide or move the subject forward toward his or her destiny.

[2] Hexagram Ø:1 Deprivation (In Zhou Yi, hexagram 23)

The title, Deprivation, means that the subject is deprived of proper rights in the relationship. In Chinese, the word for "deprivation" is "bo," meaning "peel off," "exploit" or "deprive."

Trigram Ø (⚏), Earth (adaptability), is the subject; trigram 1 (⚏), Mountain (stopping), is the object. The subject is kind and gentle, like the earth, but the object behaves in a way that is tough and arrogant, like a mountain standing in the way, depriving the subject of the freedom to move ahead. The subject should be clever and flexible, to take advantage of whatever small opportunities arise: If "there are a lot of ripe fruit and nobody eats them," the subject should take "them away with a wagon."

1 General Text

Nowhere is beneficial to go.

Neither the subject nor the object has strength or is ready to move the relationship forward. The subject is humble, agreeable, and respectful, but the object is arrogant and stubborn. The current situation of the relationship is awful and bleak: "Nowhere is beneficial to go." The subject should adapt to the bad situation, be patient, wait for a better time, and do nothing at this moment.

2 Structure

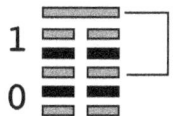

Figure 10.2 Structure of hexagram 0:1

Hexagram Ø:1 has two correct lines, yin 2 (▬ ▬) and yin 4 (▬ ▬); the others are in incorrect positions. The two middle lines and the two bottom lines are in conflict; the two top lines are complementary to each other. Hexagram Ø:1 is not favorable.

3 Texts of Lines

Yin 1

A bed with marred legs is rotting.
Staying on the current course is unfavorable.

Yin 1 indicates that the subject does not want to do something to improve the current situation in the relationship, so it remains like the rotting legs of a bed. A bed is necessary for everyone to sleep on at night, and legs are the important support for this needed rest. "A bed with marred legs" indicates that the subject's yin action is the fundamental underlying cause of the bad situation.

This line is in an incorrect position and in conflict with yin 4 (▬ ▬). The yin action of the subject is unfavorable.

Yin 2

A bed with a marred headboard is rotting.
Staying on the current course is unfavorable.

In China the headboard of a bed is separate from the feet that support the bed. It is used for people to lean on to rest. A marred headboard will not make the bed collapse, but makes people very uncomfortable and unable to relax. Yin 2 (▬ ▬) indicates that the subject's essence is like "a bed with marred headboard." The subject should make change to be more active and improve his or her essence by hard work, learning, or doing something to become stronger.

This line is in a correct position, but in conflict with yin 5 (▬ ▬). The yin essence of the subject is neutral.

Yin 3

A bed is rotting.
There is no blame.

Yin 3 indicates that the subject is pessimistic about the relationship. He or she is gentle, adaptable, agreeable and respectful — "there is no blame" — but cannot do much to improve the situation, because the object is stubborn.

This line is in an incorrect position, but is complementary with yang 6 (▬). The yin attitude of the subject is neutral.

Yin 4

A bed with a marred surface is rotting.
It is unfavorable.

Yin 4 indicates the action of the object is yin. The object does not want to improve the relationship, and even wants to retreat or terminate the relationship. The relationship is damaged severely by the yin action of the object. People cannot sleep on a "bed with marred surface."

This line is in a correct position, but in conflict with yin 1 (▬ ▬). The yin action of the object is neutral.

Yin 5

Fish are swimming with a string.
Favored court ladies go with a king.
It is beneficial.

Yin 5 (▬ ▬) indicates that the object needs help from the subject, like the fish swimming with a string seeking food, or the favored ladies following their king. That the object needs the subject keeps the relationship from falling apart. The yin essence of the object benefits the subject.

This line is central, but in an incorrect position and in conflict with yin 2 (▬ ▬). The yin essence of the object is neutral.

Yang 6

There are a lot of ripe fruit,
But nobody eats them.
A wise person moves them away with a wagon.

A foolish person is deprived of home
By the fallen fruit.

Yang 6 (▬) indicates that the object's attitude is a tree hung with a lot of ripe fruit — tall and frightening, with a sweetness that can fall to the ground at any time. The object is arrogant, reckless and careless, which possibly leaves chances open to the subject. Whether this is good or bad depends on how the subject handles the opportunities. If the subject is smart, he or she simply collects the fruit with a wagon and moves away. If the subject hesitates and lacks courage to take the chance, he or she will suffer, and be "deprived of home by the fallen fruit."

This line is in an incorrect position, but complementary with yin 3 (▬ ▬) and supported by yin 5 (▬ ▬). The yang attitude of the object is neutral.

[3] Hexagram Ø:2 Closeness (In Zhou Yi, hexagram 8)

The title, Closeness, is represented by the Chinese character, 比. The two sides of this character are the same, like a picture of two people sitting in line. Most commonly this character means "to compare," but in the case of this hexagram, it indicates a close relationship.

Trigram Ø (☷), Earth (adaptability), is the subject; trigram 2 (☵), Water (difficulty and danger) is the object. While water can be changeable and dangerous, when it flows over the earth, it penetrates and moisturizes the absorbent soil. So this hexagram symbolizes a close relationship where the subject, Earth, benefits from the object, Water.

The subject accepts this beneficial help from the object, but the object has some difficulties in dealing with the subject. The subject should take the first step to become close to the object, letting the object know what the subject needs.

1 General Text

The current situation is favorable.
The oracle suggests one should stay on the current course forever.
There is no blame.
Be close to those who were troublesome.
Acting too late is unfavorable.

The "oracle" mentioned in this text usually performed with a turtle's shell, by observing the pattern of its cracks after it has been baked above a flame.

In the current relationship, neither the subject nor the object wants to move the relationship forward. Both of them are humble, kind, graceful, and respectful. The subject is in a weak position, while the object is in a strong position. The subject benefits from the object, so the subject should stay in the current situation, remaining close to the object.

This close relationship is favorable to the subject. The subject should make an effort to maintain closeness even if the object is troublesome. If the subject is too late in establishing intimacy with the object, the subject could lose the chance to have someone take care of him or her, and the situation will be unfavorable to the subject.

2 Structure

Figure 10.3: Structure of hexagram 0:2

In this hexagram, yin 2 (--), yin 4 (--), yang 5 (—), and yin 6 (--), are in correct positions. The two middle lines are in correct positions and complementary with each other. The other two lines are in incorrect positions. The two bottom lines and the two top lines are in conflict with each other. Hexagram Ø:2 is neutral.

3 Texts of Lines

Yin 1

In forming a close relationship sincerely,
There is no blame.
Sincerity is shown
With a jug of wine.
Finally everybody comes together,
Including those who differed.
That is favorable.

Yin 1 (--) indicates that the subject does not actively choose to be close to others. If the subject goes on this way, he or she cannot get help from others. The subject should change this passive stance, and become attached to the object actively and sincerely: "In forming a close relationship sincerely, there is no blame." Even if the object is not interested in having a closer relationship, the subject should show a sincere desire to be closer: "Finally everybody comes together, including those who differed." When the subject needs help, he or she will be able to obtain it from the object: "That is favorable."

This line is in an incorrect position and in conflict with yin 4 (⚋). The yin action of the subject is unfavorable.

Yin 2

One wishes to be close to others.
Staying on the current course is favorable.

Yin 2 (⚋) indicates that the subject is sick, elderly, jobless, or having other problems, and needs help. Meanwhile, the essence of the object is yang. In a close relationship, the subject could gain from the object's strength. The subject should keep wishing to be closer to the object: "Staying on the current course is favorable."

This line is in a correct position, central, and complementary with yang 5 (⚊). The yin essence of the subject is favorable.

Yin 3

One is close to an undesirable person.

Yin 3 (⚋) indicates that the subject is kind, gentle, agreeable, and humble. That makes it possible for the subject to embark on a close relationship with an undesirable person. The subject needs to understand clearly what kind of person with whom he or she is involved. If the object is an undesirable person, the subject should not be too yielding; instead, the subject should distance himself or herself from that person.

This line is in an incorrect position and in conflict with yin 6 (⚋). The yin attitude of the subject is unfavorable.

Yin 4

One makes another happy
To be closer.
Staying on the current course is favorable.

Yin 4 (⚋) indicates that the object has become weary or frustrated in assisting the subject. The subject should strive to make the object happy in the relationship, cooperating or responding positively to the object's help. Be patient. Do not give up. "Staying on the current course is favorable."

This line is in a correct position, but in conflict with yin 1 (⚋). The yin action of the object is neutral.

Yang 5

There is a union
Based on openness and willingness.
This union is like the story of a king
Who was chasing game from three sides,
Leaving the front side open,
Giving a chance for the animals to escape.
The people in the town were impressed with king's kindness.
They lived without wariness.
It is favorable.

A similar story was recorded in the historic book Shiji: In a journey around his country, King Cheng Tang (15ØØ BC), saw a net closed on all four sides. Servant Zhu said "I catch the animals coming from all directions into my net." King Cheng Tang laughed and said, "That is too brutal. Why do you kill all of them?" and ordered three sides of the net to be opened. Zhu did this and said: "Those animals, willing to go to the right, may go to the right. Those animals willing to go to the left may go to the left. Only those animals, who do not listen to me, will enter my net and be caught." Regarding this event, the leaders from other nearby countries said, "King Cheng Tang is so kind, even kind to animals." After that those leaders supported King Cheng Tang. Later, King Cheng Tang launched a war against Xia, ended the Xia dynasty, and created a Shang dynasty.

Yang 5 (▬) indicates that the object is strong physically, financially, or spiritually, and is able to help the subject. The subject has something to gain from the object, like the prospect of animals in the hunting field.

In order to gain the benefit, the subject should respect the object, and sincerely let the object know what is desired, and why: "There is a union based on openness and willingness." The subject also should trust the object, leaving a room for the object to make decisions and handle specific issues, "leaving the front side open, giving a chance for the animals to escape." In this way, the subject could get the help needed, especially at a crucial point: "It is favorable."

This line is in a correct position, central, and complementary to yin 2 (▬ ▬). The yang essence of the object is favorable.

Yin 6

Without taking the first step

To become close to others
Is unfavorable.

Yin 6 (▬ ▬) indicates that the object is kind, gentle, agreeable, and adaptive — just like the subject. If the subject always waits for the object to help and agrees with whatever the object is doing, but does not show the object where the problems and needs are, the object cannot help. If the object also respects the subject and is waiting for the subject to feel better, but does not know what is going on from the subject's side, the object will have great difficulty in assisting the subject and become frustrated. Finally, the object could become sick of dealing with the subject and leave the subject alone: "That is unfavorable." The subject should take the first step to become close to the object, letting the object know what he or she needs.

This line is in a correct position, but in conflict with yin 3 (▬ ▬), and it suppresses yang 5 (▬▬). The yin attitude of the object is unfavorable.

4 Hexagram Ø:3 Watching (In Zhou Yi, hexagram 20)

The title, Watching, means that under current circumstances, the subject should observe the relationship objectively and fairly, from both sides, to decide how to get help from the object.

Trigram Ø (☷), Earth (adaptability), is the subject; trigram 3 (☴), Wind (flexibility) is the object. The wind changes direction frequently, so that some places on the earth are exposed to the wind, while others are harbored from it. The adaptable subject is like a sailboat on the seas, observing the wind direction and responding to its changes.

In the whole text of this hexagram, there is no word of "favorable" or "unfavorable," indicating that the development of this relationship and the subject's situation profoundly depend on subject's observations and methods of handling the relationship. The subject needs help. To get help from the object, the subject should watch the object: "Reviewing another's life is blameless."

1 General Text

After watching the persons preparing
Themselves to present an offering,
There is no need to see the offering.
The sincerity manifests reverence.

The subject should carefully watch what the object is doing. In the observation, the subject needs to pay more attention to essential issues — such as watching the person preparing to present an offering, which manifests reverence. The inessential issues in the relationship — such as the offering itself — are negligible, though interesting.

2 Structure

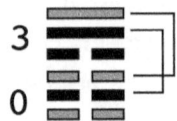

Figure 10.4: Structure of hexagram 0:3

In this hexagram, yin 2 (- -), yin 4 (- -), and yang 5 (—) are in correct positions, but other three lines are in incorrect positions. The two middle lines and the two top lines are complementary; and the two bottom lines are in conflict with each other. Hexagram Ø:3 is neutral.

3 Texts of Lines

Yin 1

There is innocence when children watch.
Foolish watching in the same way is blameless.
This naivete is regrettable in a wise person.

Yin 1 (- -) indicates that the subject does not work hard to improve the relationship, and instead is staring like a child at obvious things, ignoring the object's essential nature. In the current relationship, the subject's yin action — standing and gawking — seems innocent and foolish.

If the subject were a child, this innocence would not be blamed. If the subject were a fool, his or her naivete would not be blamed. However, the subject is a smart person, not a child or a fool, so his or her yin action is regrettable. The subject should continue to watch the object, but take more initiative in the relationship.

This line is in an incorrect position and conflicts with yin 4 (- -). The yin action of the subject is regrettable.

Yin 2

Covert watching.
It is beneficial for a woman
To stay on this course.

Yin 2 (▬ ▬) indicates that a lack of strength and courage causes the subject to be prudent, and reluctant to expose himself or herself to others, like an observer peeking from behind a door. This is a good way to protect oneself, like a woman protecting her privacy while watching others carefully through a gap of the door.

The subject is in a weak position and needs help. While the subject does not know the object very well and is not sure whether the object would help him or her, it is not necessary for the subject to expose his or her problem, and the subject should watch the object in a "covert" way.

This line is in a correct position, central, and complementary with yang 5 (▬). The yin essence of the subject is beneficial.

Yin 3

Looking at my life
Back and forth.

Yin 3 (▬ ▬) indicates that the subject is humble and prudent. When the subject needs help and is not sure whether the object would be willing to help, the subject should review his or her past behaviors in dealing with the object, and think about the possibilities: "Looking at my life, back and forth."

This line is complementary with yang 6 (▬), but in a incorrect position. The yin attitude of the subject is neutral.

Yin 4

To watch the glory of the country,
It is better to be a guest of the king.

Yin 4 (▬ ▬) indicates the action of the object is yin. The object also does not want to be exposed. To know the true situation of the object, the subject has to take advantage of every possible chance to get close to the object, and to observe the object clearly, like being a guest of the king. If the subject stays far from the object, outside of the "country" and far from the "king," it is impossible for the subject to know the object well.

This line is in a correct position, but in conflict with yin 1 (▬ ▬). That indicates the yin action of the object is neutral.

Yang 5

Being a wise person
Reviewing the course of my life
Is blameless.

Yang 5 (▬) indicates that the object is in a strong position and able to provide the help needed. To gain benefit from the object, the subject has to possess clear self-knowledge — about what the subject lacks and needs, and what the subject did in the past to help and adapt to the object, and the way of adapting to the object. If the subject examines these issues carefully, he or she should not be blamed.

This line is in a correct position, central, and complementary with yin 2 (▬ ▬). The yang essence of the object is favorable.

Yang 6

Being a wise person
Reviewing another's life
Is blameless

Yang 6 (▬) indicates that the object is arrogant, reckless, self-centered, bossy, or bullying. What kind of person is the object? What will the object possibly do to the subject? The subject should be irritated by the object's rough behavior, but also observe the object carefully, objectively, and fairly. If the subject does so, the subject could get what he or she wants.

This line is in an incorrect position, but complementary with yin 4 (▬ ▬). The yang attitude of the object is neutral.

[5] Hexagram Ø:4 Delight (In Zhou Yi, hexagram 16)

The title, Delight, is represented by the Chinese character, "Yu," also meaning "elephant." Trigram Ø (☷), Earth (adaptability), is the subject; trigram 4 (☳), Thunder (movement), is the object. The subject delightedly complies with the movement of the object, just as, after a long winter, the living things on the earth are delighted at the sound of thunder, which signals the coming rain.

1 General Text

It is beneficial to appoint a marquis.
It is beneficial to deploy the army.

Like a sleeping elephant awakened by its owner and ready to follow, the subject was living quietly and peacefully, but the object comes into his or her life and everything starts to change. At first, the subject has to do some daily housekeeping work, like an emperor appointing a marquis, or courtier, then start to do business, like the emperor deploying an army. These are the two steps after a "wakeup call." Then, the subject has to face reality and go with the object. Maybe the subject will have no difficulty getting along with the object, because both the subject and the object are humble, agreeable and respectful, but they will have a very hard time because both of them have little strength.

2 Structure

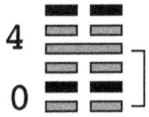

Figure 10.5: Structure of hexagram 0:4.

In this hexagram, yin 2 (- -) and yin 6 (- -) are in correct positions. The other four lines are in incorrect positions. The two bottom lines are complementary. The two middle lines and the two top lines are in conflict with each other. Hexagram Ø:4 is neutral, or less favorable.

3 Texts of Lines

Yin 1

An elephant is trumpeting.
It is unfavorable.

Yin 1 (- -) indicates that the subject only says what he or she wants to do, but does not really devote effort to improve the relationship, like an elephant that trumpets without going into motion. The subject and the object have little strength; if they do not move forward to make themselves richer in finance, health or social position, they will have a very difficult time: "It is unfavorable."

This line is complementary with yang 4 (—), but in an incorrect position. The yin action of the subject is neutral.

Yin 2

The elephant is walking along a rocky road.
The rocky road is finished before the end of day.
Staying on this course is favorable.

Yin 2 (- -) indicates that the subject's yin essence puts him or her on a difficult journey, like an elephant walking along a rocky road where there are no trees, grass, or water. The subject cannot get help on this journey from the object, because the essence of the object is yin, as well. However, the object is leading the subject along the "rocky road," which will be "finished before the end of day."

So the subject should be patient, persisting in following the object: "Staying on this course is favorable."

This line is central and in a correct position, but in conflict with yin 5 (▬ ▬). The yin essence of the subject is neutral.

Yin 3

The elephant is staring
And regrets.
Acting too late
Is regrettable.

Yin 3 (▬ ▬) indicates that the subject does not trust the object. The subject observes the object suspiciously, examining himself or herself with regret for whatever might have gone wrong, like the elephant standing and staring. The subject should quickly find a conclusion. If it is wrong to go with the object, the subject should determinedly stop the relationship; otherwise, the subject should follow the object without hesitation: "Acting too late is regrettable."

This line is in an incorrect position and in conflict with yin 6 (▬ ▬). The yin attitude of the subject is unfavorable.

Yang 4

Following others,
The elephant gains a lot.
Do not doubt
The friends gather together,
Like the hair held together by a hair clasp.

Yang 4 (▬▬) indicates that the object is pushing the relationship forward. If the subject follows the object and both work together, the subject will gain from the relationship, sharing benefits with the object like "the hair held together by a hair clasp."

This line is in an incorrect position, but complementary with yin 1 (▬ ▬). The yang action of the object is neutral.

Yin 5

Those who stay on the current course
Will be sick.
Those who persist on the current course
Will not die.

Yin 5 (- -) indicates that the object has little strength and cannot help the subject, while the subject needs help badly: "Those who stay on the current course will be sick." However, the object is leading and the subject is advancing, so progress is being made. If the subject follows the object persistently, they will go through this difficult time: "Those who persist on the current course will not die."

This line is central, but in an incorrect position and in conflict with yin 2 (- -). The yin essence of the object is less favorable.

Yin 6

Closing its eyes,
The elephant enjoys.
Making change is blameless.

Yin 6 (- -) indicates that the object is humble. Both sides respect each other. They get along very well and together walk through difficulties. The subject enjoys the change, like the elephant closing its eyes. The subject did the right thing in following the object. Change is blameless.

This line is in a correct position, but in conflict with yin 3 (- -). The yin action of the object is neutral.

[6] Hexagram Ø:5 Promotion (In Zhou Yi, hexagram 35)

The title, Promotion, is a translation from the Chinese "Jin," meaning a promotion in position, or stressing graciousness while visiting others.

Trigram Ø (☷), Earth (adaptability), is the subject; trigram 5 (☲), Fire (brightness and clinging) is the object. Fire in the upper position and earth in the lower position form an image of sunrise, the symbol of promotion. While the sun rises from the horizon, the field becomes bright.

When the subject adapts to the brightness of the object, the object clings to the subject, but also uses or manipulates the subject, promoting the subject "to a high position," "and then" sending the subject "to battle." So the fire's brightness can burn: "Staying on the current course is mean" to the subject.

1 General Text

Duke Kang was honored.
He was presented with many horses
And interviewed three times in a single day.

The subject is in a weak position, adaptive and humble. The object wants to advance but has little strength, intending to use the subject to serve his or her own purpose. The object is arrogant and bossy, manipulating the subject, just as King Wen honored his son, Duke Kang, presenting him with many horses and interviewing him three times in a single day.

The text uses a particular historic event to illustrate the current situation of the relationship, but the words "favorable" and "unfavorable" are not used explicitly. This neutrality implies that the subject should not be satisfied with the achievement without remaining alert to potential danger.

 STRUCTURE

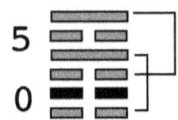

Figure 10.6: Structure of hexagram 0:5.

In this hexagram, yin 2 (▬ ▬) is the only line in a correct position. The other five lines are in incorrect positions. The two bottom lines and the two top lines are complementary to each other, but the two middle lines are in conflict with each other. Hexagram Ø:5 is neutral or less favorable.

3 Texts of Lines

Yin 1

The promotion is like a torture.
Staying on the current course is favorable.
Be relaxed and calm even when sincerity is lacking.
There is no blame.

Yin 1 (▬ ▬) indicates that the subject does not want to be promoted, but he or she is nevertheless promoted by the object: "The promotion is like a torture." Apparently the promotion is not sincere, but the situation is favorable to the subject because of his or her weak position: "Be relaxed and calm." Anyway, the subject should enjoy the promotion; it is the object's tactic, and the subject should not be blamed.

This line is in an incorrect position, but complementary to yang 4 (▬). The yin action of the subject is neutral.

Yin 2

The promotion seems worrisome.

Staying on the current course is favorable.
The grandmother might do
A big favor.

Yin 2 (∎∎) indicates that the subject has less ability to work well at a higher position: "The promotion seems worrisome." But it is the object who promoted the subject, so if there is a problem, the object should take care of it. The object is "the grandmother," who "might do a big favor."

This line is central and in a correct position, but conflicts with yin 5 (∎∎). The yin essence of the subject is neutral, or a little favorable.

Yin 3

The majority of people support the promotion.
Regret vanishes.

Yin 3 (∎∎) indicates that the subject is kind, humble, agreeable, and respectful. This attitude makes the subject easier to get support from the object and others: "Regret vanishes."

This line is complementary to yang 6 (▬), but in an incorrect position. The yin attitude is neutral.

Yang 4

Being promoted, like a mole cricket, and then
Staying on the current course is dangerous.

Yang 4 (▬) indicates that the object wants to advance, but lacks essential strength. So the object promotes the subject and uses the subject for further advancement.

Being promoted, the subject feels like a mole cricket, which has five skills, none of which are excellent: it can fly, but never high enough to get over a house. It can climb, but can never reach the top of a tree. It can swim, but would never get across a river. It can dig holes, but never even cover its own body. It can walk, but never fast enough to pass a person. With such limited skills, the subject's position is insecure: "Staying on the current course is dangerous."

This line is in an incorrect position, but complementary to Yin 1 (∎∎). The yang action of the object is neutral.

Yin 5

Regret vanishes.

Do not worry about loss and gain.
Moving ahead is favorable.
It is beneficial.

Yin 5 (- -) indicates that the object does not have enough strength and has to cling to the subject. The subject benefits from the promotion without severe loss. The subject does not have to worry about the gain or loss: "Regret vanishes." The subject does not want advancement and promotion, but it happens anyway. The subject should yield to this forward movement, following the stream: "Do not worry about loss and gain."

This line is central, but in an incorrect position and in conflict with yin 2 (- -). The yin essence of the object is neutral.

Yang 6

Being promoted to a high position,
Like on a tip of a horn, and then
Being sent to battle against another country
Are blameless, dangerous, but favorable.
Staying on the current course is mean.

Yang 6 (—) indicates that the object is so self-centered, bossy, and demanding that there is little room left for the subject to turn around. After being promoted to a high position, the subject feels like being "on a tip of a horn," without any other choice but that of going to battle for the object. The situation is blameless but dangerous, and it offers a chance for the subject to benefit. However, being manipulated by others is not a happy state of affairs: "Staying on the current course is mean."

This line is in an incorrect position but complementary to yin 3 (- -) and supported by yin 5. The yang attitude of the object is neutral.

[7] Hexagram Ø:6 Gathering (In Zhou Yi, hexagram 45)

The title, Gathering, refers to the act of bringing people together.

Trigram Ø (☷), Earth (adaptability) is the subject; trigram 6 (☱), Lake (pleasure), is the object. The lake above the earth gathers streams and rivers together, primarily for replenishing itself. The earth might benefit from the moisture and irrigation that attend this flow, but also could be disappointed sadly, "weeping and sniveling." Because the object is seeking pleasure, the adaptable object may share in this pleasure, but also might not.

1 General Text

Things are going smoothly.
A king comes to a temple.
It is beneficial to visit a great person.
Things are going smoothly.
Staying on the current course is beneficial.
Offering a big animal is favorable.
It is beneficial to do something.

While the subject is weak, the object is strong and able to help the subject. The subject does not want to improve the relationship, but the object does, pushing the subject forward. Both the subject and the object respect each other. Generally, "things are going smoothly."

The subject is sick, or has some other problems, and needs help, in the same way that "a king comes to a temple" to pray for an ancestor's blessing. The object is healthy, or has other strengths or powers. The subject should be close to the object: "It is beneficial to visit a great person." The object meets with the subject and helps him or her: "Things are going smoothly." Despite reluctance, the subject should keep in touch with the object: "Staying on the current course is beneficial." The subject should show sincerity and respect for the object: "Offering a big animal is favorable."

With the object's help, the subject should do something to improve his or her situation: "It is beneficial to do something." However, whatever is done must be done correctly. Here is an implication: if the subject does not respect the object enough, offering a small or middle-sized animal instead of a big one, the situation could become unfavorable. And without the help from the object, the subject could have nowhere to go.

2 Structure

Figure 10.7: Structure of hexagram 0:6.

In this hexagram, three lines, yin 2 (━ ━), yang 5 (━━) and yin 6 (━ ━), are in correct positions. The other three lines, yin 1 (━ ━), yin 3 (━ ━), and yang 4 (━━), are in incorrect positions. The two middle lines and the two bottom lines are complementary to each other. The two top lines are in conflict. Hexagram Ø:6 is neutral.

3 Texts of Lines

Yin 1

There is a sincerity,
But not enduring.
The people are in discord at some times
And in agreement at other times.
Somebody behaves inappropriately,
Making loud noises,
But returns to acceptable behavior, smiling,
After stern criticism.
Then everybody feels happy.
Nothing is disquieting.
Going ahead is blameless.

Yin 1 (− −) indicates that the subject does not want to improve the relationship, but is compelled by the object who is offering to help: "There is a sincerity, but not enduring." The object wants to have a better relationship — but because the object seeks greater power, not because of the subject's essential qualities: "The people are in discord at some times and in agreement at other times." When feeling unhappy with the situation, the subject might enter into a dispute with the object, "making loud noises." But when the object responds with "stern criticism," the subject yields to the object — "Then everybody feels happy." The object keeps helping the subject, and all is well: "Nothing is disquieting." In gathering together with the object and "going ahead," the subject should not be blamed.

This line is in an incorrect position, but complementary to yang 4 (—). The yin action of the subject is neutral.

Yin 2

Being led by the other is favorable.
There is no blame.
Being sincere is beneficial,
Even with a simple sacrifice.

Yin 2 (− −) indicates that the subject is sick, jobless, or has other problems in life and needs help. The object is strong, and can lead the subject through a difficult time. The subject should accept this help: "Being led by the other is favorable. There is no blame." To please the object for offering such assistance, "being sincere is beneficial, even with a simple sacrifice."

This line is central, in a correct position and complementary with yang 5 (▬). The yin essence of the subject is favorable.

Yin 3

While people gather together,
Someone sighs with dissatisfaction.
It doesn't benefit anybody.
To go ahead is blameless.
It is a little mean.

Yin 3 (▬ ▬) indicates that the subject respects the object because the subject seeks the object's help. The object is agreeable, kind, and graceful, because the object wants to get support from others to expand his or her own interests. So the two sides have different goals: "While people gather together, someone sighs with dissatisfaction." The subject, who truly needs help, should overcome this reluctance, which "doesn't blame anybody," and should not be blamed for following the object. However, "it is a little mean," when the subject follows the object reluctantly, without sincerity.

This line is in an incorrect position and in conflict with yin 6 (▬ ▬). The yin attitude of the subject is less favorable.

Yang 4

It is very favorable.
There is no blame.

Yang 4 (▬) indicates that the object approaches and helps the subject: "It is very favorable." The subject accepts the object's offer, and "there is no blame."

This line is in an incorrect position, but complementary with yin 1 (▬ ▬) and supported by yin 3 (▬ ▬). The yang action of the object is neutral, or a little favorable.

Yang 5

When people gather together,
Everybody has a position.
There is no blame.
There is a lack of sincerity.
From the beginning it always is this way.
Regret vanishes.

Yang 5 (▬) indicates that the object is in a strong position physically, financially, or spiritually, and is able to help the subject. The subject accepts the help because he or she really needs it. The object helps the subject out of a moral duty or some other obligations, and wants to expand his or her own interests: "When people gather together, everybody has a position." If the subject can keep this reality in mind, "there is no blame." But the subject should not think that the object is offering help for the subject's sake: "There is lack of sincerity." From the beginning, the subject sees the need to follow the object, and then follows persistently, because of the benefits of this course: "Regret vanishes."

This line is in a correct position, central and complementary to yin 2 (⚋). The yang essence of the object is favorable.

Yin 6

Weeping and sniveling.
There is no blame.

Yin 6 (⚋) indicates that the object looks gentle, kind, and agreeable, but, in reality, lacks sincerity. That makes the subject feel unhappy, giving in to weeping and sniveling. However, because the subject does benefit from the object, even if it's not enough, it is right for the subject to be gathered into the object's forces: "There is no blame."

This line is in a correct position, but in conflict with yin 3 (⚋). The yin attitude of the object is neutral.

8 Hexagram Ø:7 Denial (In Zhou Yi, hexagram 12)

The title, Denial, in Chinese is "Pi," also meaning "false" or "negative."

Trigram Ø (☷), Earth (adaptability), is the subject; trigram 7 (☰), Heaven (strength), is the object. The subject adapts to the powerful object like earth adapts to heaven, receiving energy and yielding to its power. It is not imaginable that living things on earth could survive without the light and heat from heaven; in the same way it is not imaginable that the subject can live — except in misery — without the object's assistance or permission.

1 General Text

Dealing with a wrong person
Is the cause of sadness.
It is not beneficial to stay on this course.
What is lost is large.
What is gained is small.

The subject is weak, and wants to stay in a quiet and peaceful environment, living with others in a friendly way. The object approaches the subject and actively helps the subject. This seems like a good chance for the subject, but the object is self-centered and a bully, not the right person for the subject, but a "wrong person." This relationship brings sadness to the subject. The subject gains some benefit from the object, but loses freedom and dignity: "What is lost is large. What is gained is small."

2 Structure

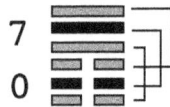

Figure 10.8: Structure of hexagram 0:7

In this hexagram, only two lines, yin 2 (- -) and yang 5 (—), are in correct positions. The other four lines, yin 1 (- -), yin 3 (- -), yang 4 (—), and yang 6 (—), are in incorrect positions. Although all the lines in this hexagram are complementary to the corresponding lines, the four incorrect positions indicate that this hexagram is unfavorable.

3 Texts of Lines

Yin 1

When a reed is pulled out of the ground,
All the reeds come out together.
Staying on this course is favorable.
Things are going smoothly.

Yin 1 (- -) indicates that the subject does not want to be deeply involved in the relationship, but the object is pushing the relationship forward. The subject is unable to resist the object, and follows along, entangled in the relationship like reeds bundled together. On the other hand, this tie benefits the subject, because if "a reed is pulled out of the ground, all the reeds come out together," so "staying on this course is favorable."

This line is in an incorrect position, but complementary to yang 4 (—). The yin action of the subject is neutral.

Yin 2

Flattery is disguised.
It seems favorable to a wicked person,
But not to the nice people.

Things are going smoothly.

Yin 2 (▬ ▬) indicates that the subject is sick, having financial difficulty or other troubles in life. The subject needs help. However, while the subject tries to gain from the object, the subject should not feel flattered; otherwise, even though the subject could get what he or she needs — caring, money, or other assistance — the subject will lose rights, freedom or dignity. "It seems favorable to a wicked person, but not to the nice people." Actually, because the subject and the object are tied together, sharing common interests, without the distraction of flattery, things will still go smoothly.

This line is central, in a correct position and complementary to yang 5 (▬▬). The yin essence of the subject is favorable.

Yin 3

Covering a problem up is shameful.

Yin 3 (▬ ▬) indicates that the subject is humble and adaptive. Facing the rough, rude, and bossy object, the subject may want to cover problems up. If the subject behaves dishonestly, the object could control and use the subject: "Covering a problem up is shameful."

This line is in an incorrect position, but complementary to yang 6 (▬▬). The yin attitude of the subject is neutral.

Yang 4

There is a commission.
There is no blame.
Share benefit with others.

Yang 4 (▬▬) indicates that the object is pushing the relationship forward out of duty or obligation, or to use the subject to reach the object's own goal. "There is a commission" that ties the subject and the object together, making the subject able to share some benefit with the object.

This line is in an incorrect position, but complementary to yin 1 (▬ ▬). The yang action of the object is neutral.

Yang 5

The bad time is over.
The situation favors the nice person.
"Disaster is coming, disaster is coming,"
This warning is posted on a mulberry tree.

Yang 5 (—) indicates that the object is strong and helps the subject. The situation favors the subject. However, the subject should be aware of the danger from the object's tendency to supervise, manipulate, and control others. Anytime the object feels unhappy with the subject, the object could put the subject in jeopardy. The subject should remember: "Disaster is coming, disaster is coming" on the signs posted on a "mulberry tree," which is mostly planted in China for feeding silk worms with its leaves.

This line is central, in a correct position and complementary to yin 2 (− −). That indicates the yang essence of the object is favorable.

Yang 6

The bad situation has turned over,
Starting with sadness,
Ending in happiness.

Yang 6 (—) indicates that the object is arrogant, harsh, demanding, and bossy. At first, under the harsh control of the object, the situation for the subject is very bad. However, things are always changing, and the yang attitude of the powerful object finally leads the object into trouble and forces the object to change. If the subject waits for the situation to evolve, the subject will enjoy happiness. While the object remains in power, the subject should be patient, following the object and waiting for the favorable change to happen.

This line is in an incorrect position, but complementary to yin 3 (− −). The yang attitude of the object is neutral.

CHAPTER 11
When Mountain (⛰) is the Subject

This chapter contains yi text of eight hexagrams from 1:Ø to 1:7. Their subject trigrams are trigram 1, Mountain. The typical characteristic of mountain is to stop or block. Mountains are tall, and they stop everything that approaches. Mountains are stable, never changing position.

1 Hexagram 1:Ø Modest (In Zhou Yi, hexagram 15)

The title, Modest, describes what Chinese people see as an important virtue.

Trigram 1 (⛰), Mountain (stopping), is the subject; trigram Ø (☷), Earth (adaptability), is the object. Unlike water — which flows over the land to make rivers, lakes and oceans; unlike wind — which blows across the fields, displaying great power; and also unlike fire — which burns forests and threatens animals — the mountain stands quietly on the earth, not boasting about its tallness or taking advantage of neighbors. It constrains itself, showing honesty, fairness and respect.

In the text of this hexagram, you will not read such negative, judgmental words such as "blame," "regret," "mean," "danger," or "unfavorable." This is because, for more than five thousand years, the Chinese people have been endorsing the virtue of modesty.

1 General Text

Things are going smoothly.
A modest person has a good ending.

Both the subject and the object are weak, but the subject is a little stronger. While the object yields to the subject, the subject does not take advantage of the object, but stands firmly beside the object, like a faithful person taking care of a friend when both of them are trapped in a very difficult situation. Since they are working together, "things are going smoothly." The subject is modest and gives confidence to the object, so the subject "has a good ending."

2 Structure

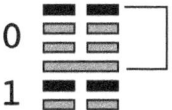

Figure 11.1: Structure of hexagram 1:0

In hexagram 1:Ø, four lines, yin 2 (--), yang 3 (—), yin 4 (--) and yin 6 (--), are in correct positions. The other two lines, yin 1 (--) and yin 5 (--), are in incorrect positions. The two top lines are complementary, and the two bottom lines and the two middle lines are in conflict. Hexagram Ø:1 is neutral, or a little favorable.

3 Texts of Lines

Yin 1

A truly modest person demonstrates
Modesty when taking adventures
Like crossing big rivers.
It is favorable.

Yin 1 (--) indicates that the subject is not inclined to move forward in the relationship. If the subject changes his or her action from yin to yang, "crossing big rivers," and demonstrates modesty while fulfilling these significant missions, the situation will be favorable for the subject.

This line is in an incorrect position and in conflict with yin 4 (--). The yin action of the subject is unfavorable.

Yin 2

Be modest in communication.
Staying on the current course is favorable.

Yin 2 (--) indicates that the subject is sick, has difficulties in finance, business, or social issues, or suffers from other disadvantages in life as does the object. If the subject honestly tells the truth to the object, without boasting, both of them will work together and the situation will be favorable.

This line is central and in a correct position, but in conflict with yin 5 (--). The yin essence of the subject is neutral.

Yang 3

Be modest in taking credit.
A nice person has a favorable ending.

Yang 3 (—) indicates that the subject seems arrogant, demanding and bossy, but is modest about taking credit. When something has been done, the subject always counts the contributions of the others first, objectively and fairly. The object feels the subject is honest and truthful. This modesty brings a favorable ending for the subject.

This line is in a correct position and complementary to yin 6 (- -). The yang attitude of the subject is favorable.

Yin 4

Nothing is detrimental.
Be modest in dealing with everything.

Yin 4 (- -) indicates that — like the subject — the object is self-protective and not inclined to go too far in the relationship. "Nothing is detrimental" for the subject in this. If the subject is modest in dealing with everything, the object will reward the subject with confidence, trust and respect.

This line is in a correct position, but in conflict with yin 1 (- -). The yin action of the object is neutral.

Yin 5

A modest person does not try
To become rich by taking advantage of neighbors.
It is beneficial to be modest during a war.
Nothing is detrimental.

Yin 5 (- -) indicates that the object is essentially in a weak position and needs help. So the subject helps, not taking advantage of the object, but working together with the object to get through the difficulties, being modest during the "war." The object supports the subject, so "nothing is detrimental."

This line is central, but in an incorrect position and in conflict with yin 2 (- -). The yin essence of the object is neutral.

Yin 6

Be modest in communication.
It is beneficial to be modest during
Advancing and conquering another country.

Yin 6 (− −) indicates that the object is humble, agreeable, and respectful. Now, both the subject and the object are working together to go through a challenging time, like "advancing and conquering another country." If the subject honestly tells the truth to the object, without boasting, the object is more likely to understand and cooperate with the subject. That makes their path together easier.

This line is in a correct position and complementary to yang 3 (▬). The yin attitude of the object is favorable.

2 Hexagram 1:1 Stop (In Zhou Yi, hexagram 52)

The title of hexagram 1:1, Stop, indicates that the relationship is in an awkward situation.

Hexagram 1:1 consists of double trigram 1 (− −), Mountain (stopping). A mountain blocks what is coming toward it and also keeps its own position unchanged. The two sides involved in this relationship are like two mountains: neither of them shifting position, yielding, communicating, or interacting.

1 General Text

She holds his back,
But cannot keep his body.
She comes over to his courtyard,
But cannot see him.
There is no blame.

Both the subject and the object have little strength, and neither one attracts the other. Both have no interest in improving the relationship, and both are stubborn. There is no touching or communication between the two, and yet they persist in the relationship. Now the subject is trying to find a way out of this dilemma: "She holds his back, but cannot keep his body. She comes over to his courtyard, but cannot see him." Here, "she" refers to the subject and "he" refers to the object. The subject does try to solve the problems, so "there is no blame." If nobody tries to address the problems, all should be blamed.

2 Structure

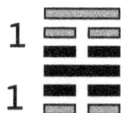

Figure 11.2: Structure of hexagram 1:1

In this hexagram, yin 2 (▬ ▬), yang 3 (▬▬▬), and yin 4 (▬ ▬) are in correct positions, but all the corresponding lines of the two component trigrams conflict with each other. Hexagram 1:1 is a little unfavorable.

3 Texts of Lines

Yin 1

She holds his toes.
There is no blame.
It is good to stay on the current course forever.

Yin 1 (▬ ▬) indicates that the subject has no interest in improving the relationship. But now the subject is trying to find a way out. So a little effort is put forth, as described in the phrase "she holds his toes": The subject is willing to make a small gesture. Since the toe is the lowest part of body, holding the toes is not a strong enough act to stop someone from running away. It is just a test of the object's attitude, to see how easy it would be to persuade the object to stay. Since the subject is doing his or her best, "there is no blame." This small, modest gesture of testing should continue until the two sides find a way to talk and solve their problems: "It is good to stay on the current course forever."

This line is in an incorrect position and in conflict with yin 4 (▬ ▬). The yin action of the subject is unfavorable. This means the subject should persist in as much action as possible, even if it's only "holding his toes," and seek the chance to change his or her action from yin to yang.

Yin 2

She holds his calves,
But he goes away.
Since she cannot follow him,
She feels unhappy.

Yin 2 (▬ ▬) indicates that the subject has very little power to control the object. "She holds his calves," but cannot stop the object from running away. That she is unable to follow the object makes her unhappy.

This line is central and in a correct position, but in conflict with yin 5 (▬ ▬). The yin essence of the subject is neutral.

Yang 3

When she holds his waist,

He strikes, even splitting his muscle.
That is dangerous.
She feels her heart is burning.

Yang 3 (━) indicates that the subject's stubborn attitude inspires a dramatic, desperate gesture: "she holds his waist." This succeeds in keeping the object from escaping from the relationship, but results in a dangerous struggle: "He strikes, even splitting his muscle. That is dangerous. She feels her heart is burning." This situation is difficult, possibly painful for the subject.

This line is in a correct position, but in conflict with yang 6 (━). The yang attitude of the subject is neutral.

Yin 4

She holds his body.
There is no blame.

Yin 4 (╌) indicates that when the subject tries to stop the problems in the relationship from getting worse, the object yields to the subject's efforts without resistance. When "she holds his body," the object does not run away. Because the subject is trying to hold the relationship together, the subject should not be blamed.

This line is in a correct position, but in conflict with yin 1 (╌). The yin action of the object is neutral.

Yin 5

She holds his cheek,
And talks with him patiently.
Regret vanishes.

Yin 5 (╌) indicates that the object is weak physically, financially, or spiritually, and needs help. When the subject engages in a sincere and direct conversation, and "holds his cheek," it seems he does not resist. This is the starting point for solving the problems: "Regret vanishes."

This line is central, but in an incorrect position and in conflict with yin 2 (╌). The yin essence of the object is neutral.

Yang 6

She urges him to stop uncongenial behavior.
That is favorable.

Yang 6 (—) indicates that the object's behavior is "uncongenial" — arrogant or rude or destructive, perhaps involving drugs, alcohol, or violence. Urging the object to stop this behavior is favorable for the subject.

This line is in an incorrect position and in conflict with yang 3 (—). The yang attitude of the object is unfavorable.

3 Hexagram 1:2 Lame (In Zhou Yi, hexagram 39)

The title, Lame, in Chinese also means difficulty in walking.

Trigram 1 (☶), Mountain (stopping) is the subject; trigram 2 (☵), Water (danger or difficulty) is the object. A mountain may block the flow of the water. The subject is arrogant and stubborn, like the mountain, blocking the object's effort to improve the relationship or help the subject. This frustrates the object and makes the relationship awkward. Indeed, the subject is weak, like a lame animal, but still limps away from the object, who is a "great person" and could offer help.

1 General Text

The current situation benefits southwest,
But not northeast.
It is beneficial to see the great person.
Staying on the current course is favorable.

At the time when King Wen revised the Yijing text, he was living in the "southwest," so this term refers to the homeland. The northeast refers to the foreign country. The subject should maintain the relationship, not break it up: "The current situation benefits southwest, but not northeast." The object is strong and able to help the subject: "It is beneficial to see the great person." If the subject can maintain the relationship and become closer to the object, "staying on the current course is favorable."

2 Structure

Figure 11.3: Structure of hexagram 1:2

In this hexagram, five lines are in correct positions, except yin 1 (- -). The two middle lines and the two top lines are complementary to each other. The two bottom lines are in conflict with each other. Hexagram 1:2 is neutral, or a little favorable.

3 Texts of Lines

Yin 1

Compared to limping away,
Limping back is honorable.

Yin 1 (▬ ▬) indicates that the subject, while having a severe difficulty, has no interest in improving the relationship and even wants to withdraw from it, "limping away." But, actually, it would be better to recommit to the relationship: "Compared to limping away, limping back is honorable." The subject should stay with the object because the object will help the subject.

This line is in an incorrect position and conflicts with yin 4 (▬ ▬). The yin action of the subject is unfavorable.

Yin 2

As a servant to the king,
I am limping around with a single leg.
That is not my fault.

Yin 2 (▬ ▬) indicates that the subject is in a weak position, "limping around with a single leg." The situation is difficult, but it is not the subject's fault, because the subject is trying to work with the object, "as a servant to the king." With help from the object, the situation will be better. If the subject yields to the difficulty and breaks up with the object, the situation will become worse. That will be the fault of the subject.

This line is central, in a correct position and complementary to yang 5 (▬▬). The yin essence of the subject is favorable.

Yang 3

Compared to limping away,
Limping back makes the situation reverse.

Yang 3 (▬▬) indicates that the subject's attitude is stubborn, but also truthful and honest, firmly dedicated to the relationship and insistent about accepting assistance from the object. In conflict with his or her own actions of seeking distance from the object, the subject firmly desires to be closer, revealing problems to the object truthfully and honestly. That makes helping the subject easier for the object. In this way, the subject's disadvantageous situation could be reversed.

This line is in a correct position and complementary to yin 6 (▬ ▬). The yang attitude of the subject is favorable.

Yin 4

Compared to limping away,
Limping back makes the connection stronger.

Yin 4 (∎ ∎) indicates that the object is frustrated with the relationship and is even ready to leave. In this difficult time, if the subject struggles to make the relationship closer, that will enhance the connection between the two sides: "Limping back makes the connection stronger."

This line is in a correct position, but in conflict with yin 1 (∎ ∎). The yin action of the object is neutral.

Yang 5

A big limp.
The friend comes to help.

Yang 5 (▬) indicates that the object is in a strong position — healthy or enjoying financial or social support — and is able to help the subject. When the subject has a severe difficulty, "a big limp," the object, "the friend," comes to help.

This line is central, in a correct position and complementary to yin 2 (∎ ∎). The yang essence of the object is favorable.

Yin 6

Compared to limping away,
Limping back is much more favorable.
It is beneficial to see a great person.

Yin 6 (∎ ∎) indicates the attitude of the object is yin. The object is kind, humble, agreeable, respectful and graceful. If the subject manages not to leave the object, and instead limps back to the object with "a single leg," the object will help the subject. The situation will be much better. The subject should make the effort to approach the object, the "great person," who has the ability to help.

This line is in a correct position and complementary to yang 3 (▬). The yin attitude of the object is favorable.

[4] Hexagram 1:3 Gradual (In Zhou Yi, hexagram 53)

The title, Gradual, indicates that the relationship develops gradually.

Trigram 1 (☶), Mountain (stopping) is the subject; trigram 3 (☴), Wind (flexibility), is the object. The mountain can stop the blowing wind, or divert the wind's direction when it is close to the mountain, but it cannot change the wind's volatile behavior. The subject would like to be able to control the object, so that the object does not simply go around the subject as if he or she were an obstacle in the way, but remains nearby — a gentle breeze instead of a fickle wind. But under the current circumstance, the subject has to be patient, "staying on the current course."

The text of this hexagram manifests a particular relationship, marriage. A woman is the subject, her husband is the object. A wild goose serves as the image of the husband, underlining his mobility. But when the hexagram applies to a real situation, the relationship is not necessarily a marriage relationship, and the subject is not necessarily a woman.

1 General Text

The marriage is favorable to the lady.
Staying on the current course is beneficial.

The subject is weak, sick, elderly, or having financial, social, or spiritual difficulties, and needs help. But the subject acts firmly, like a mountain standing still, without advancing. The object has a great physical, financial, social or spiritual strength, and is able to help the subject: "The marriage is favorable to the lady." However, the object is volatile, like a wind blowing in unpredictable directions. The subject should be patient, waiting for the object to become stable gradually, like a wind dying down: "staying on the current course is beneficial."

2 Structure

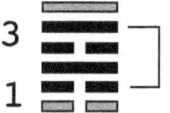

Figure 11.4: Structure of hexagram 1:3

In this hexagram four lines are in correct positions, except yin 1 (⚋) and yang 6 (⚊). The two middle lines are complementary with each other. The two bottom lines and the two top lines are in conflict. Hexagram 1:3 is neutral.

3 Texts of Lines

Yin 1

A wild goose approaches the shore.
A man comes to a lady.
There are rumors that
Going with this man could be dangerous.
There is no blame.

Yin 1 (**- -**) indicates that the subject, the lady, does not actively approach the object, the man, but remains still and worries about the danger of going out with the man. The subject is protecting himself or herself, courteously paying attention to the "rumors that going with this man could be dangerous." The subject should not be blamed.

This line is in an incorrect position and in conflict with yin 4 (**- -**). The yin action of the subject is unfavorable.

Yin 2

A goose lands on a boulder.
A man comes to a lady.
They eat and drink in peace and harmony.
It is favorable.

Yin 2 (**- -**) indicates that the subject does not have great power, but the object approaches the subject to "eat and drink" with her "in peace and harmony." The current situation is favorable for the subject, because the object has much to offer.

This line is central, in a correct position and complementary to yang 5 (**—**). The yin essence of the subject is favorable.

Yang 3

A goose flies to a field.
Her husband goes away to war.
He does not return.
The lady conceives from another man.
The lady cannot nurture the baby.
It is good for her husband far away
Fighting with an invader.
It is unfavorable to the lady.

Yang 3 (**—**) indicates that the subject is like a lady who does not patiently wait for her husband to return home, but has an affair with another man. Her yang attitude results in "conceiving from another man" and she "cannot nurture the baby." This yang attitude is unfavorable to the subject, because it can cause rash actions in a position of weakness.

This line is in a correct position, but in conflict with yang 6 (━). The yang attitude of the subject is neutral.

Yin 4

A goose lands on a tree
And perhaps finds a place to roost.
It is not a comfortable place
For the goose to stay.
The lady is expecting her husband back home.
There is no blame.

Yin 4 (━ ━) indicates that the object is not enthusiastic about moving the relationship forward, but is perched nearby for the moment. "A goose lands on a tree," instead of the land where it came from, and this tree "is not a comfortable place for the goose to stay." The subject is sincerely hoping the relationship will improve, and should not be blamed.

This line is in a correct position, but in conflict with yin 1 (━ ━). The yin action of the object is neutral.

Yang 5

A goose flies to a hill.
Her husband goes far away with the army.
She does not conceive for three years.
The enemy is unable to conquer the army.
Finally, it is favorable.

Yang 5 (━) indicates that the object possesses strength. However, the object has to use his strength for fulfilling his mission, not for helping the subject: "Her husband goes far away with the army." It will take some time before the object's strength is available to help the subject: "She does not conceive for three years." If the subject is patient, the situation will improve: "Finally, it is favorable."

This line is central, in a correct position and complementary to yin 2 (━ ━). The yang essence of the object is favorable.

Yang 6

The goose flies back to the land,
And stays there leaving a lot of feathers.

*The feathers are very beautiful
And can be used as ornaments.
It is favorable.*

Yang 6 (▬) indicates that the object is arrogant, rough, bossy, or self-centered. The object is also boastful, like the goose showing off its beautiful feathers. Like the object, the subject is also bossy and demanding. But since the subject is weak and needs help, they might get along very well in the end — after the object is through fighting other battles and "flies back to the land." The object has something of value to offer the subject: "The feathers are very beautiful and can be used as ornaments. It is favorable." However, the value of the feathers is superficial, not significant. The favorable result of this relationship also could be insignificant.

This line is in an incorrect position and in conflict with yang 3 (▬). The yang attitude of the object is unfavorable.

5 Hexagram 1:4 Tolerance (In Zhou Yi, hexagram 62)

The title, Tolerance, in Chinese consists of two characters: "small" and "pass." That means, "let the small one pass through." The implication is: Do not let the big one pass through.

Trigram 1 (☶), Mountain (stopping), is the subject; trigram 4 (☳), Thunder (movement) is the object. Tolerance occurs when a mountain muffles the rumblings of thunder but allows a small portion of the sound to pass through. The title implies that in this relationship, the subject should solve the problems when they are small and manageable, like the sound of thunder in the distance. Letting the problems pile up, out of control, can give rise to "catastrophe, or ailment."

1 General Text

*Things are going smoothly.
It is beneficial to stay on the current course.
One may do something unimportant,
But not important.
A voice of flying bird says:
"It is not good to soar up, but down."
It is very favorable.*

The subject does not want to move forward in the relationship, but the object does. The subject is pushed by the object until they work together: "Things are going smoothly. It is beneficial to stay on the current course."

On the other hand, both subject and object possess little strength, and can only attempt modest achievements: "One may do something unimportant, but not important." The object is humble, respectful and prudent, while the subject is arrogant and reckless. So they are getting along very well, but may be neglecting the conflict that is building up. The subject should heed "a voice of flying bird," that says, "It is not good to soar up, but down." The subject should not just go along with the object, like the bird soaring ever higher in the sky, but also should be looking down, finding out the problems when they remain under control and swooping down to solve them. If the subject can follow this advice, the situation is favorable to the subject.

2 Structure

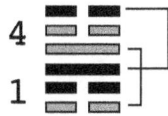

Figure 11.5: Structure of hexagram 1:4

In this hexagram, yin 2 (- -), yang 3 (—), and yin 6 (- -) are in correct positions, but the other three are in incorrect positions. The two bottom lines and the two top lines are complementary to each other. The two central lines are in conflict. Hexagram 1:4 is neutral.

3 Texts of Lines

Yin 1

Acting like a flying bird is unfavorable.

Yin 1 (- -) indicates that the subject does not seek to move like a bird at the sound of thunder, but to stay in place like a mountain. The object pushes the subject to move, but while yielding to the object's force, the subject should carefully observe changes in the situation and do something to prevent trouble — not in the flighty manner of a bird that neglects what happens on the ground.

This line is in an incorrect position, but complementary to yang 4 (—). The yin action of the subject is neutral.

Yin 2

*One does not meet with the grandfather
Who passed through,*

But meets with the grandmother.
One does not reach the king
Who went too far,
But reaches the minister.
There is no blame.

Yin 2 (==) indicates that the subject has less strength and needs help. In seeking assistance from others, the subject should tolerate disappointments and make compromises. If the subject does not succeed in reaching his or her primary goal — "does not meet with the grandfather" or "reach the king who went too far" — but gains something beneficial — "meets with the grandmother" or "reaches the minister" — the subject should not be blamed.

This line is central, in a correct position, but in conflict with yin 5 (==). The yin essence of the subject is neutral.

Yang 3

If the animal does not go beyond the fence,
Prevent it from doing so.
If it appears to be going beyond the fence,
No matter, letting it go or killing it.
That is unfavorable.

Yang 3 (—) indicates that the subject is arrogant, bossy, and demanding, which is helpful for maintaining control. Since both the subject and the object have little strength, no resources, no experience, or no support, it is important to keep any problems contained, like an animal that "does not go beyond the fence." If this prevention fails, and the problem gets out of control, it doesn't matter what the subject does at that point, "letting it go or killing it." If this happens, the relationship can become a lost cause: "That is unfavorable."

This line is in a correct position, complementary to yin 6 (==), and supported by yin 2 (==). The yang attitude of the subject is favorable.

Yang 4

There is no blame.
Meet with the animal, which does not pass yet.
Be aware of the danger from letting it going away.
Do not let it go.
Stay on this course forever.

Yang 4 (—) indicates that the object pushes the relationship forward, while the subject follows: "There is no blame." However, the subject should pay attention to anticipate problems before they happen: "Meet with the animal, which does not pass yet." "Be aware of the danger" when problems get out of hand. "Stay on this course forever," remaining courteous and watchful as the relationship develops.

This line is in an incorrect position, but complementary to yin 1 (==). The yang action of the object is neutral.

Yin 5

There are the dense clouds,
But it is not rain yet.
The clouds come from our west suburbs.
The lord shoots an animal in a cave
And catches it.

Yin 5 (==) indicates that the object pushes the relationship forward, but has no experience, resources, or support for his or her actions. The subject follows the object, but is weak and unable to help the object. In this relationship, there could be problems, but they have not surfaced: "There are the dense clouds, but it is not rain yet." In the middle of this insecure situation, the subject should be realistic and pragmatic, and stick to actions that are possible and useful, like a lord who "shoots an animal in a cave and catches it" while the clouds are gathering outside.

This line is central, but in an incorrect position and in conflict with yin 2 (==). The yin essence of the object is neutral.

Yin 6

One does not meet with the animal,
Which passes the fence.
A bird flies away,
It is unfavorable.
It is called catastrophe,
Or ailment.

Yin 6 (==) indicates that the object is humble, agreeable, respectful and graceful, while the subject is arrogant, rough, reckless, and bossy. The subject gets along well with the object, but the problems in the relationship could be easily neglected. When problems come to the surface, they are already out of control and cannot be faced: "One does not meet with the animal, which passes the fence." When this happens, the relationship suffers damage and is very hard to restore to its original state, like a bird that "flies away." "It is unfavorable" — amounting to a "catastrophe, or ailment."

This line is in a correct position and complementary to yang 3 (▬). The yin attitude of the object is favorable.

6 Hexagram 1:5 Travel (In Zhou Yi, hexagram 56)

The title, Travel, suggests that the relationship between the subject and the object resembles that of a landlord and travelers. The landlord receives the booking requests from the travelers, provides services, and receives payment; then the travelers go on their way.

Trigram 1 (☶), Mountain (stopping), is the subject; trigram 5 (☲), Fire (brightness and clinging) is the object. The bright object flickers, and needs the subject to cling to, just as a traveler needs a hotel to stay in at night. The subject does not stand to gain too much from the object, and also cannot hurt the object, because the object is a moving target: "The travelers are like pheasants. If I shoot a pheasant, it flies away with my arrow. I get nothing, but lose an arrow."

1 General Text

Things are going a little smoothly.
The travelers always stop by me.
Staying on the current course is favorable.

The object comes to the subject, advancing the relationship further, but both sides have little strength, and their arrogant and bullying attitudes conflict. The situation is acceptable, but not great: "Things are going a little smoothly." The subject is in a weak position and needs help. If the object comes to the subject frequently, the subject benefits, like a landlord with a full house: "The travelers always stop by me. Staying on the current course is favorable."

2 Structure

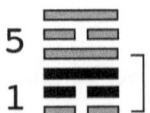

Figure 11.6: Structure of hexagram 1:5

In this hexagram, only yin 2 (▬ ▬) and yang 3 (▬) are in correct positions; other lines are in incorrect positions. Only the two bottom lines are complementary to each other. The other lines are in conflict. Hexagram 1:5 is neutral, or less favorable.

3 Texts of Lines

Yin 1

The travelers are petty.
They cause me trouble.

Yin 1 (━ ━) indicates that the subject does not want to improve the relationship, but the object does. The object pushes the subject to advance further. However, the essence of the object is yin, so the object cannot help the subject too much: "The travelers are petty." And in attitude, the object as well as the subject is arrogant, self-centered, and bossy: "They cause me trouble."

This line is in an incorrect position, but complementary to yang 4 (━). The yin action of the subject is neutral.

Yin 2

Travelers stop by my house.
I receive payment,
And hire a child servant.
Stay on the current course.

Yin 2 (━ ━) indicates that the subject is in a weak position and needs help. The object comes to the subject and helps a little, like a traveler paying for a night's lodging: "Travelers stop by my house. I receive payment, and hire a child servant." Because of this benefit, the subject should keep in contact with the object: "Stay on the current course."

This line is central and in a correct position, but in conflict with yin 5 (━ ━). The yin essence of the subject is neutral.

Yang 3

The travelers burn my house.
I lose my child servant.
It is dangerous.

Yang 3 (━) indicates that the subject is arrogant, rough, and bossy. And so is the object, so the two sides could become entangled in a conflict that is destructive for the subject: "The travelers burn my house. I lose my child servant." This rough and bossy behavior could damage the relationship: "It is dangerous."

This line is in a correct position, but in conflict with yang 6 (▬). The yang attitude of the subject is neutral, or less favorable.

Yang 4

The travelers stay in my house.
I get a lot of money in axe-shaped currency.
I feel unhappy.

Yang 4 (▬) indicates that the object wants to have a better relationship, and is willing to contribute: "The travelers stay in my house. I get a lot of money in axe-shaped currency" — which was a kind of highly valuable cash used in ancient times. However, the object is arrogant and demanding, so the subject is less than pleased with this exchange: "I feel unhappy."

This line is in an incorrect position, but complementary to yin 1 (▬ ▬). The yang action of the object is neutral.

Yin 5

The travelers are like pheasants.
If I shoot a pheasant,
It flies away with my arrow.
I get nothing, but lose an arrow.
I have to keep my dignity and live to the end.

Yin 5 (▬ ▬) indicates that the object is essentially weak, but mobile. While the subject tries to hurt the object, the object cannot fight against the subject, but can flee: "The travelers are like pheasants. If I shoot a pheasant, it flies away with my arrow. I get nothing, but lose an arrow." The subject cannot gain from the object's weakness. The subject is also weak and arrogant. Though there is no way to make the situation better, "I have to keep my dignity and live to the end."

This line is in an incorrect position and in conflict to yin 2 (▬ ▬), but central. The yin essence of the object is neutral, or less favorable.

Yang 6

A bird has its nest burned.
The travelers are excited and laughing at first,
But cry for their tragedy at the end.
"The oxen were lost in the country of Yi."
It is unfavorable.

Yang 6 (▬) indicates that the object is arrogant, rough, rude, and demanding.

So is the subject, which causes problems in the relationship. The object's yang attitude can mean that he or she enjoys causing trouble, but is not essentially a cruel person: "A bird has its nest burned. The travelers are excited and laughing at first, but cry for their tragedy at the end."

In this text, Yi is a name of a country in ancient times. "The oxen were lost in the country of Yi," refers to a story that originated around 1900 B.C. Duke Hai, with his brother Heng, drove a group of wagons and a big flock of sheep and oxen into the country of Yi. The oxen drew the wagons. The inhabitants of Yi had never seen that method of transportation. Duke Mianchen, the leader of Yi, entertained Duke Hai and his entourage and asked if they would teach him to train oxen in this manner, and Duke Hai agreed.

During his stay, Duke Hai discovered Duke Mianchen's very beautiful daughter. He met with her secretly, but his brother Heng discovered their secret. Heng was also interested in this beautiful young girl, and disclosed the affair to Duke Mianchen out of jealousy. Duke Mianchen, outraged, killed Duke Hai and confiscated all the wagons, oxen and sheep.

By citing this story, the text suggests the yang attitude of the object is not good for the object.

But it is not good for the subject either, who is like the landlord whose travelers get themselves into trouble; this means the landlord loses business and suffers loss as well.

This line is in an incorrect position and in conflict to yang 3 (▬). The yang attitude of the object is unfavorable.

[7] Hexagram 1:6 Enjoyable (In Zhou Yi, hexagram 31)

The title, Enjoyable is represented in Chinese by the word "Gan," meaning "to feel" or "to sense."

Trigram 1 (☶), Mountain (stopping), is the subject; trigram 6 (☱), Lake (pleasure), is the object. The lake is above the mountain, like a reservoir at the peak that sends refreshing waterfalls cascading down the mountain. To enjoy the relationship, the subject has to understand the object, to feel or sense the object. Meanwhile, the object presents the subject with pleasure, like a friend whose presence is perfectly in tune with one's inner longings: "The companion follows your thought."

1 General Text

Things are going smoothly.
It is beneficial to stay on the current course.
To marry a woman is favorable.

The subject does not deliberately pursue a better relationship, but the object does. The object pushes the subject to move forward in the relationship, helps the subject with any difficulties, and respects the subject, while the subject is arrogant and bossy. "Things are going smoothly," because the current situation favors the subject: "It is beneficial to stay on the current course." The subject should allow the object to come closer: "To marry a woman is favorable." Here, marriage is a metaphor for an enjoyable, beneficial state; the relationship does not have to be marital. And while the text for this hexagram describes the progress of an intimate, sensual encounter, it can apply to any relationship where pleasure and enjoyment deepen as the subject and object get to know each other better.

2 Structure

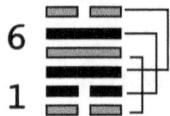

Figure 11.7: Structure of hexagram 1:6

In this hexagram, yin 2 (━ ━), yang 3 (━━), and yang 5 (━━) are in correct positions; the other three lines are in incorrect positions. All the lines are complementary to the corresponding lines. Hexagram 1:6 is favorable.

3 Texts of Lines

Yin 1

Feel the toes.

Yin 1 (━ ━) indicates that the subject does not want to do much to push the relationship forward. "Feel the toes" means the subject can only appreciate the object in a limited way. What the subject is doing for the relationship is insignificant.

This line is in an incorrect position, but complementary to yang 4 (━━). The yin action of the subject is neutral.

Yin 2

Feel the calves.
Going further is unfavorable.
Keeping the current situation is favorable.

Yin 2 (--) indicates that the subject is essentially incapable of knowing the object well. "Feel the calves" describes a situation where the subject starts really getting to know the object better, but what the subject senses is not significant. Because of the subject's limited perceptions, going forward will create a situation unfavorable to the subject. The subject should be patient and persistent, remaining at this level of intimacy: "Keeping the current situation is favorable" to the subject.

This line is central, in a correct position and complementary to yang 5 (—). The yin essence of the subject is favorable.

Yang 3

Feel the thighs.
Persist in following others.
Moving away is mean.

Yang 3 (—) indicates that the subject is straightforward, frank and open to the object, which makes mutual understanding easier. "Feel the thighs" means that, thanks to a yang attitude, the subject is getting to know the object better, even sensing private aspects of the object's situation. The subject should follow the object's lead in advancing the relationship: "Persist in following others." A yang attitude allows the subject to enjoy significant happiness in the relationship, but could also cause the subject to become arrogant or reckless, moving away rather than following the object. This could make the object unhappy: "Moving away is mean."

This line is in a correct position and complementary to yin 6 (--). The yang attitude of the subject is favorable.

Yang 4

Staying on this course is favorable.
Regret vanishes.
Flickering back and forth, the companion follows your thought.

Yang 4 (—) indicates that the object is actively pushing the relationship forward, with the inevitability and enjoyment of a lake's water cascading down a mountainside: "Staying on this course is favorable. Regret vanishes." Since the subject is passive, and resistant to progress, the object is doing what the subject wants, like water changing its course among rocks and crevices: "Flickering back and forth, the companion follows your thought."

This line is in an incorrect position, but complementary to yin 1 (--). The yang action of the object is neutral.

Yang 5

Feel the flesh.
There is no regret.

Yang 5 (━) indicates that the object has strength and could benefit the subject. The subject perceives the warmth and liveliness of the object: "Feel the flesh." The situation is gratifying and enjoyable: "There is no regret."

This line is central, in a correct position and complementary to yin 2 (╌). The yang essence of the object is favorable.

Yin 6

Feel the cheeks,
Jaw and tongue.

Yin 6 (╌) indicates that the object behaves gently, speaking nicely and approaching respectfully, making it easier for the subject to sense, feel, and understand. The subject is listening to what the object is saying and enjoys the object's graceful, yielding ways: "Feel the cheeks, jaw and tongue."

This line is in a correct position and complementary to yang 3 (━). The yin attitude of the object is favorable.

[8] Hexagram 1:7 Flee (In Zhou Yi, hexagram 33)

The Chinese word for the title, Flee, shares the same pronunciation with "Fly" and "Fat." Its multiple meanings appear in the title and the texts of this hexagram.

Trigram 1 (☶), Mountain (stopping) is the subject; trigram 7 (☰), Heaven (strength), is the object. The subject behaves roughly, but lacks power, like the disobedient subject of an almighty ruler. The best course for the subject in this situation is to escape from the object's control: "Flying away. Nothing is detrimental."

1 General Text

Things are going smoothly.
Staying on the current course is slightly beneficial.

The subject is weak and needs help, while the object is strong and able to help, control or destroy the subject. The subject does not want to become deeply involved in the relationship, but the object approaches the subject and seeks to control him or her, like the sun rising above the mountain and shining down on it relentlessly. The object is arrogant, rude, self-centered, and bullying, but instead of yielding to the object's power, the subject stubbornly maintains his or her dignity, freedom, and independence. Facing strong pressures, the stubborn subject struggles to maintain the current situation. At this moment, no trouble has yet occurred; the subject is standing still like a mountain, bearing up under the heat: "Things are going smoothly." But there is little to be gained from this stance: "Staying on the current course is slightly beneficial." Fleeing may be a better choice.

2 Structure

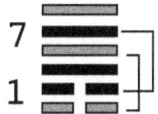

Figure 11.8: Structure of hexagram 1:7

In this hexagram, three lines, yin 2 (━ ━), yang 3 (━━), and yang 5 (━━) are in correct positions. The two bottom lines and the two middle lines are complementary to each other. The two top lines are in conflict with each other. Hexagram 1:7 is neutral.

3 Text of Lines

Yin 1

Fleeing too late,
As at the tail of an incident, is dangerous.
It is not a good time to do something.

Yin 1 (━ ━) indicates that the subject hesitates, does not want to flee, and instead sticks to routine behaviors. This will delay and possibly prevent an escape: "Fleeing too late, as at the tail of an incident, is dangerous." But now, under a direct threat from the object, "it is not a good time to do something."

This line is in an incorrect position, but complementary to yang 4 (━━). The yin action of the subject is neutral.

Yin 2

A leather belt
Made from the hide of a yellow ox binds one.

One cannot get away.

Yin 2 (− −) indicates that under the current situation, the subject should flee, but cannot do so. The subject's yin essence has created a reliance on the powerful object, like "a leather belt made from the hide of a yellow ox." This tie that binds works both ways: The subject can get help from the object, even though this requires a sacrifice of freedom.

This situation might not be too bad for the subject. The line is central, in a correct position and complementary to yang 5 (—), so the yin essence of the subject is favorable. To gain benefits, the subject has to be complementary to the object, which in this case calls for remaining in one place, under the object's power.

Yang 3

When one is involved in several positions,
Fleeing is dangerous
And troublesome.
Keeping servants and concubines is favorable.

Yang 3 (—) indicates that the subject's stubborn attitude leads him or her to believe that fleeing is humiliating, or that it is too difficult to escape from complicated entanglements with others: "One is involved in several positions." Under the current situation the subject should flee, but fleeing could be dangerous, because success is not certain. Before fleeing, the subject should simplify his or her position, severing connections with others and traveling as lightly as possible, carrying only the necessities: "Keeping servants and concubines is favorable."

This line is in a correct position, but in conflict with yang 6 (—). The yang attitude of the subject is neutral.

Yang 4

Fleeing is a good action.
It is favorable for an intelligent person.
It is not favorable for the foolish.

Yang 4 (—) indicates that the object is aggressively pushing the subject. That encourages the subject to leave without hesitation: "Fleeing is a good action." The intelligent person is able to assess the situation and is willing to flee. Taking a yin action in response to the yang action of the object is favorable to the subject. However, a foolish person may take a yang action to resist the object. That is unfavorable.

This line is in an incorrect position, but complementary to yin 1 (− −). The yang action of the object is neutral, depending on how the subject responds. If the subject is smart, the yang action of the object makes the subject flee at the right moment, avoiding major loss. If the subject resists, the yang action of the object could cause the subject to suffer severe damage.

Yang 5

Fleeing is an honorable action.
Staying on this course is favorable.

Yang 5 (━) indicates that the object is strong, powerful, or wealthy. If the subject stays on the current course, he or she could get help from the object. However, if the subject flees, this could mean missing the chance for benefit from the object, but it is "an honorable action" in the interests of freedom and dignity.

This line is central, in a correct position and complementary to yin 2 (╌). The yang essence of the object is favorable.

Yang 6

One flees,
Flying away with whatever is valuable.
Nothing is detrimental.

Yang 6 (━) indicates that the object is arrogant, harsh, rude, bossy, self-centered, or demanding. This compels the subject to flee, "flying away with whatever is valuable," including family members and money. Fleeing means that the subject retains freedom and dignity, avoids loss, and possibly meets with a new chance: "Nothing is detrimental."

This line is in an incorrect position and conflicts with yang 3 (━). The yang attitude of the object is unfavorable. If the subject flees, leaving this unfavorable situation behind, the situation could become beneficial.

CHAPTER 12
When Water (☵) is the Subject

THIS CHAPTER CONTAINS YI TEXT of eight hexagrams from 2:Ø to 2:7. Their subject trigrams are trigram 2, Water. The typical characteristics of water are danger and difficulty. This can be danger and difficulty that one faces or that one imposes on others.

1 Hexagram 2:Ø Army (In Zhou Yi, hexagram 7)

The title, Army, gives a sense of the subject and object working together, like an army fighting a common enemy. Trigram 2 (☵), Water (difficulty and danger), is the subject; trigram Ø (☷), Earth (adaptability), is the object. The object is very weak, needing help and yielding to the subject. The subject is strong and able to help, but has some difficulties in dealing with the object — like water encountering obstacles in its movement over the earth. So the water must make its own course: To win the war, the subject has to solve his or her own problems and become a qualified commander: "To create a new country, or to build an inherited family, never use an unqualified person."

1 General Text

Stay on the current course.
It is favorable to an older person.
There is no blame.

The object is weak and needs help, while the subject is strong and able to help the object. The subject should "stay on the current course," like an army fighting a common enemy. Currently, the subject and object are both passive and unfocused, like an army with a poor administration. Neither subject nor object behaves truthfully and frankly, so they resemble an army that lacks good communication. To win, the subject has to solve these problems, being stronger than the object, and become a qualified commander: "It is favorable to an older person." If the subject makes this effort, "there is no blame."

2 Structure

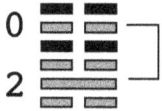

Figure 12.1: Structure of hexagram 2:0

In this hexagram, only two lines, yin 4 (▬ ▬) and yin 6 (▬ ▬), are in correct positions. The two central lines are complementary to each other, but the two bottom lines and the two top lines are in conflict with each other. Hexagram 2:Ø is less favorable.

3 Texts of Lines

Yin 1

After departure,
The army must be highly disciplined,
Otherwise there will be a tragedy.

Yin 1 (▬ ▬) indicates that the subject is tired, or somehow frustrated in the relationship. But the object is weak and needs help, and the subject is a proper person to help the object. So the subject must rise to this occasion. If the subject does not change his or her action from yin to yang, the subject will not be able to lead the object through the difficult time: "After departure, the army must be highly disciplined." If the subject maintains a passive action, the army will continue to lack organization and will lose the war: "There will be a tragedy."

This line is in an incorrect position and in conflict with yin 4 (▬ ▬). The yin action of the subject is unfavorable.

Yang 2

During the expedition,
The situation is favorable.
There is no blame.
The king assigns a mission three times.

Yang 2 (▬▬) indicates that the subject is essentially strong and able to help the object. When the subject helps the object, the situation improves and the subject's efforts could be repaid, morally or materially: "During the expedition, the situation is favorable. There is no blame." That encourages the subject to assist the object, fulfilling a duty toward friendship, family, love, or business: "The king assigns a mission three times."

This line is central and complementary to yin 5 (==), but in an incorrect position. The yang essence of the subject is neutral, or a little favorable.

Yin 3

When the army puzzles,
There are so many casualties,
The soldiers' bodies are removed with wagons.
It is unfavorable.

Yin 3 (==) indicates that the subject is humble, kind, agreeable, and respectful. Meanwhile, the object is just as humble, kind, agreeable, and respectful as the subject. They respect each other, but may be unable to communicate with each other in a frank, straightforward way. They puzzle at what they should do, and that could be harmful for both: "When the army puzzles, there are so many casualties, the soldiers' bodies are removed with wagons." The subject should change his or her attitude from yin to yang, talking to the object truthfully and honestly, finding a way out; otherwise, the situation could be unfavorable to the subject.

This line is in an incorrect position and in conflict with yin 6 (==). The yin attitude of the subject is unfavorable.

Yin 4

The army retreats.
There is no blame.

Yin 4 (==) indicates that the object does not want to move forward in the relationship, and even wants to yield to the common enemy, because he or she is close to losing heart from the failure of progress: "The army retreats." The subject understands the seriousness of this situation and is doing his or her best, so "there is no blame."

This line is in a correct position, but in conflict with yin 1 (==). The yin action of the object is neutral.

Yin 5

There is game in a field.
It is beneficial to facilitate the communication.
There is no blame.
While an older son leads the armies into the battle,
A younger son removes the corpses with wagons.
Staying on this course is unfavorable.

Yin 5 (− −) indicates that the object is in a weak position and needs help. The subject is strong and helps the object. Two of them work together, with the chance of making progress: "There is game in a field." To catch the game, they have to cooperate, communicating with each other: "It is beneficial to facilitate the communication."

Knowing what is going on with the object, the subject is able to help the object effectively: "There is no blame." But if there is a lack of communication, that causes more casualties: "while an older son leads the army into the battle, a younger son removes the corpses with wagons." "Staying on this course is unfavorable," because removal of corpses with wagons should take place after the battle is won. The subject should do the things for the object at the right time, in the right way, and cooperation is vital.

This line is central, in an incorrect position, but complementary to yang 2 (−). The yin essence of the object is neutral.

Yin 6

The great leader taught,
That to create a new country, or
To build an inherited family,
Never use an unqualified person.

Yin 6 (− −) indicates that the object may be obedient, adaptive, humble, or respectful, accepting the demands of the subject and following his or her instructions. Meanwhile, the subject is humble like the object, and this could pose problems. Without clear instruction and a determined commander, the object could be confused and lose confidence in the subject. The subject has to learn, to study, to understand the real situation and acquire the ability to win the war. The subject has to make himself or herself into a qualified person.

This line is in a correct position, but in conflict with yin 3 (− −). The yin attitude of the object is neutral.

2 Hexagram 2:1 Ignorance (In Zhou Yi, hexagram 4)

The title of hexagram 2:1, Ignorance, is depicted by a Chinese character that has multiple meanings: cover, ignorant, illiterate, receive, cheat, and unconscious. It is often used in the sense of enlightening, as illustrated by the relationship between a teacher and pupils.

Trigram 2 (☵), Water (difficulty and danger) is the subject; trigram 1 (☶),

Mountain (stopping), is the object. The subject encounters difficulty, like flowing water that has been stopped by a mountain as it washes down its path toward the ocean.

In a relationship, when a sluggish person does not respond to the actions of other people, it may be considered like a mountain, getting in the way of the flow. In this case, the subject has difficulty overcoming the sluggishness of the object, like a teacher frustrated with the task of teaching an ignorant student. The subject should not go to great lengths to accommodate a resistant object: "It is not I seeking pupils, but the pupils beg me."

1 General Text

Things are going smoothly.
The teacher says,
"It is not I seeking pupils,
But the pupils beg me.
The question will be answered the first time.
The repeated questions,
Which show impertinence,
Will not be answered."
It is beneficial to stay on the current course.

The object is weak and needs help. The subject is strong, and able to help the object, so there is a potential for success: "Things are going smoothly." But the object is arrogant, rough and demanding. The subject respects the object, but the object does not come willingly to the subject, and this is frustrating because the object is the needy one: "It is not I seeking pupils, but the pupils beg me." Regardless, the subject proceeds to offer some help to the object: "The question will be answered the first time."

But the ultimate solution to the object's problems are in the object's own hands; there is a limit to what the subject can do. Only the object can finally solve the problems through hard work, which the subject should not be asked to do: "The repeated questions, which show impertinence, will not be answered." While helping the object, the subject should encourage the object to do his or her own work. That will make the progress easier and relieve the subject from stress: "It is beneficial to stay on the current course," and not yield to unreasonable demands from the object.

2 Structure

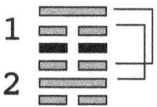

Figure 12.2: Structure of hexagram 2:1

In this hexagram, yin 4 (- -) is the only line in a correct position. The other five lines are in incorrect positions. The two bottom lines are in conflict with each other. The two middle lines and the two top lines are complementary to each other. Hexagram 2:1 is neutral, or less favorable.

3 Texts of Lines

Yin 1

The teacher shows the ignorant
The model,
Who feels the freedom
Gained from learning,
Like getting rid of fetters and handcuffs.
It is mean to ask pupils to do too much.

Yin 1 (- -) indicates that the subject does not want to do anything for the object. Regardless of this reluctance, the subject should make an effort for the object, even if it's very limited — like a teacher exposing an ignorant student to the "model, who feels the freedom gained from learning, like getting rid of fetters and handcuffs." Then it is up to the object to learn from this example; the subject should not push the object too forcefully: "It is mean to ask pupils to do too much."

This line is in an incorrect position and in conflict with yin 4 (- -). The yin action of the subject is unfavorable.

Yang 2

Taking care of an ignorant person is favorable.
To marry a woman is favorable.
The woman might give birth to a child
Who will grow up and become a householder.

Yang 2 (—) indicates that the subject is in a strong position and able to do something for the object: "Taking care of an ignorant person is favorable." Despite the fact that the object is weak, stubborn, and uncooperative, this care could turn out to be valuable: If you marry an ignorant woman, she may be not smart, but her child might prove capable of being a householder.

This line is central and complementary to yin 5 (∎∎), but in an incorrect position. The yang essence of the subject is neutral.

Yin 3

Do not marry a woman,
Who seeks a wealthy man,
And loses possession of herself.
It is not beneficial.

Yin 3 (∎∎) indicates that the subject is modest and agreeable. However, if the subject is too humble and agreeable, the situation may not be desirable, as when a powerful person stoops too low in hopes of helping someone who will not benefit: "Do not marry a woman, who seeks a wealthy man, and loses possession of herself." If the subject behaves too humbly and agreeably, "it is not beneficial."

This line is in an incorrect position, but complementary to yang 6 (∎). The yin attitude of the subject is neutral.

Yin 4

Dealing with weary ignorance
Is mean.

Yin 4 (∎∎) indicates that the object does not want to move the relationship forward, like a tired, ignorant student who just wants to sleep or leave the class. If the subject pushes the object to move forward, but the object does not respond, trying to overcome this sluggishness makes the subject seem mean.

This line is the only line in a correct position, but in conflict with yin 1 (∎∎). The yin action of the object is neutral.

Yin 5

Teaching youthful ignorance
Is favorable.

Yin 5 (∎∎) indicates that the object is in a weak position, like anyone who displays "youthful ignorance." The object needs help from the subject. While the subject helps the object, the subject also gains. That is favorable for the subject.

This line is central, complementary to yang 2 (∎), but in an incorrect position. The yin essence of the object is favorable, even though the subject has to help the object.

Yang 6

Teach violent ignorance
That it is beneficial not to be a robber,
But to be a defender against robbers.

Yang 6 (▬) indicates that the object is in the grips of "violent ignorance." The subject should help the object change this rough attitude, and bring out the best in the object, teaching that "it is beneficial not to be a robber, but to be a defender against robbers."

This line is in an incorrect position, but complementary to yin 3 (▬ ▬). The yang attitude of the object is neutral.

[3] Hexagram 2:2 Pitfall (In Zhou Yi, hexagram 29)

The title, Pitfall, indicates a difficulty in the relationship, like the sensation of being trapped in a pitfall, with no way out. In ancient times, a pitfall might be used as a prison.

Both subject and object of this hexagram are trigram 2 (☵), Water (danger or difficulty.) In the current relationship, both subject and object have dangers and difficulties, the kind that stem from a particular environmental situation. For example, if you are in the waiting room of an airport with millions of dollars in your pocket and the airplane is ready to be boarded, but the airport is hit with a major power blackout, suddenly you are trapped in a "pitfall." What should you do? You "should be more prudent, doing nothing."

1 General Text

Being trapped in a pitfall,
If one is sincere from the heart with others,
Things will be going smoothly.
One's effort will be rewarded.

Both the subject and the object have strength, but no one can use this strength to push the relationship forward. They are "trapped in a pitfall." Both of them are humble and yielding to each other, but they suffer from a lack of communication, without truthful talking: "If one is sincere from the heart with others, things will be going smoothly." If the subject actively talks with the object and inspires the object's cooperation, the subject's effort will be rewarded."

2 Structure

Figure 11.3: Structure of hexagram 2:2.

In this hexagram, all the three lines of the object trigram are in correct positions, but the three lines of the subject trigrams are in incorrect positions. There is no line complementary with the other line. Hexagram 2:Ø is neutral, less favorable.

3 Texts of Lines

Yin 1

There is a deep pitfall.
One is trapped in the pitfall.
It is unfavorable.

Yin 1 (⚋) indicates that the subject does not do something to improve the relationship because he or she is in a difficult time, like being trapped in a deep pitfall: "It is unfavorable."

This line is in an incorrect position and in conflict with yin 4 (⚋). The yin action of the subject is unfavorable. It is very hard for the subject to make a change in this aspect, since the subject is like being trapped in a deep pitfall.

Yang 2

The pitfalls are dangerous.
Seek a little gain, not big gain.

Yang 2 (⚊) indicates that the subject has strength. However, at this very difficult time, the subject is unable to gain a significant benefit by using this strength. What the subject can do is insignificant. Meanwhile, the object possesses strength, just as the subject does. The subject cannot help the object, because the object does not want the help.

This line is central, but in conflict with yang 5 (⚊) and in an incorrect position. The yang essence of the subject is neutral.

Yin 3

One comes to a hazardous pitfall,
Which is dangerous and deep.

One is trapped in the pitfall
And should be more prudent, doing nothing.

Yin 3 (- -) indicates that the subject is humble, adaptive, and agreeable. Meanwhile, the object has the same attitude as the subject does. That makes mutual understanding difficult. However, in the current difficult and dangerous situation, the subject should not make a change in attitude. The subject should be "more prudent" and do nothing, waiting for a better chance.

This line is in an incorrect position and in conflict with yin 6 (- -). The yin action of the subject is unfavorable.

Yin 4

One receives a simple meal
From a high window with two baskets.
In one basket there is a cup of wine.
In another basket there is a jar of food.
There is no blame in the end.

Yin 4 (- -) indicates that the object does not want to push the relationship ahead, and does not want to help the subject. That is unfavorable for the subject.

However, the subject should carefully watch any changes in the situation, even a subtle change, like "a simple meal" for a prisoner dropping from a high window of the prison. That little change helps the subject going through the difficult time, and possibly results in a good ending.

This line is in a correct position, but in conflict with yin 1 (- -). The yin action of the object is neutral.

Yang 5

The pitfall is not full.
Only its hilly bottom is covered by dirt.
There is no blame.

Yang 5 (—) indicates that the object has strength and is able to make a contribution to the relationship, like filling in the pitfall with dirt. However, the action of the object is yin, and the object does not want to do much for the relationship, so the "pitfall" may be filled with dirt, but not enough to allow escape. Only its hilly bottom is covered by the dirt. That is not the subject's fault, because the subject cannot alter the action of the object: "There is no blame."

This line is in a correct position, but in conflict to yang 2 (—). The yang essence of the object is neutral.

Yin 6

One is bound to the other by rope
And trapped in the bramble bush.
They find no way out for three years.
It is unfavorable.

Yin 6 (▬ ▬) indicates that the object is as humble, adaptive, and agreeable as the subject is. This is not good for mutual understanding, or for resolving the tough problems in their relationship. The subject feels as though he or she is bound to the object "by rope and trapped in the bramble bush." They are in a stalemate, feeling hopeless, as if there were "no way out for three years."

This line is in a correct position, but in conflict with yin 3 (▬ ▬). The yin action of the object is neutral.

4 Hexagram 2:3 Flood (In Zhou Yi, hexagram 59)

In Chinese, the title of hexagram 2:3 is "Huan," meaning "melt" or "vanish," but it is hardly ever used alone. Frequently this character is doubled, as in "Huan huan," describing a huge flood. Sometimes this character combines with another character "san," as "Huansan," meaning "lax" or "slack." The flood this hexagram refers to could wash away houses, crops, trees, animals, inundate fields, even kill a lot of people.

Trigram 2 (☵), Water (difficulty and danger), is the subject; trigram 3 (☴), Wind (flexibility), is the object. The direction of the wind changes easily, making it difficult for the subject to keep up. The situation in this relationship could be like a flood for the subject, an overwhelming disaster. However, this flood is avoidable, if the subject takes appropriate action.

1 General Text

Things are going smoothly.
A king comes to a temple.
It is beneficial to cross a big river.
It is beneficial to stay on the current course.

In this relationship, both the subject and the object are strong. The subject yields easily to the object's bullying: "Things are going smoothly." However, neither of the two sides wants to improve the relationship. This alienates each from the other, damaging the relationship and its benefits, like a dangerous flood that washes everything away. The subject's situation is insecure. To avoid deterioration and collapse, the subject should have courage to take a big step forward in the relationship: "It is beneficial to cross a big river. It is beneficial to stay on the current course," maintaining and improving the relationship.

2 Structure

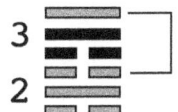

Figure 12.4: Structure of hexagram 2:3

In this hexagram, yin 4 (╍) and yang 5 (━) are in correct positions. The other four lines, yin 1 (╍), yang 2 (━), yin 3 (╍), and yang 6 (━), are in incorrect positions. The two top lines are complementary, but the two bottom lines and the two middle lines are in conflict with each other. Hexagram 2:3 is less favorable.

3 Texts of Lines

Yin 1

A strong horse saves one from danger.
It is favorable.

Yin 1 (╍) indicates that the subject does not want to push the relationship forward. Meanwhile, the action of the object is also yin. This will cause the relationship to fall apart, like the water and wind flowing forcefully in separate directions. That would be unfavorable to the subject. To avoid this unfavorable development, the subject should change the action from yin to yang. The yang action is like a strong horse, that would carry the subject above the flood, away from danger.

This line is in an incorrect position and in conflict with yin 4 (╍). The yin action of the subject is unfavorable.

Yang 2

Ahead of flood,
One runs to a high place.
Regret vanishes.

Yang 2 (━) indicates that the subject has essential strength, which can save the subject from the dangerous changing situation. The subject should call on this strength, like someone "ahead of flood" running to a "high place." If the subject does so, "regret vanishes." The subject does not need help from the object, and, since the essence of the object is yang as well, the subject does not have to help the object. The yang essence of the subject does not improve the relationship but does save the subject from disaster.

This line is central, but in conflict with yang 5 (━) and in an incorrect position. The yang essence of the subject is neutral.

Yin 3

The flood approaches one's own position.
There is no regret.

Yin 3 (━ ━) indicates that the subject is adaptive, agreeable and humble. However, the yielding attitude of the subject is powerless to make the situation better, because the actions of both sides are yin. This places the subject in a situation where "the flood approaches one's own position," but this is not the fault of the subject's yin attitude: "There is no regret."

This line is in an incorrect position, but complementary with yang 6 (━ ━). The yin attitude of the subject is neutral.

Yin 4

The flood inundates a residential area.
It seems there is a hill in the flooded area.
It is very favorable
It is unbelievable.

Yin 4 (━ ━) indicates that the object does not want to move the relationship forward. Since the subject does not desire this either, the problems in the relationship become very severe, like a flood that "inundates a residential area," damaging not only the subject's prospects, but also those of the object. If the object realizes the danger of this situation and makes a change in his or her action, the change will save the relationship, and will be very favorable, like "a hill in the flooded area." This change is not something that would be expected as a matter of course. If it happens, "it is unbelievable."

This line is in a correct position, but in conflict with yin 1 (━ ━). The yin action of the object is neutral.

Yang 5

There is a broad flood.

The residents are yelling.
The flood inundates the king's palace.
There is no blame.

Yang 5 (██) indicates that the object has essential strength. Since neither of the two sides in the relationship wants to improve the situation, the situation can deteriorate into catastrophe, so that "there is a broad flood," and "the residents are yelling." The strength of the object is overwhelmed, as when "the flood inundates the king's palace." Since the object does not want to improve the relationship, his or her loss of strength is not the subject's fault. "There is no blame" for the subject.

This line is in a correct position, but in conflict with yang 2 (██). The yang essence of the object is neutral.

Yang 6

The flood washes away blood,
Drawn bodies appear in a far remote area.
There is no blame.

Yang 6 (██) indicates that the object is rude, harsh, arrogant, bossy, or self-centered. Knowing this helps the subject to understand the object and eliminate fantasies about the relationship, like "the flood washes away blood." "Blood" indicates that the problem in the relationship is fatal. "The flood washes away blood" suggests that the problems in the relationship will result in a violent and painful upheaval. "Drawn bodies" refer to the loss that results. Their appearance "in a far remote area" implies that yang attitude of the object damages the relationship, perhaps beyond recovery. This is not the subject's fault. "There is no blame" for the subject.

This line is in an incorrect position, but complementary with yin 3 (██). The yang attitude of the object is neutral.

[5] Hexagram 2:4 Solution (In Zhou Yi, hexagram 40)

The title, Solution, indicates that although in the current situation of the relationship there are many sorts of problems, there are also solutions to these problems.

Trigram 2 (☵), Water (difficulty and danger), is the subject; trigram 4 (☳), Thunder (movement), is the object. The subject has strength, but is tied by the problems, and unable to move. The object comes and unties the subject. The subject should grasp this chance to find a solution, as when "the duke shoots the hawk and takes it" after it "lands above a wall."

1 General Text

The current situation benefits the southwest.
When there is no interesting place to go,
Coming back is favorable.
When there is an interesting place to go,
Going swiftly is favorable.

The "southwest" refers to the area of Country Zhou, where King Wen was the leader.

The subject is strong, but has difficulty in relationship. The subject cannot use his or her strength to benefit from the object or help the object, because the subject does not want to improve the relationship. The subject hesitates and behaves excessively humble and adaptive because he or she worries about the danger in dealing with the object.

In fact, the object is weak and needs help; the situation benefits the subject, the "southwest." The object actively approaches the subject, bringing a chance for the subject to solve his or her problems. The solution depends on which direction to go. "When there is no interesting place to go, coming back is favorable": in this instance, the object actively seeks the subject's help, and the subject has the opportunity to consolidate his or her strong position and follow the object. "When there is an interesting place to go, going swiftly is favorable": in this instance, while the object is humble and yielding, trusting and respecting the subject, the subject should talk with the object truthfully and honestly, and firmly lead the object in an advance.

2 Structure

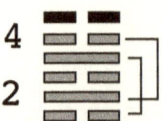

Figure 12.5: Structure of hexagram 2:4

In this hexagram, there is only one line, yin 6 (⚋), in a correct position. The other five lines, including all three lines of the subject trigram, are in incorrect positions. The two top lines are in conflict with each other. The two bottom lines and the two middle lines are complementary. Hexagram 2:4 is neutral, or less favorable.

3 Texts of Lines

Yin 1

There is no blame.

Yin 1 (▬ ▬) indicates that the subject does not want to push the relationship forward. There are some reasons, such as, the subject is not ready to go farther with the object, there is no benefit for the subject to go farther, or the subject was hurt by the object. The problems in the relationship are not the fault of the subject. "There is no blame" for the subject.

This line is in an incorrect position, but complementary to yang 4 (▬▬). The yin action of the subject is neutral.

Yang 2

In a field one captured three foxes,
And found a yellow arrow.
Staying on this course is favorable.

Yang 2 (▬▬) indicates that the subject has strength and is able to achieve some gains: "in a field one captured three foxes, and found a yellow arrow." There are some problems in the relationship, but the subject should not be frustrated. When in a difficult situation, the subject should hold on to his or her strong position: "Staying on this course is favorable" for the subject.

This line is in an incorrect position, but complementary to yin 5 (▬ ▬) and supported by yin 1 (▬ ▬). The yang essence of the subject is neutral, or a little favorable.

Yin 3

One carries a load,
While riding a horse,
That entices a robber to come.
Staying on this course is mean.

Yin 3 (▬ ▬) indicates that the subject is excessively polite or prudent, like a person who "carries a load, while riding a horse." While riding a horse, one should normally put the load on the horse's back; but here, on the contrary, one carries the load. One looks like a rich and clumsy person, which makes the robber think one is a good target for an attack. Being excessively polite or prudent is being mean to the subject. The subject should change his or her attitude from yin to yang, and behave more firmly and frankly.

This line is in an incorrect position and in conflict to yin 6 (- -), and suppressing yang 2. The yin attitude of the subject is unfavorable.

Yang 4

Friends untie one's toes.
Friends come to help one.
The friends are sincere.

Yang 4 (—) indicates that the object is taking an action to improve the relationship. While the subject is tied by problems, the object comes to help the subject solve the problems. "Friends untie one's toes." The object does this because he or she is sincere in wanting to pursue a better relationship with the subject.

This line is in an incorrect position, but complementary to yin 1 (- -) and supported by yin 3 (- -). The yang action of the object is neutral, or a little favorable.

Yin 5

One was tied.
One is released.
It is favorable.
There is sincerity.
One gets the help from normal people.

Yin 5 (- -) indicates that the object has less strength, being like a person who is normal, not great. However, while the subject is tied with troubles, the object comes and is able to help, with little strength but enough to release the subject from trouble. What the object is doing demonstrates the sincerity. The subject also should be sincere.

This line is in an incorrect position, but complementary to yang 2 (—). The yin essence of the object is neutral, or a little favorable.

Yin 6

A hawk lands above a wall.
The duke shoots the hawk and takes it.
Nothing is detrimental.

Yin 6 (- -) indicates that the object is humble, flexible and adaptive, like a hawk that lands above a wall, not soaring in the sky. The hawk wants to stay, not fly. The yin attitude of the object makes it easier for the subject to touch and talk with the object. The subject should change his or her attitude from yin to yang, and take the chance, as when "the duke shoots the hawk and takes it." If he or she makes this change, the subject will be able to control the situation and work together with the object: "Nothing is detrimental."

This line is in correct position, but in conflict to yin 3 (⚋). The yin attitude of the object is neutral. Moreover, the solution is not to change the object's attitude from yin to yang, but to change the subject's attitude. If the subject changes his or her attitude from yin to yang, the hexagram becomes hexagram 3:4, Persistence.

6 Hexagram 2:5 Imperfect (In Zhou Yi, hexagram 64)

The title, Imperfect, consists of two Chinese characters, "wei," meaning "not yet," and "ji," meaning cross, referring to a story of a small fox, which is forced to cross a river, and gets its tail wet.

Trigram 2 (☵), Water (difficulty and danger), is the subject; trigram 5 (☲), Fire (brightness and clinging), is the object. The object clings to the subject, manipulating the subject in his or her interests. The subject is strong, but yields to manipulation by the object and loses control of his or her own interests. The situation is imperfect. If the subject sacrifices dignity, and lets himself or herself be used by the object, "making his or her own head wet," that is not right.

1 General Text

Things are going smoothly.
A little fox tries to cross a river,
And gets its tail wet.
That is not beneficial.

The subject is strong, while the object is weak. The subject is able to protect his or her interests and help the object, so "things are going smoothly." However, the malleable subject yields to the object, like a little fox that is forced to cross a river and gets its tail wet. The situation is "not beneficial."

2 Structure

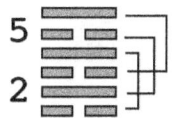

Figure 12.6: Structure of hexagram 2:5

In hexagram 2:5, all lines are complementary to the corresponding lines, but their positions are wrong. Hexagram 2:5 is unfavorable.

3 Texts of Lines

Yin 1

The little fox gets its tail wet.
It is mean.

Yin 1 (━ ━) indicates that the subject does not want to move forward in the relationship, but yields to the desire of the object. The little fox that gets its tail wet, when it shouldn't have to cross the river, illustrates a situation that "is mean" for the subject.

This line is in an incorrect position, but complementary to yang 4 (━). The yin action of the subject is neutral.

Yang 2

A fox drags the wheels of a wagon to cross the river.
Staying on the current course is favorable.

Yang 2 (━) indicates that the subject has strength and is able to make whatever effort it takes to fulfill the mission, like the little fox dragging the wheels of a wagon to cross a dry riverbed. Meanwhile, the essence of the object is yin, so the subject can do what the object needs. Staying on the current course, maintaining and using this superior strength, is favorable to the subject. If the subject loses this advantage of essential strength, the subject is in danger of becoming insignificant to the object, who could then cause harm to the subject. The situation could become unfavorable.

This line is complementary to yin 5 (━ ━), but in an incorrect position. The yang essence of the subject is neutral.

Yin 3

The fox fails to cross the river.
Launching an expedition is dangerous.
It is beneficial to cross a big river.

Yin 3 (━ ━) indicates that the subject is humble, adaptive, and agreeable. A lack of confidence or self-esteem can cause the subject to fail in his or her mission, like the little fox that "fails to cross the river." Without a strengthening of attitude, trying something ambitious, like "launching an expedition," can be dangerous. The subject should make a big change in his or her attitude, like switching from one side of a river to the other.

This line is complementary to yang 6 (▬), but in an incorrect position. The yin attitude of the subject is neutral.

Yang 4

Staying on this course is favorable.
Regret vanishes.
Unexpectedly used to fight against Guifang,
One gets a reward from a big country in the third year.

"Fighting against Guifang" refers to a war conducted by King Wen, who was leader of Country Zhou and revised the Yijing text. After being released from prison by Emperor Shangzhou of the central government of Shang (a "big country"), King Wen was authorized by Emperor Shangzhou to wage war against the small countries that were not yielding to the central government. In the third year after his release from prison, King Wen was rewarded by Emperor Shangzhou for fighting against Guifang, which was one of the small countries north of Shang.

Yang 4 (▬) indicates that the object uses the subject for his or her own interests, just as Emperor Shangzhou used Kin Wen to fight Guifang. If the subject follows the object's desires, as Kin Wen did, the subject will be rewarded: "Staying on this course is favorable" for the subject. If the subject properly uses his or her strength to pursue this goal, "regret vanishes."

This line is in an incorrect position, but complementary to yin 1 (▬ ▬). The yang action of the object is neutral.

Yin 5

Staying on this course is favorable.
There is no regret.
With his essential offer,
The gentleman shows sincerity.
That is favorable.

Yin 5 (▬ ▬) indicates that the object has little strength and needs the subject's yang essence to succeed. The subject helps the object and is rewarded: "Staying on this course is favorable. There is no regret."

The help from the subject is essential, and the subject is sincerely doing just what the object wants. So the object trusts the subject and depends on the subject: "That is favorable."

This line is in an incorrect position, but complementary to yang 2 (▬). The yin essence of the object is neutral.

Yang 6

Showing sincerity
By drinking
Is blameless.
Showing sincerity
By making his or her own head wet
Is not right.

Yang 6 (▬) indicates that the object is arrogant, reckless, bossy, or bullying. If the subject wants to show sincerity and openness, in the way that two people show their trust by sharing a drink together, this is useful for keeping a good relationship. The subject should not be blamed. But if the subject behaves too humbly, allowing the arrogant object to abuse his or her good nature, like the little fox who is forced to cross a river and gets in over its head, that is not right.

This line is in an incorrect position, but complementary to yin 3 (▬ ▬). The yang attitude of the object is neutral.

7 Hexagram 2:6 Adversity (In Zhou Yi, hexagram 47)

The title, Adversity, indicates that subject is in for a bad time and has to fight hard to deal with the situation.

Trigram 2 (☵), Water (difficulty and danger), is the subject; trigram 6 (☱), Lake (pleasure), is the object. Water on the land flows to the lake, generally unable to change its course, while the lake enjoys the pleasure of putting all the water under its control. The subject is in a difficult situation, being controlled, manipulated, or used by the object.

1 General Text

Things are going smoothly.
Persistently striving to be a good person is favorable, and blameless.
Do not believe the promises of others.

The subject is strong and prudent in the relationship, so "things are going smoothly." But the object is strong as well and very aggressive, and wants to place the subject under his or her control, while the subject reacts very passively. The subject has to strive persistently to be a good person, protecting his or her own interests and maintaining freedom, independence, and dignity. Both the subject and the object are humble, agreeable and respectful. In the face of the object's aggression, the subject should be prudent and cautious: "Do not believe the promises of others."

2 Structure

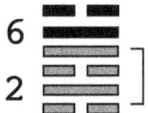

Figure 12.7: Structure of hexagram 2:6

In this hexagram, yang 5 (—) and yin 6 (— —) are in correct positions; the other four lines are in incorrect positions. The two bottom lines are complementary to each other. The two middle lines and the two top lines are in conflict with each other. Hexagram 2:6 is less favorable.

3 Texts of Lines

Yin 1

Straying in a forest of bare trees,
Or falling into a secluded valley,
One disappears for three years.

Yin 1 (— —) indicates that the subject does not want to push the relationship forward, but the object does. The subject is pushed and controlled by the object, like "straying in a forest of bare trees," which is a place without cover and food, very hard to survive in, "or falling into a secluded valley," which is very deep and hard to escape. Under the control of the object, the subject feels as though he or she is disappearing in such a forest or valley for three years. The situation is very difficult and is likely to remain that way for a long period of time.

This line is in an incorrect position, but complementary to yang 4 (—). The yin action of the subject is neutral.

Yang 2

Lacking food and drink,
Suffering adversity,
One comes into a prison in red clothes.
Praying is the only thing one can do.
Advance is unfavorable.
There is no blame.

Yang 2 (—) indicates that the subject has strength, but cannot use it, because he or she is under the object's control, like someone in a prison, lacking food and drink and wearing a prisoner's red uniform. Under this constrained situation, the subject can do nothing but pray. "Advance is unfavorable" to the subject. The subject should maintain confidence and patience, waiting for a better chance. The subject is doing his or her best, so "there is no blame."

This line is central, but in an incorrect position and in conflict with yang 5 (▬). The yang essence of the subject is less favorable.

Yin 3

Being trapped among rocks,
Tied to a thorny vine,
Or unable to see his wife
When he enters his home,
He is in an unfavorable situation.

Yin 3 (▬ ▬) indicates that the subject is humble, adaptive, or agreeable. The subject yields to the object, like "being trapped among rocks," or "tied to a thorny vine." And the subject is helpless, like a man who cannot "see his wife, when he enters his home."

This line is in an incorrect position and in conflict with yin 6 (▬ ▬). The yin attitude of the subject is unfavorable.

Yang 4

One is imprisoned in a metal cage on a wagon.
The wagon moves very slowly.
It is mean.
There is an end.

Yang 4 (▬) indicates that the object is pushing the relationship forward, but the subject is not ready to go along willingly. The subject is forced to follow the object, like "being imprisoned in a metal cage on a wagon," which "moves very slowly." The yang action of the object is mean to the subject. However, this is an unstable situation and things will change: If the subject remains patient and strong, there is an end to the adversity.

This line is in an incorrect position, but complementary to yin 1 (▬ ▬). The yang action of the object is neutral.

Yang 5

One's nose and feet are cut off.

One is dressed in red clothes.
Later on, one is released.
It is beneficial for one
To make an offering and to sacrifice.

Yang 5 (▬) indicates that the object has strength and power. The subject suffers from the object's impact, like one being tortured, as "one's nose and feet are cut off" and "dressed in red clothes," which is a prisoner's uniform. On the other hand, the object does not want to be too harsh to the subject, because he or she wants to make use of the subject. Finally, the subject will be "released." And this adversity, in the end, will prove favorable in some ways for the subject: "It is beneficial for one to make an offering and to sacrifice."

This line is central, in an incorrect position, and in conflict with yang 2 (▬). The yang essence of the object is less favorable.

Yin 6

Being stranded in the vines and weeds,
One reminds oneself to regret what is regrettable.
Moving ahead is favorable.

Yin 6 (▬ ▬) indicates that the object is adaptive, agreeable, or flexible. This yin attitude makes the object slippery. It is hard for the subject to get away from the object's control, so the feeling is like "being stranded in the vines and weeds." It is time for the subject to think through the rights and wrongs of this situation, "to regret what is regrettable." If the subject can learn a lesson from this adversity and submit to a change in action, or attitude, or both, from yin to yang, then "moving ahead is favorable."

This line is in an incorrect position and in conflict with yin 3 (▬ ▬). The yin attitude of the object is unfavorable.

[8] Hexagram 2:7 Sue (In Zhou Yi, hexagram 6)

The title, Sue, indicates the subject is seeking protection, like a plaintiff who turns to the courts of law for justice.

Trigram 2 (☵), Water (difficulty and danger), is the subject; trigram 7 (☰), Heaven (strength), is the object. The object is so powerful and so bullying that the subject has to "sue" the object to protect his or her interests. The position of the subject is insecure and vulnerable, like water that is exposed to the full strength of the sun. The outcome is uncertain: The subject could lose the case, or gain a protection that may not last, like someone who "is awarded a leather belt," and then "the belt is withdrawn three times in a day."

1 General Text

There is sincerity,
But no communication.
One is vigilant.
It is favorable at a mid-stage,
But unfavorable at the end.
It is beneficial to consult a wise person.
It is not beneficial to cross a big river.

Both subject and object are strong, but the object is stronger. The subject does not want to move forward in the relationship, but the object does. The subject is pushed by the object, an arrogant, bossy bully. The subject yields to the object.

The subject deals with the object sincerely, but remains passive and unwilling: "There is sincerity, but no communication." Under the control of the object, the subject "is vigilant," ready to defend himself or herself with essential strength. At a mid-stage, when the subject does not communicate with the object, but is sincere and respectful, the object appreciates the subject's obedience, and can ignore minor problems: "It is favorable at a mid-stage." But at the end, when the problems become so severe that they are unacceptable to the object, the situation becomes unfavorable. Even if the subject remains sincere and vigilant, a lack of communication can cause the object to misunderstand and hurt the subject.

When the power of the object is overwhelming, the subject should not stand alone, but seek help from a wise person, such as a parent, teacher, boss, or friend. The subject should consult the wise person and look for appropriate settlement of the conflict. The subject should not embark alone on a major action, like switching from one side of a big river to the other.

2 Structure

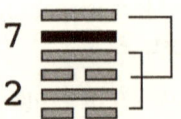

Figure 12.8: Structure of hexagram 2:7

In this hexagram, yang 5 (▬) is the only line in a correct position; the others are in incorrect positions. The two bottom lines and the two top lines are complementary to each other. However, the two middle lines are in conflict with each other. Hexagram 2:7 is less favorable.

3 Texts of Lines

Yin 1

Do not always enter into litigation.
Discussion with others frequently
Leads to a favorable ending.

Yin 1 (- -) indicates that the subject does not want to move the relationship forward, but the object does. The subject cannot pursue a peaceful life in this situation. However, it is not always a good idea to enter into litigation. It is better to talk with the object whenever a problem happens, before the problem becomes severe: "Discussion with others frequently leads to a favorable ending."

This line is in an incorrect position, but complementary to yang 4 (—). The yin action of the subject is neutral.

Yang 2

Having failed in a lawsuit,
One comes back and hides in his home.
To avoid being tortured he offers the land of three hundred families for the fine.

There was a story about King Wen, who was the leader of a small country, Zhou. At that time, the central government of China was Country Shang, headed by Emperor Shangzhou. While Country Shang was declining, Country Zhou was rising, becoming stronger and stronger. To contain the growing power of Country Zhou, the Emperor Shangzhou put King Wen in prison for seven years. King Wen offered the land of three hundred families in order to avoid torture and a possible death penalty, and to be released.

Yang 2 (—) indicates that the subject has strength. However, being contained by the powerful object, the subject cannot exercise this strength and has to strike a compromise with the object, as King Wen did. When the situation is bad, as with a failure in a lawsuit, the subject should deploy his or her essential strength for self-protection, like King Wen offering "the land of three hundred families."

This line is in an incorrect position and in conflict with yang 5 (—), but supported by yin 1 (- -). The yang essence of the subject is neutral, or less favorable.

Yin 3

Living on past achievements is dangerous,
But the ending will be favorable.
If one serves the country,
There will be no success.

Yin 3 (− −) indicates that when being contained and threatened by the strong object, the subject must be polite and prudent. "Living on past achievements is dangerous," because this will not serve the subject well in the current circumstance; neither is a new success likely in this situation. However, if the subject keeps the yin attitude persistently, waiting until the object declines naturally in power, the ending will be favorable.

The "country" refers to the object. Even if the subject is very polite and respectful, the subject should not expect to be repaid by the object, because the attitude of the object is yang. The object is arrogant, stubborn, and tough: "If one serves the country, There will be no success."

This line is in an incorrect position, but complementary to yang 6 (—). The yin attitude of the subject is neutral.

Yang 4

After failing in a lawsuit,
One turns to a peaceful life.
Staying on this course is favorable.

Yang 4 (—) indicates that the object is pushing the subject to move forward, like an injustice that spurs one to file a lawsuit. Since the object is very strong, the subject fails "in a lawsuit" and may suffer a loss. Since the object is too strong to prevail against, the subject should not seek revenge or keep fighting; instead, the subject should embark on a "peaceful life." "Staying on this course is favorable" to the subject.

This line is in an incorrect position, but complementary to yin 1 (− −). The yang action of the object is neutral.

Yang 5

The lawsuit is very favorable.

Yang 5 (—) indicates that the object is wealthy or in a powerful position. If the subject fights with the object, the subject could be defeated. When the problems become severe, the subject should attempt litigation to protect his or her rights and possibly reclaim losses. The conflict between the subject and the object could be eliminated and the subject could be able to live in peace: "The lawsuit is very favorable" for the subject.

This line is the only line in a correct position, but in conflict with yang 2 (━). The yang essence of the object is neutral. If the subject acts properly, such as seeking a litigation, the situation possibly favors the subject.

Yang 6

Sometimes, one is awarded a leather belt.
The belt is withdrawn three times in a day.

The "leather belt" refers to a belt presented as a symbol of honor to an official in ancient times.

Yang 6 (━) indicates that the object is arrogant, harsh, or frank. The object cannot tolerate humiliation or defeat. The subject should be careful to hold onto anything gained. Even if the object loses once in a while, the object will try to deprive the subject of his or her winnings: "The belt is withdrawn three times in a day."

This line is in an incorrect position, but complementary to yin 3 (━ ━). The yang attitude of the object is neutral.

CHAPTER 13
When Wind (☴) is the Subject

THIS CHAPTER CONTAINS YI TEXT of eight hexagrams from 3:Ø to 3:7. Their subject trigrams are trigram 3, Wind. The typical characteristic of wind is flexibility. This can mean adaptability or a willingness to yield, but also a threatening blow and a great power.

1 Hexagram 3:Ø Rising (In Zhou Yi, hexagram 46)

The title, Rising, indicates that the relationship is growing, advancing, progressing — a situation favorable to the subject.

Trigram 3 (☴), Wind (flexibility), is the subject; trigram Ø (☷), Earth (adaptability), is the object. Facing an adaptable, yielding object, the subject is able to move freely, like the wind blowing over a vast, open field, but there is no real gain.

1 General Text

Things are moving very smoothly.
It is beneficial to visit a great person.
Do not worry.
Expedition toward the south is favorable.

In ancient times, the "south" referred to a warm region, less developed than the central area of China. "Expedition toward the south" indicates that if the subject heads in the right direction, moving forward is favorable.

In the current relationship, "things are moving very smoothly." It is a time for the subject to advance. There might be some problems, and if they occur, the subject should seek help from a "great person" — a boss, leader, parent, friend or teacher. When the subject gets help from a "great person," there will be no worry, and "moving forward is favorable" to the subject.

2 Structure

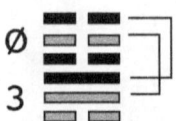

Figure 13.1: Structure of hexagram 3:0

There are three lines in correct positions — yang 3 (▬), yin 4 (▬ ▬), and yin 6 (▬ ▬). The other three are in incorrect positions. The two middle lines and the two top lines are complementary, but the two bottom lines are in conflict with each other. Hexagram 3:Ø is neutral, or a little favorable.

3 Texts of Lines

Yin 1

Advancing is allowable,
And very favorable.

Yin 1 (▬ ▬) indicates that the subject does not want to move forward. Meanwhile, the action of the object is also yin; the object does not want to move forward either. If the subject continues to insist on a yin action, then the relationship will not be improved and the situation will not benefit the subject.

The subject should realize that since the object is adaptable, an advancing action will meet with no resistance. The current situation invites the subject to advance. The subject should take advantage of this very favorable chance to make progress.

This line is in an incorrect position and in conflict with yin 4 (▬ ▬). The text advises the subject very clearly to take a yang action.

Yang 2

Be sincere.
It is good to keep offerings simple.
There is no blame.

Yang 2 (▬) indicates that the essence of the subject possesses strength and is able to help the object. At the same time, the essence of the object is yin; the object is in a weak position and needs the help. When helping the object, the subject should be sincere. If the subject is sincere, even a little help will be gratifying for the object. The subject should make the offer simple, and easy for the object to accept; then "there is no blame" for the subject.

This line is in an incorrect position, but complementary to yin 5 (▬ ▬). The yang essence of the subject is neutral.

Yang 3

One advances in an empty town.

Yang 3 (▬) indicates that the attitude of the subject is arrogant, harsh, or reckless. When the subject advances with a yang attitude and encounters no resistance, it is like advancing in an empty town. On the other hand, since the town is empty, there is no friendly, warm welcome for the subject's advance. The subject obtains no real gain; it is merely passing through.

This line is in a correct position and complementary to yin 6 (━ ━), but suppresses yang 2 (━━). The yang attitude of the subject is neutral, or a little favorable.

Yin 4

The king makes an offering on Mount Qi.
It is favorable.
There is no blame.

This passage refers to King Wen, the leader of Country Zhou, who revised the Yijing text. Mount Qi was in Zhou.

By citing the story of King Wen making an offering, the text emphasizes the yin action of the object, which puts up no opposition to the advance of the subject. This yin action of the object is favorable and blameless for the subject, so the subject should take the chance to advance.

This line is in a correct position, but in conflict with yin 1 (━ ━). The yin action of the object is neutral.

Yin 5

Staying on this course is favorable.
One is ascending a stairway.

Yin 5 (━ ━) indicates that object is in a weak position and needs the subject's help. This need of the object gives the subject an invitation to move forward, like an ascending stairway for the subject to climb. The subject should use this chance: "Staying on this course is favorable."

This line is in an incorrect position, but central and complementary to yang 2 (━━). The yin essence of the object is neutral, or a little favorable.

Yin 6

Advance in silence.
It is beneficial to stay on this course indefinitely.

Yin 6 (━ ━) indicates that the attitude of the object is humble, adaptive, agreeable, or obedient. There is no quarrel, no protest, no fight. The subject advances peacefully, in silence, and should "stay on this course indefinitely."

This line is in a correct position, and complementary to yang 3 (━━). The yin attitude of the object is favorable.

2. Hexagram 3:1 Bugs (In Zhou Yi, hexagram 18)

The title, Bugs, suggests that there are troubles, or complications in the relationship.

Trigram 3 (☴), Wind (flexibility), is the subject; trigram 1 (☶), Mountain (stop), is the object. The blowing wind is stopped by the mountain, which causes problems. The subject wants to be flexible in the relationship, but the object prevents the subject from moving freely.

1 General Text

Things are going very smoothly.
It is beneficial to cross a big river,
In a cycle of three days back
And three days forward.

There are problems in the relationship. However, when the troubles are identified, the solutions will arrive in due course; then things will go very smoothly and it will be beneficial for the subject to move ahead. Things are always changing, "in a cycle of three days back and three days forward." The flexible subject should yield to the changes and find ways to solve the problems, like switching back forth from one shore of a wide river to the other.

2 Structure

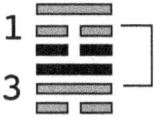

Figure 13.2: Structure of hexagram 3:1

Two lines, yang 3 (▬) and yin 4 (▬ ▬) in correct positions. The others are in incorrect positions. The two middle lines are complementary; the bottom lines and the top ones are in conflict. This hexagram demonstrates the negative nature of the current situation.

3 Texts of Lines

Yin 1

As a son,

He solves the problems inherited from his father.
That is blameless, but dangerous.
That has a favorable ending.

"Problems inherited from his father" refers to masculine problems — perhaps such as conflicts in business, finances or work, or involving colleagues and friends.

Yin 1 (▬ ▬) indicates that the subject does not want to solve these tough problems that have accumulated in the relationship. But if the problems remain unsolved, the situation is unfavorable.

The text advises the subject to change the action from yin to yang, working on resolving the problems as a duty — "as a son, solving the problems left by his father." It could be dangerous to solve the problems, but if the problems are solved, the situation will end well, without blame for the subject.

This line is in an incorrect position and in conflict with yin 4 (▬ ▬). The yin action of the subject is unfavorable. The text advises the subject to take a yang action.

Yang 2

Do not stay too long
In solving the problems inherited from his mother.

"Problems inherited from his mother" refers to feminine problems, such as domestic or personal issues.

Yang 2 (▬▬) indicates that the subject has enough strength to solve these domestic or personal problems. The subject should approach the problems seriously, as a son might regard an inheritance from his mother; but should also solve them quickly: "Do not stay too long."

This line is in an incorrect position, but complementary to yin 5 (▬ ▬). The yang essence of the subject is neutral.

Yang 3

He is solving the problems
Inherited from his father,
There is regret on trivial issues,
But no blame on important issues.

Yang 3 (▬▬) indicates that the attitude of the subject is arrogant, rough, or rude. Meanwhile, the attitude of the object is also yang, so the object could be just as stubborn. Trying to resolve so many tough problems, the subject might make mistakes. Such mistakes could be a little regrettable, but if the subject makes a sincere effort at resolution, there will be no major repercussions.

This line is in a correct position, but in conflict with yang 6 (▬). The yang attitude of the subject is neutral.

Yin 4

A delay in solving the problems
Left by his father is mean.

Again, the reference here is to masculine types of problems — those outside the home and the personal realm.

Yin 4 (▬ ▬) indicates that the object's lack of commitment to solve these tough problems could create delays in finding a solution. The object's tendency to obstruct the subject's efforts is mean — petty and counterproductive.

This line is in a correct position, but in conflict with yin 1 (▬ ▬). The yin action of the object is neutral.

Yin 5

Solving the problems left by his father
Is honorable.

Yin 5 (▬ ▬) indicates that the object is in a weak position and needs the subject's help. This creates a good opportunity for the subject to solve these thorny problems and be appreciated for the honorable effort.

This line is in an incorrect position, but complementary to yang 2 (▬). The yin essence of the object is neutral.

Yang 6

Do not serve a king.
Be respectable.

Yang 6 (▬) indicates that the object's attitude is arrogant, snobbish, harsh, reckless, or domineering, like a "king." The subject should not be too obedient and servile, but should steer clear of the object's bullying tendencies, in order to maintain self-respect.

This line is in an incorrect position and in conflict with yang 3 (▬). The yang attitude of the object is unfavorable.

3 Hexagram 3:2 Well (In Zhou Yi, hexagram 48)

The title, Well, symbolizes the dependent relationship between subject and object: Water in the well is a vital source of life for the residents nearby, who need it for drinking, cooking and washing.

Trigram 3 (☴), Wind (flexibility), is the subject; trigram 2 (☵), Water (difficulty and danger), is the object. The object causes problems that the subject needs to solve, like citizens of a town making repairs to their old well.

1 General Text

A town might change.
The location of a well never changes.
The level of water inside a well does not decrease, nor does it increase.
People come and go to get water.
Before reaching the top of the well
The jar turns over.
It is unfavorable.

"People" refers to both the subject and the object, involved in the relationship symbolized by a well. Despite a lot of problems, the relationship is useful and beneficial for both sides. However, sometimes the problems are frustrating, as when a jar being hauled upward turns over and empties before reaching the top of the well. Such problems are unfavorable to the subject, who is in need of the water.

2 Structure

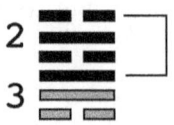

Figure 13.3: Structure of hexagram 3:2

In this hexagram, two lines, yin 1 (− −) and yang 2 (—) are in incorrect positions, and the other four lines are in correct positions. The two top lines are complementary to each other, but the bottom and middle lines are in conflict.

Hexagram 3:2 is neutral, with a favorable situation being offset by problems. The two lines in incorrect positions and the conflicts between the two bottom lines and the two middle lines symbolize the problems.

3 Texts of Lines

Yin 1

The water in the well is muddy,
Not drinkable,
Even birds refuse to drink it.

Yin 1 (- -) indicates that the subject does not want to solve the problems in the relationship. Meanwhile, the object's yin action shows that the object is equally reluctant to make an effort. The problems stagnate, like muddy water in the well. The current situation is not enjoyable, even for birds.

This line is in an incorrect position and in conflict with yin 4 (- -). The yin action of the subject is unfavorable.

Yang 2

The wall of the well collapsed.
There are fish in the water at the bottom.
People throw stones at the carp.
The jar leaks.

Yang 2 (—) indicates that the subject has a strong essence and is able to solve the problems in the relationship, despite initial reluctance. The strength of the subject has not yet been wielded, and lies still, like water in the well. The wall of the well has collapsed, so water cannot be maintained at a useful level, and becomes instead a shallow carp pool. The jar leaks and cannot be used for fetching water. Instead of getting water for life, people throw stones at the fish for their amusement. The situation of the relationship is awful, even though the essence of the subject is yang.

This line is in an incorrect position and in conflict with yang 5 (—). The yang essence of the subject is unfavorable.

Yang 3

The mud in the well has been removed.
The water still cannot be taken out for drink.
I feel sad.
This well could provide drinking water.
If the king is bright,
The people may be favored.

Yang 3 (—) indicates that the attitude of the subject is arrogant, reckless, rough, or bullying, but also frank and honest. Usually people do not like to deal with an arrogant person, and are unlikely to cooperate. Even if the subject does something to improve the relationship, a lot of problems remain unsolved: "The mud has been removed. The water still cannot be taken out for drink." Before the water can be drinkable, more needs to be done; the wall of the well needs to be fixed and the rope and jar have to be ready for use. To solve the problems in the relationship, the subject and object need to work together.

"I" refers to the subject, and "the king" refers to the object. In this awful situation, the subject feels sad, and wants the object to cooperate intelligently, so they can work toward a favorable outcome.

This line is in a correct position and complementary to yin 6 (∎∎). The yang attitude of the subject is favorable.

Yin 4

The wall of the well has been tiled.
There is no blame.

Yin 4 (∎∎) indicates that the object does not want to solve the problems in the relationship, but might yield if pushed by the subject to cooperate, as in repairing the lining of the well with new tiles.

If the subject pushes the object to move forward and gets the cooperation of the object, this will be a blameless act.

This line is in a correct position, but in conflict with yin 1 (∎∎). The yin action of the object is neutral.

Yang 5

The well provides clean and cool spring water,
Drinkable water.

Yang 5 (∎) indicates that the object, like the subject, has sufficient strength to solve problems. If cooperation can be achieved, there is a potential for "clean and cool spring water, drinkable water." But if the subject and object do not cooperate, nothing will happen.

This line is in a correct position, but in conflict with yang 2 (∎). The yang essence of the object is neutral.

Yin 6

People come and get water from the well.
The well remains uncovered.
Being sincere is very favorable.

Yin 6 (∎∎) indicates that the object's attitude is humble, adaptable, or agreeable, which should make solving the problems easier. Once the problems are solved, a useful relationship can be restored: "People come and get water from the well."

In order to keep the relationship harmonious and open — as in, "The well remains uncovered." — the subject should be sincere in dealing with the object. If the subject accomplishes this, the situation is very favorable.

This line is in a correct position, and complementary to yang 3 (━). The yin attitude of the object is favorable.

4 Hexagram 3:3 Yield (In Zhou Yi, hexagram 57)

The title, Yield, suggests a relationship where both sides are equally flexible, and the subject must find a way to yield to the object where appropriate.

Both the subject and object are represented by trigram 3 (☴), Wind (flexibility). The subject should find out the "wind direction" of the object and flexibly yield to the "wind" — either sheltering from it, or hoisting a sail to harness its power.

1 General Text

Things are going a little smoothly.
It is beneficial to do something.
It is beneficial to consult a great person.

The object is volatile, and it is not easy for the subject to keep up with all the changes on the object's part. So there are problems in the relationship, but they are not very severe: "Things are going a little smoothly." The subject is flexible, and ready to follow the object; the difficulty lies in anticipating what the object intends to do. The subject should make an effort to know, to understand, and to follow the object. The subject should not stand alone in this, but should consult a great person — perhaps a boss, parent, teacher, or advisor — for advice on how to proceed with caution.

2 Structure

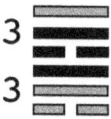

Figure 13.4: Structure of hexagram 3:3

In this hexagram, yang 3 (━), yin 4 (╌ ╌), and yang 5 (━) are in correct positions, and the other three lines are in incorrect positions. No line is complementary. Hexagram 3:3 is neutral, or a little unfavorable.

3 Texts of Lines

Yin 1

Move back and forth.
It is beneficial to stay on the way
A warrior follows.

Yin 1 (▬ ▬) indicates that the subject does not want to move forward in the relationship, and neither does the object. If the both sides keep on in this way, the problems will never be solved; the relationship will never be improved. The subject should make a change, moving back and forth, demanding and compromising, offering and withdrawing — trying to find what works. The warrior attacks the enemy, and also protects himself from being hurt. The warrior advances at some times and retreats at others. The subject should stay alert like a warrior, keeping a yang action and performing flexibly.

The text clearly advises the subject to change the action from yin to yang, while remaining flexible.

This line is in an incorrect position and in conflict with yin 4 (▬ ▬). The yin action of the subject is unfavorable.

Yang 2

One hides under a bed,
Giving way to others,
Like priests and magicians
Yielding to god or fate.
It is favorable and blameless.

Yang 2 (▬▬) indicates that the essence of the subject is strong, but using this strength reduces flexibility. Since the object is equally strong, the subject should not compete directly, but yield to the object instead, like priests and magicians yielding to god or fate. If the subject does so, the situation will be favorable, and if something goes wrong, the subject should not be blamed.

This line is in an incorrect position and in conflict with yang 5 (▬▬). The yang essence of the subject is unfavorable.

Yang 3

Yielding unwillingly and reluctantly

Is mean.

Yang 3 (━) indicates that the attitude of the subject is arrogant or bossy. When the situation requires yielding, the subject should react spontaneously and graciously. With a yang attitude, the subject is unwilling and reluctant. It is good to yield, but mean to do so without genuine humility.

This line is in a correct position, but in conflict with yang 6 (━). The yang attitude of the subject is neutral.

Yin 4

Regret vanishes.
During field hunting
One kills three kinds of game.

Yin 4 (━ ━) indicates that the object does not want to move forward, which offers a good chance for the subject to advance. If the subject takes this chance, he or she will not regret it. The subject could move forward like a hunter in a field, obtaining three kinds of game. But if the subject does not seize this chance, there will be regret and nothing gained.

This line is in a correct position, but in conflict with yin 1 (━ ━). The yin action of the object is neutral.

Yang 5

Staying on this course is favorable.
Regret vanishes.
It is beneficial.
Do not initiate a thing.
But end it.
Making a change every three days
Is favorable.

Yang 5 (━) indicates that the essence of the object is strong. The subject should not challenge this strength: "Staying on this course is favorable" and "regret vanishes." It is beneficial for the subject to conserve strength and refrain from initiating anything. Let the object start it, using his or her strength until it ebbs. When the object weakens, it will be time for the subject to end the conflict favorably. The subject should frequently change strategies, to keep up with the changes in the object's side: "Making a change every three days is favorable."

This line is in a correct position, but in conflict with yang 2 (━). The yang essence of the object is neutral, but the text tells the subject how to make this situation favorable.

Yang 6

He hides under a bed.
One gives up a sharp axe for self-defense.
Staying on this course is unfavorable.

Yang 6 (▬) indicates that the object is arrogant, bullying, or bossy. If the subject is submissive and fearful, like someone hiding under a bed and giving up a sharp axe that could have been used for self-defense, then the object will take advantage of this and inflict more damage. "Staying on this course is unfavorable" — and also avoidable, because being flexible does not mean giving up one's own strength. The subject possesses enough strength — the sharp axe — so he or she can yield to the object to an appropriate extent, and wait for a good chance to proceed.

This line is in a correct position, but in conflict with yang 3 (▬). The yang attitude of the object is neutral.

[5] Hexagram 3:4 Persistence (In Zhou Yi, hexagram 32)

The title, Persistence, suggests the subject should be persistent in keeping a good relationship with the object.

Trigram 3 (☴), Wind (flexibility), is the subject; trigram 4 (☳), Thunder (move), is the object. The subject has to persist in yielding to a moving object, in order to keep the relationship beneficial.

1 General Text

Things are going smoothly.
There is no blame.
It is beneficial to stay on the current course.
It is beneficial to do something.

The subject is not interested in moving the relationship forward, but the object is. While the object does not have strength, the subject does. The subject is arrogant; the object is respectful. The subject and the object are complementary in all aspects: "Things are going smoothly." The subject helps the object with strength, and gains momentum from the object. The subject should not be blamed; the current course is beneficial. If the subject actively does something instead of merely reacting to a push from the object, the subject could gain more from the change.

2 Structure

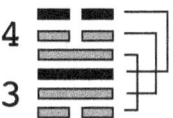

Figure 13.5: Structure of hexagram 3:4

In this hexagram, yang 3 (—) and yin 6 (- -) are in correct positions. The other four lines are in incorrect positions. All pairs of lines are complementary. Hexagram 3:4 is neutral, or a little favorable.

3 Texts of Lines

Yin 1

Dredge mud persistently.
Staying on this course is unfavorable
And not beneficial.

Yin 1 (- -) indicates that the subject does not want to persist in the relationship, but the object pushes the subject to move. Though the subject's strength helps the object, the object may be dissatisfied. That could cause problems and jeopardize the relationship. The subject has to persist in doing something to avoid trouble, like dredging mud to keep a waterway open. "Staying on this course is unfavorable and not beneficial" for the subject — so something must change. The text stresses the negative aspect of the yin action of the subject, urging the subject to a more determined action that can improve the relationship.

This line is in an incorrect position, but complementary with yang 4 (—). The yin action of the subject is neutral.

Yang 2

Regret vanishes.

Yang 2 (—) indicates that the subject's essence is strong, which is beneficial to the relationship and not a cause for regret.

This line is in an incorrect position, but complementary to yin 5 (- -). The yang essence of the subject is neutral.

Yang 3

Be virtuous or face humiliation.

Staying on this course is mean.

Yang 3 (▬) indicates that the attitude of the subject is arrogant, bossy, rude or domineering, but also truthful and honest, while the object's complementary attitude is modest, respectful, trusting, and willing to compromise. However, to keep a good relationship with the object, the subject must be persistently virtuous, truthful and honest: "Be virtuous or face humiliation." If not tempered with truth and sincerity, the object's pushiness can come across as mean.

This line is in a correct position and complementary to yin 6 (▬ ▬). The yang attitude of the subject is favorable.

Yang 4

There is no game in the field.

Yang 4 (▬) indicates that the object is fighting for his or her own interests, without considering the subject. The situation is like a hunt where the object bags all of the animals, leaving nothing for the subject: "There is no game in the field." Meanwhile, because the subject's action is yin, the subject is content to let the object win this contest. Even if there is no gain from the object's aggressive ways, neither is the subject hurt by them.

This line is in an incorrect position, but complementary to yin 1 (▬ ▬). The yang action of the object is neutral.

Yin 5

Be virtuous persistently.
Staying on this course favors women,
But not men.

Yin 5 (▬ ▬) indicates that the object has less strength and needs help from the subject, who has a yang essence and is fully able to offer that help.

The subject should persistently be truthful and honest while extending this help: "Be virtuous persistently." The outcome of the relationship depends on how the subject deals with the object. If the subject gently, flexibly offers support to the object, as a woman might do, the subject will be rewarded favorably for the gesture. But if the subject forces the object to accept help, in a rough or tactless manner, the object will not care about the subject's good intentions, and will, in fact, resent the subject.

This line is in an incorrect position, but complementary to yang 2 (▬). The yin essence of the object is neutral.

Yin 6

When others are vacillating,
It is hard to be persistent.
It is unfavorable.

Yin 6 (- -) indicates that the object's attitude is humble, agreeable, polite, or respectful, but could also be deceptive or obsequious. Since the attitude of the subject is yang, it is easy to misinterpret the sweet smiles and compromises of the object. If the object is wavering, the subject has to be careful: "When others are vacillating, it is hard to be persistent." Since persistence is highly important for the subject, this situation could be unfavorable.

This line is in a correct position, and complementary to yang 3 (—). The yin attitude of the object is favorable. But the text warns the subject to be on guard for a possible negative side of the object's yin attitude.

6 Hexagram 3:5 Cauldron (In Zhou Yi, hexagram 50)

The title, Cauldron, takes its imagery from the vessels that ancient people used for cooking or for rituals, as we see today in Buddhist temples. Hexagram 3:5 describes the subject's position in a relationship where the object is bright and also clinging.

Trigram 3 (☴), Wind (flexibility) is the subject, and trigram 5 (☲), Fire (brightness or clinging) is the object. When the subject serves his or her intended purpose, like a cauldron used for cooking and ritual, the object needs the caldron, uses it and decorates it. Even the object dislikes the cauldron, but cannot hurt it.

1 General Text

The situation is very favorable.
Things are going smoothly.

The object is bright and clings to the subject, like a flame caressing the surface of a cauldron. When the subject behaves appropriately, using the object's brightness to a good purpose, "the situation is very favorable" to the subject and "things are going smoothly." If not, the subject could get burned.

2 Structure

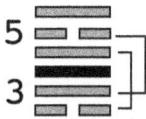

Figure 13.6: Structure of hexagram 3:5

Yang 3 (▬) is the only line in correct position. The other lines are in incorrect positions. The two bottom lines and the two middle lines are complementary, while the top lines are in conflict. Hexagram 3:5 is neutral, or a little favorable. The text stresses the positive side of the current situation, but the structure suggests that there may be problems — as indicated by the many lines in incorrect positions.

3 Texts of Lines

Yin 1

When a cauldron is upset,
That is a chance to empty things from it.
Marrying a concubine.
The concubine gives birth to a child.
There is no blame.

Yin 1 (▬ ▬) indicates that the subject does not want to move ahead in the relationship, although the object does — as shown by the yang action of the object. The subject has been pushed, like "a cauldron upset." This toppling could actually be a change to resolve problems in the relationship, like a chance to empty debris from an upset cauldron. The subject could feel uncomfortable being pushed — like a man marrying a concubine when there are no children with the wife — but the end result is not bad. The beneficial situation occurs naturally — like a concubine giving birth to a child — and the subject should not be blamed.

This line is in an incorrect position, but complementary to yang 4 (▬). The yin action of the subject is neutral.

Yang 2

The cauldron is full of food.
My rival hates me,
But cannot hurt me.
That is favorable.

Yang 2 (▬) indicates that the essence of the subject is strong, wealthy, well-educated, successful in business, experienced, professional, powerful, or backed by others. Some people might dislike, and even hate, the subject. They are represented by the object, the enemy of the subject, or others who are envious or in disagreement. All of them could make trouble for the subject, but could not seriously hurt the subject, because the subject is in a strong position. The situation is favorable for the subject.

This line is in an incorrect position, but central and complementary to yin 5 (▬ ▬). The yang essence of the subject is neutral, or a little favorable. The text stresses the positive side of the yang essence, encouraging the subject to maintain this aspect.

Yang 3

The cauldron could not be moved,
For its handle is damaged.
The delicious pheasant's meat inside it
Could not be enjoyed.
When the rain comes,
All the regrets are washed away.
The ending is favorable.

Yang 3 (▬▬) indicates that the subject's attitude is arrogant, self-centered, rough, rude, or bossy. This yang attitude hinders others from being close to the subject, like a cauldron that cannot be made use of because of a damaged handle. The subject has an inner strength that it cannot wield, like "the delicious pheasant meat inside" the cauldron that "could not be enjoyed."

It would be favorable for the subject's attitude to change from yang to yin — to be humble, respectful, agreeable, gentle and graceful. This would change the situation to arrive at a favorable ending, like the gentle rain that washes all regrets away. If the subject's attitude cannot change, it will be like a beneficial rain that never comes.

This line is in a correct position, but it conflicts with yang 6 (▬▬). The yang attitude of the subject is neutral.

Yang 4

The leg of the cauldron is broken,
And the gentlemen's meal is spilled out,
Making a big mess.
That is unfavorable.

Yang 4 (▬▬) indicates that the object is pushing the subject farther than the subject is ready to go. The pushing makes the subject uncomfortable and awkward, like a cauldron with a broken leg. This could result in a big mess for the subject in the realm of business—disrupting a schedule, plan, routine, or budget, or upsetting the people engaging in business, such as customers, clients, colleagues, boss, parents and friends: "The gentlemen's meal is spilled, making a big mess." That is unfavorable.

The text stresses the negative side of the yang action of the object. But if the subject responds quickly and gracefully to the object's push, then the mess is avoidable.

This line is in an incorrect position, but complementary to yin 1 (▬ ▬). The yang action of the object is neutral.

Yin 5

The cauldron gets a yellow handle,
Attached with a golden stick.
It is beneficial to stay on this course.

Yin 5 (▬ ▬) indicates that the object has less strength, and needs help from the subject. The subject is in a strong position to help the object. If the subject offers what the object wants, the relationship will be improved, like a cauldron that has been repaired, with "a yellow handle attached with a golden stick." The subject will be rewarded for these contributions and enjoy the relationship: "It is beneficial to stay on this course." But if the subject does not want to help the object, the subject will gain nothing.

This line is in an incorrect position, but central and complementary to yang 2 (▬). The yin essence of the object is neutral, or a little favorable.

Yang 6

The cauldron is attached with a jade stick.
That is beneficial and very favorable.

Yang 6 (▬) indicates that the attitude of the object is arrogant, bossy, and rude, but also may be truthful and honest.

The attachment of a stick made of the precious material jade makes the cauldron more useful. If the subject offers help in a genuine way, the subject could be rewarded fairly — although the object could be arrogant and rude.

This text stresses the positive nature of the object's yang attitude of the object, and does not mention its negative nature. The subject has to be careful dealing with an object whose attitude is yang. Because the object has less strength and clings to the subject, the favorability to the subject is variable. But the situation can still be beneficial to the subject, as indicated by the useful and beautiful jade handle.

This line is in an incorrect position and in conflict with yang 3 (▬), but it is supported by yin 5 (▬ ▬). The yang attitude of the object is neutral, or a little favorable.

[7] Hexagram 3:6 Overburden (In Zhou Yi, hexagram 28)

The title, Overburden, consists of two Chinese characters: "big" and "pass," — meaning "too much," "overwhelming." It implies that the situation is a heavy burden for the subject, but not a disaster.

Trigram 3 (☴), Wind (flexibility), is the subject, and trigram 6 (☱), Lake (pleasure) is the object. The subject wants to take it easy, with no interest in advancing, while the object actively pursues pleasure and excitement. This makes the subject feel overburdened.

1 General Text

The main support beam is bent.
Going ahead is beneficial.
Things are going smoothly.

The subject does not want to progress in the relationship, but the object wants to go farther, so pushes the subject — so forcefully that the subject feels as though "the main support beam is bent." But the subject is essentially strong enough to handle this relationship, and should change to a yang action: "Going ahead is beneficial." If the subject advances actively, instead of being pushed by the object, the subject would not feel pressure, and "things" will go "smoothly."

2 Structure

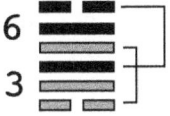

Figure 13.7: Structure of hexagram 3:6

In this hexagram, three lines, yang 3 (▬), yang 5 (▬), and yin 6 (▬ ▬), are in correct positions; the other three are in incorrect positions. The two bottom lines and the two top lines are complementary. The two middle lines are in conflict with each other. Hexagram 3:6 is neutral.

3 Texts of Lines

Yin 1

Making a pad with a layer of white grass is blameless.

Yin 1 (— —) indicates that the action of the subject is yin. The subject does not want to move ahead in the relationship, while the object does. Being pushed by the object, the subject tries to protect him/herself, as if "making a pad with a layer of soft white grass" before lying on the ground. Under pressure, trying to act cautiously, the subject is blameless.

This line is in an incorrect position, but complementary to yang 4 (——). The yin action of the subject is neutral.

Yang 2

The withering willow produces a sprout.
An old man marries a young wife.
The situation is beneficial.

Yang 2 (——) indicates that the subject has essential strength — being healthy, well-educated or well-trained, powerful, or supported by others — but does not want to advance; so he or she is like a "withering willow," like an "old man." Because the subject is pushed by the object to move, the situation is similar to the withering willow producing a sprout, or the old man marrying a young wife.

This can be a beneficial situation, when everything is considered: the willow may be withering, but the sprout could grow big to become a new tree; the man is old, but his young wife might give birth to a baby who could grow to adulthood. The subject has been pushed by the object to move forward, but yielding to the push can be rewarding: "The situation is beneficial."

This line is in an incorrect position, and in conflict with yang 5 (——), but supported by yin 1 (— —). The yang essence of the subject is neutral, or a little favorable.

Yang 3

The main support beam bends.
The situation is unfavorable.

Yang 3 (——) indicates that the attitude of the subject could be arrogant, bossy, bullying, rude, reckless, or truthful and honest. The subject is under pressure, but has strength and is in a solid position, like the main support beam of a building. The subject should earn respect by doing what he or she thinks is right, by not "bending." If the subject heeds the warning in the text, and keeps being truthful, honest and upright, then the situation will be favorable.

This line is in a correct position and complementary to yin 6 (▬ ▬). The yang attitude of the subject is favorable.

Yang 4

The main support beam bulges.
The situation is favorable.
Being involved with another is regrettable.

Yang 4 (▬) indicates that the object wants to push the relationship forward. This pushing solves some of the problems in the relationship, relieving the subject of a heavy burden. "The main support beam bulges," but does not collapse, so "the situation is favorable" for the subject. However, the subject should be vigilant, avoid being deceived or trapped, conserve strength, and remain respectable, upright and independent: "Being involved with another is regrettable."

This line is in an incorrect position, but complementary to yin 1 (▬ ▬). The yang action of the object is neutral.

Yang 5

A withering willow produces flowers.
An old lady marries a young man.
There is no blame,
Nor honor.

Yang 5 (▬) indicates that the essence of the object has vitality, like a young man, or a fresh flower. By contrast, the subject also has strength, but because he or she has no interest in advancing, the subject resembles a withering willow, or an old lady. Now the subject and the object come together in a productive relationship: "A withering willow produces flowers," and "an old lady marries a young man."

The flowers on the withering willow are beautiful, but cannot last long. When an "old lady" marries a young man, they may feel happy, but cannot have children. Their family cannot last long. Being humble, agreeable, in a strong position, and pushing the relationship along, the object is only concerned about his or her own benefit, and might leave once an action is not beneficial. If this happens, "there is no blame, nor honor" for the subject.

This line is in a correct position, but in conflict with yang 2 (▬). The yang essence of the object is neutral.

Yin 6

Wading across a river,
With the top of the head submerged in water,
Is unfavorable,
But blameless.

Yin 6 (− −) indicates that the attitude of the object is yin. The object is humble, agreeable, adaptive, respectful, or graceful, but elusive to the subject. While the object is pushing the subject forward, the subject does not know the object well, so making progress in the relationship is like crossing a river when the bottom is invisible. The subject should be prudent in responding to the object, and aware that "wading across a river with the top of the head submerged in water is unfavorable." The deceptive nature of the object causes trouble. But that is not the subject's fault; the subject should not be blamed.

This line is in a correct position, complementary to yang 3 (—), but suppressing yang 5. The yin attitude of the object is neutral.

[8] Hexagram 3:7 Encounter (In Zhou Yi, hexagram 44)

The title, Encounter, describes a current situation where the subject encounters an object the subject does not want to meet.

Trigram 3 (☴), Wind (flexibility), is the subject, and trigram 7 (☰), Heaven (strength), is the object. The subject wants to take things easily, and has no interest in advancing. By contrast, the object is very aggressive and very powerful. The subject does not want to see this object, but they happen to meet.

1 General Text

Do not marry a woman
Who is too strong.

This text offers a very clear warning. In the current relationship, the object is very aggressive, very strong and arrogant, like the sun shining down from heaven. The subject just wants to survive, and has no interest in becoming involved or competing with the object. However, in reality the subject must deal with the object, like it or not: The "marriage" between the subject and the strong "woman" already exists. The subject should be prudent and watchful, in order to handle the problems that come with this encounter.

2 Structure

Figure 13.8: Structure of hexagram 3:7

In this hexagram, yang 3 (▬) and yang 5 (▬) are in correct positions, but the other four lines are in incorrect positions. The two bottom lines are complementary, while the top and middle lines are in conflict. Hexagram 3:7 is less favorable.

3 Texts of Lines

Yin 1

A wagon is stopped with a metal brake.
Staying on this course is favorable.
Moving ahead looks unfavorable,
Pacing up and down like a lean sow.

Yin 1 (▬ ▬) indicates that the subject does not want to move forward in the relationship. While the object is pushing hard, the subject should stand still, like "a wagon" that "is stopped with a metal brake." "Staying on this course is favorable" to the subject. Since the object is very strong and arrogant, "moving ahead is unfavorable" for the subject. The subject should stop moving and remain still and calm, not pacing nervously up and down the road like a lean sow.

This line is in an incorrect position, but complementary to yang 4 (▬). The yin action of the subject is neutral.

Yang 2

In the kitchen there is a fish,
But serving a guest that fish
Is not beneficial.
There is no blame.

Yang 2 (▬) indicates that the essence of the subject is wealthy, well-educated or well-trained, healthy, desirable, or supported by others. This advantage is like having a "fish" in the kitchen, or eggs in your basket. The object is very aggressive and wants to approach the subject as a "guest" on a visit. The object is not only very greedy, but also very strong and arrogant: the object will take advantage of the subject, eating or taking away the "fish" for free. Treating the object too kindly — serving the "guest" the "fish" — is not beneficial. The subject is guarding his or her own privacy and independence, and should not be blamed.

This line is in an incorrect position and in conflict with yang 5 (▬), but supported by yin 1 (▬ ▬). The yang essence of the subject is neutral.

Yang 3

It is very hard to walk
Without skin on the buttocks.
This situation is dangerous,
But blameless.

Yang 3 (▬) indicates that the subject could be arrogant, rough, rude, bullying, bossy, or truthful and honest. The attitude of the object is also yang. When the subject is arrogant, the object fights back, giving the subject a hard time. It is very hard for the subject to get along with the object, and the discomfort makes the subject feel vulnerable, as if walking "without skin on the buttocks." There may be quarrels and fights — "This situation is dangerous" — but there is no blame in sticking up for the subject's rights.

This line is in a correct position, but in conflict with yang 6 (▬). The yang attitude of the subject is neutral.

Yang 4

The fish in the kitchen is missing.
That causes an unfavorable consequence.

Yang 4 (▬) indicates that the subject suffers loss from the yang action of the object. The object could be very aggressive, taking advantage of the subject, stealing the "fish" from the subject's kitchen. The yang action of the object creates discord in the relationship.

This line is in an incorrect position, but complementary to yin 1 (▬ ▬). The yang action of the object is neutral. The text stresses its negative nature, but the yang action of the object could also solve some of the problems in the relationship.

Yang 5

A melon was under the leaves of a wolfberry tree.
Talent has been hidden.
A chance is coming,
Like meteorites crossing the sky.

Yang 5 (▬) indicates that the object could be as brilliant as the subject. Because of yin action, the subject's talent has been hidden. When the subject encounters the object, the object exposes the talent of the subject. This encounter creates an unexpected chance for the subject, like meteorites crossing the sky.

This line is in a correct position, but in conflict with yang 2 (▬). The yang essence of the object is neutral.

Yang 6

The encounter happens at an intersection.
It is unkind but blameless.

Yang 6 (▬) indicates that the attitude of the object is yang. The object may be arrogant, rough, rude, domineering, bossy, or simply truthful and honest like the subject. The subject's action is yin; the subject does not want to meet the object. But this undesirable encounter may happen anyway, merely because the subject and object are "at an intersection." It may be unpleasant for the subject, but it is not his or her fault.

This line is in an incorrect position and in conflict with yang 3 (▬). The yang attitude of the object is unfavorable.

CHAPTER 14
When Thunder (☳) is the Subject

This chapter contains Yi text of eight hexagrams from 4:Ø to 4:7. Their subject trigrams are trigram 4, Thunder. The typical characteristic of thunder is movement. It does not refer to specific kinds of movement, such as running, flying, or throwing, but rather to the impulse of movement itself: starting, initiating, or setting out to accomplish something. The image of thunder stresses the vibrating, shocking impact of this force on others; and also implies an associated weakness, such as that of a newborn, a newly emerging force.

1 Hexagram 4:Ø Return (In Zhou Yi, hexagram 24)

The title, Return, evokes the time after winter, when spring comes and the seasons start a new yearly cycle. After a divorce, one starts a new relationship with another person; that is a return. After being laid off, one starts a new job; that is also a return. One walks out of a house, then, after a while, comes back to the house; that is also a return. Hexagram 4:Ø symbolizes a new start of a relationship after completing an old relationship.

Trigram 4 (☳), Thunder (movement), is the subject; trigram Ø (☷), Earth (adaptability), is the object. When starting a new relationship, the subject wants to move ahead, to take a chance. The object adapts to the subject's initiation, providing a vast field in which the subject may advance. But the subject is lacking in strength and cannot go too far; after the initial attempt, he or she must come back.

1 General Text

Things are going smoothly.
Going back and forth is harmless.
Friends are visiting without blame.
Things are moving around a cycle of a week.
It is beneficial to do something.

The start of this new relationship proceeds smoothly: the subject wants to move forward, but lacks strength and experience. Vacillating is harmless. The object responds to the initiative of the subject. The subject initiates the interaction and should not be blamed.

Patience is called for here. Things in the world are always developing along spiral tracks, and a relationship cannot be expected to proceed quickly along a straight path. The reference to a "cycle of a week" suggests that there will be a resolution in good time. While waiting for the cycle to complete, the subject should keep moving, "It is beneficial to do something."

2 Structure

Figure 14.1: Structure of hexagram 4:0

Yang 1 (▬), yin 2 (▬ ▬), yin 4 (▬ ▬), and yin 6 (▬ ▬), are in correct positions; the other two lines are in incorrect positions. The two bottom lines are complementary to each other. The two middle lines and the two top lines are in conflict. Hexagram 4:Ø is neutral.

3 Texts of Lines

Yang 1

Turning back
After not going very far
Is harmless, not regrettable,
Possibly, very favorable.

Yang 1 (▬) indicates that the subject wants to move ahead, but lacks strength and experience. "Turning back after not going very far" could be a way to reserve strength, with lessons having been learned from the last cycle. Turning back is harmless, not regrettable; it can even be very favorable for preparing to begin the next cycle.

This line is in a correct position, and complementary with yin 4 (▬ ▬). The yang action of the subject is favorable.

Yin 2

Turning back after resting
Is favorable.

Yin 2 (▬ ▬) indicates that the essence of the subject is yin. The subject does not have enough strength to move very far. When the subject has inadequate strength to keep advancing, he or she should stop and take a break, avoiding mistakes and loss, then return to the original place. If the subject ignores this lack of strength and presses on without resting and retreating, the subject might fail to progress to the next cycle, and the situation could become unfavorable.

This line is in a correct position, but in conflict with yin 5 (- -). The yin essence of the subject is neutral.

Yin 3

Worrying about turning back
Is dangerous
Yet blameless.

Yin 3 (- -) indicates that the subject's attitude may be modest, flexible and respectful. After advancing a certain distance, it is time to turn back, but the subject succumbs to the object and agrees to his or her demands, for which the subject really does not have enough strength. "Worrying about turning back is dangerous," because to have a better relationship in the future, the subject must retreat.

This line is in an incorrect position and in conflict with yin 6 (- -). The yin attitude of the subject is unfavorable.

Yin 4

Turn back alone at the halfway point.

Yin 4 (- -) indicates that the object does not want to initiate an action, and prefers to follow the subject. In the process of advancing, the subject controls the situation and gains. This is favorable for the subject. When it is time to retreat, the subject should turn back alone, leaving the object and not letting the object follow. If the object is allowed to follow, the subject may not be able to control the situation and could suffer loss. The subject should remember the rule, "Turn back alone at the halfway point."

This line is in a correct position, and complementary with yang 1 (—). The yin action of the object is favorable.

Yin 5

Turning back after being urged to
Is not regrettable.

Yin 5 (- -) indicates that the object's essence has less strength and needs help from the subject. Because the subject feels tired and needs to rest and retreat, the object urges the subject to turn back. If the subject does not retreat, the demand of the object is not met and this may result in trouble for the subject.

This line is in an incorrect position and in conflict with yin 2 (▬ ▬). The yin essence of the object is unfavorable.

Yin 6

Turning back with confusion
Is unfavorable and troublesome.
It is especially unfavorable for the king of a country conducting a war.
The king will be unable to subdue the enemy in ten years and suffer a terrible defeat at the end.

Yin 6 (▬ ▬) indicates the object's attitude could prove tricky, confusing the subject when it is time for a retreat. The subject does not really know what the object is doing. This creates trouble for the subject on the way back or during the next advance.

In ancient times, China was split into more than one hundred small countries. Frequently, the king of one country launched a war against another country. After an advance, if the king was uncertain of the circumstances, and did not take appropriate measures to turn back at the right time, he would be "unable to subdue the enemy in ten years and would suffer a terrible defeat in the end."

On the other hand, the object could be humble, adaptive and agreeable. After advancing, if the subject works hard to secure the situation, takes a rest, gets the object to cooperate, and makes the status clear, then during the retreat and in the future, the subject could benefit from the cooperation of the object.

This line is in a correct position, but in conflict with yin 3 (▬ ▬). The yin attitude of the object is neutral.

⟦2⟧ Hexagram 4:1 Care (In Zhou Yi, hexagram 27)

The title, Care, suggests that the subject should take care of himself or herself. In Chinese, the character "care" also means cheek, the area on the face around the mouth, implying nourishment.

Trigram 4 (☳), Thunder (movement), is the subject; the object is trigram 1 (☶), Mountain (stopping). The subject wants to move, to pursue adventure, but is delayed or blocked by the object. Instead of trying to benefit from others, the subject should depend on his or her own resources.

1 General Text

Staying on the current course is favorable.
When watching others eating,
Seek food yourself.

The subject wants to push the relationship forward. The object is flexible, following the subject, so that "staying on the current course is favorable." The subject is weak and wants to improve his or her situation with help from the object. The subject envies the object, like a hungry person watching others eat. But the object is stubborn, refusing to share any advantage with the subject. "Seek food yourself" is advice for the humble and obedient subject; after being refused, he or she must attempt to improve the situation alone.

2 Structure

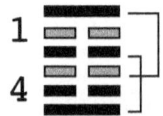

Figure 14.2: Structure of hexagram 4:1

Yang 1 (▬), yin 2 (▬ ▬), and yin 4 (▬ ▬) are in correct positions; the others are in incorrect positions. The two bottom lines and the two top lines are complementary to each other, and the two middle lines are in conflict. Hexagram 4:1 is neutral.

3 Texts of Lines

Yang 1

You abandoned a divine tortoise,
Looking at my mouth chewing
A big piece of meat.
That is unfavorable.

With a yang action, the subject wants to take advantage of others, taking them for granted, or even cheating, robbing or stealing for personal gain. This way "is unfavorable" to the subject. The subject should seek improvement through his or her own efforts, such as going to college to get a better education, doing exercise to be healthier or saving money.

This line is in a correct position, and complementary to yin 4 (▬ ▬). The yang action of the subject is neutral.

Yin 2

You want to eat others' food.
This is the wrong way to seek nourishment.
They have food piling up like a hill.
Assaulting others is unfavorable.

The subject's essence is weak, but it cannot gain strength from the object, "You want to eat others' food; this is the wrong way to seek nourishment." Even if the object is better off, with "food piling up like a hill," the subject should not take advantage of the object's wealth. "Assaulting others is unfavorable," meaning that there is nothing to be gained by exploiting the good fortune of the object.

This line is in a correct position, but in conflict with yin 5 (==). The yin essence of the subject is neutral.

Yin 3

You are not taking care of yourself.
Staying on the current course is unfavorable.
Do not live this way for ten years.
Nothing is beneficial.

The subject's attitude is compliant and yielding, not self-supporting. When the subject tries to get help from the object, he or she is rejected. The subject is admonished not to let this situation go on indefinitely, because it does no good.

This line is in an incorrect position, but complementary with yang 6 (—). The yin attitude of the subject is neutral.

Yin 4

You eat other's food.
That is favorable.
Your desire for care
Resembles a stalking tiger.
That is blameless.

The object's action is yin, indicating that there will be little resistance to the subject. The subject is blameless, like a hungry tiger in search of food, and will be treated favorably by the object.

This line is in a correct position, and complementary to yang 1 (—). The yin action of the object is neutral.

Yin 5

Even though it is the wrong way
Staying on this course is favorable.
Do not cross a big river.

The object's essence is weak, so the subject's desire to gain from the object can have favorable results. But the subject is warned not to go too far, and take advantage of the object's tendency to yield, "Do not cross a big river."

This line is in an incorrect position and in conflict with yin 2 (▬ ▬). The yin essence of the object is unfavorable.

Yang 6

Being taken care of by others
Is dangerous but favorable.
It is beneficial to cross a big river.

The object may be submissive in action and essence, but his or her attitude is yang. This means that the object may be arrogant, bossy, rude, truthful or honest. The subject gains from the object, "being taken care of by others," and this dependency can be dangerous but also favorable. The subject should be humble, agreeable, and respectful, remaining close to the object and pursuing this dependency. "It is beneficial to cross a big river,".

This line is in an incorrect position, but complementary to yin 3 (▬ ▬). The yang attitude of the object is neutral.

3 Hexagram 4:2 Prospect (In Zhou Yi, hexagram 3)

The title, Prospect, indicates hope in a relationship. In Chinese, the title of this hexagram also means "store up."

Trigram 4 (☳), Thunder (movement) is the subject, and trigram 2 (☵), Water (difficulty and danger) is the object. The subject's desire to move will lead to difficulties in keeping up with the object. The prospect of this relationship depends on how the subject deals with this difficulty.

1 General Text

Things are going very smoothly.
It is beneficial to stay on the current course.
Do not go too far.

It is beneficial to appoint a minister.

The subject wants to move the relationship forward, and can do so "very smoothly." "It is beneficial to stay on the current course," moving forward at a pace that is good for the subject, and also manageable to the object. The object has strength and is able to help the subject. However, the object does not trust the subject because the subject is not straightforward. The subject should stay close to the object, but "not go too far." The relationship should be negotiated and formalized, in the way that a king appoints a "minister," assigning missions and relying on the minister. This gives the object confidence in the subject; both of them can work together to develop a favorable prospect for the relationship.

2 Structure

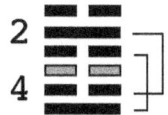

Figure 14.3: Structure of hexagram 4:2

Yang 3 (▬) is the only line in an incorrect position, and the two bottom lines and two middle lines are complementary to each other. Hexagram 4:2 tends to be favorable.

3 Texts of Lines

Yang 1

One is pacing up and down.
It is beneficial to stay on this course
And to appoint a minister.

The subject's action is yang, indicating a desire to push the relationship forward. But progress is subject to delays, "One is pacing up and down." The subject should be patient and persistent in dealing with the object, "It is beneficial to stay on this course." The subject should be close to and reliant on the object, building the relationship like a king appointing a minister and assigning increasingly substantial missions.

This line is in a correct position and complementary with yin 4 (▬ ▬). The yang action of the subject is favorable.

Yin 2

Vacillating and wavering,

A band of riders are wandering around.
They aren't robbers,
But are seeking marriage.
There is no woman willing to be married
Until ten years later.

The essence of the subject is yin. The subject has less strength and needs help from the object. The object does not know or understand the subject very well and is unwilling to do favors for the subject. The subject is troubled, like a band of riders, "vacillating," "wavering," and "wandering around." The subject should deal with the object truthfully and honestly, showing that the "band of riders" "aren't robbers," "but are seeking marriage." Then, in time, the situation will change, "Ten years later," there will be a "woman willing to be married."

This line is in a correct position and complementary to yang 5 (▬). The yin essence of the subject is favorable.

Yin 3

Without a guide,
Chasing deer into a forest
Is not beneficial.
It is better to give up,
Or else there will be trouble.

The attitude of the subject may be humble and yielding, a mirror image of the object's attitude. The subject is suspicious of the object and of the prospects for the relationship, because too much is unknown. Pursuing the relationship is like "chasing deer into a forest." The subject has no "guide." Going further is not beneficial. The subject should adopt a truthful attitude. Otherwise, the prospects will be dim.

This line is in an incorrect position and in conflict with yin 6 (▬ ▬). The yin essence of the subject is unfavorable.

Yin 4

A band of riders are wandering around.
They are seeking marriage.
Going ahead is favorable and beneficial.

The yin action of the object yields to the subject. The subject is pushing the relationship forward, like "a band of riders wandering around." "They are seeking marriage." The object acquiesces. "Going ahead is favorable and beneficial" for the subject.

This line is in a correct position and complementary with yang 1 (▬). The yin action of the object is favorable.

Yang 5

One is making progress like storing grease.
Staying on this course for a short time is favorable.
Staying on this course too long is unfavorable.

The object's yang essence offers strength and help to the subject. The subject reaps the benefits of the object's essence, like "storing grease." But since the object is suspicious of the subject, "staying on this course too long is unfavorable." The subject should be truthful and straightforward, giving the object confidence.

This line is in a correct position and complementary to yin 2 (▬ ▬). The yang essence of the object is favorable.

Yin 6

A band of riders are wandering around.
They are weeping with bloody tears
That flow down their faces like rivulets.

The object's yin attitude is what makes the object suspicious of the subject. Even though the subject comes with good will, "seeking marriage," there is no progress, "A band of riders are wandering around." The subject cannot get what he or she wants, so the riders "are weeping with bloody tears."

This line is in a correct position, but in conflict with yin 3 (▬ ▬). The yin attitude of the object is neutral, even though the text stresses the negative nature of this line. If the subject's attitude can become more truthful and straightforward, the object's suspicion can be overcome, and the wandering and tears can come to an end.

[4] Hexagram 4:3 Gain (In Zhou Yi, hexagram 42)

The title, Gain, promises benefits for the subject.

Trigram 4 (☳), Thunder (movement), is the subject, and the object is trigram 3 (☴), Wind (flexibility), suggesting the fluid and pleasing relationship of a dance, where one partner leads and the other follows. Without question, the subject gains.

1 General Text

It is beneficial to go further.
It is beneficial to cross a big river.

The subject wants to push the relationship forward. The object consents, following along and doing what the subject wants. The subject should take advantage of this opportunity, "It is beneficial to go further." The current situation favors risk-taking, "It is beneficial to cross a big river."

2 Structure

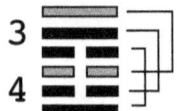

Figure 14.4: Structure of hexagram 4:3

In this hexagram, four lines, yang 1 (▬), yin 2 (▬ ▬), yin 4 (▬ ▬), and yang 5 (▬) are in correct positions. All the lines are complementary with the corresponding lines. Hexagram 4:3 is favorable.

3 Texts of Lines

Yang 1

This situation is promising for great work,
It is very favorable and blameless.

The action of the subject is yang. The subject wants to move forward in the relationship. The object is supportive and yielding. The subject should take this exceptional chance, "It is very favorable and blameless."

This line is in a correct position, and complementary to yin 4 (▬ ▬). The yang action of the subject is favorable.

Yin 2

It is impossible to refuse the contribution of
A tortoise worth ten pairs of seashells.
It is favorable to stay on this course forever.
The king performs a ritual
Praying to his ancestors for favor.
It is favorable.

Because of a yin essence, the subject has little strength and needs help. The object has strength, as shown with yang 5 (▬) and is willing to help the subject, contributing "a tortoise worth ten pairs of seashells." A pair of seashells was a kind of ancient currency. The relationship between the subject and the object resembles that of a "king" and "his ancestors," where favor is asked for and received.

This line is in a correct position, and complementary to yang 5 (▬). The yin essence of the subject is favorable.

Yin 3

Receiving help at a bad time
Is blameless.
Holding a jade tablet and
Speaking gingerly,
Like walking in the middle of a road,
One advises the lord.

With a yin attitude, the subject treats the object as a "lord" and talks to the object in a polite and serious manner. The subject is very polite, like a servant holding a jade tablet, which was used by the servants of the emperor as a symbol of their sincerity and trustworthiness. The subject chooses words and actions deliberately, like walking carefully in the middle of a road. When the subject has a bad time, it is blameless to receive help from the object, as a servant would from a lord.

This line is in an incorrect position, but complementary to yang 6 (▬). The yin attitude of the subject is neutral.

Yin 4

Like walking in the middle of a road,
One speaks with the lord gingerly.
The lord accepts one's advice.
Based on that,
The capital is relocated.

The object follows the subject and does what the subject wants. The subject respects the object as a "lord" and speaks with the object very carefully, like walking in the middle of a road. The object listens to the subject and follows his or her suggestion, even on very significant issues, like a "lord" following the advice of a servant and relocating the capital of the country.

This line is in a correct position, and complementary to yang 1 (▬). The yin action of the object is favorable.

Yang 5

Sincerity makes people feel better.
Certainly it is very favorable.
Sincerity makes me want to be more virtuous.

The essence of the object is yang, so the object is strong enough to help the subject. The subject deals with the object sincerely, making the object feel willing to help. "Certainly it is very favorable" for the subject. The sincerity expressed in the relationship encourages the subject to be "more virtuous."

This line is in a correct position, and complementary to yin 2 (⚋). The yang essence of the object is favorable.

Yang 6

Do not help
But beat.
Not persistently being virtuous
Is unfavorable.

The attitude of the object is yang, which means the object may be rude and bossy in an unfavorable situation. When the subject is not sincere or not polite, the object does not help, but instead beats the subject. If the subject wants to move the relationship forward and benefit, he or she must be sincere and polite, being virtuous persistently. Otherwise, the situation is unfavorable to the subject.

This line is in a correct position, and complementary to yin 3 (⚋). The yang attitude of the object is favorable.

5 Hexagram 4:4 Shock (In Zhou Yi, hexagram 51)

The title, Shock, implies that something suddenly happens in the relationship, like a clap of thunder.

Both the subject trigram and the object trigram are trigram 4 (☳), Thunder (movement). The subject wants to get something done, and the object wants to do something else. They do not synchronize with each other, and sometimes clash, like thunderheads coming together. However, neither the subject nor the object has great power. The problems are not fatal.

1 General Text

Things are going smoothly.

Even though horrible thunder blasts,
The noisy chatting and laughing remain.
The thunder scares people over a hundred miles.
No one loses a spoon or a cup.

The subject and the object are weak and polite. They get along well. "Things are going smoothly." They are very active. Sometimes, while the subject wants to do something, the object is working on something else. Without coordination, they clash with each other, but they are not really intending to hurt each other, "Even though horrible thunder blasts, the noisy chatting and laughing remain." The subject, as well as the object, has little strength, and is humble. Problems occur in various cases, but do not damage the relationship severely, "The thunder scares people over a hundred miles; no one loses a spoon or a cup."

2 Structure

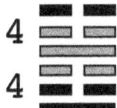

Figure 14.5: Structure of hexagram 4:4

In this hexagram, three lines, yang 1 (━), yin 2 (━ ━), and yin 6 (━ ━), are in correct positions, and the other three are in incorrect positions. No lines are complementary. Hexagram 4:4 is neutral, or less favorable.

3 Texts of Lines

Yang 1

After horrible thunder,
Noisy chatting and laughing resume.
It is favorable.

The subject takes a yang action to improve the relationship. The object does not anticipate it. They clash with each other like "horrible thunder." Then each realizes the good will of the other and they respond politely, "Noisy chatting and laughing resume." "It is favorable" for the subject.

This line is in a correct position, but in conflict with yang 4 (━). The yang action of the subject is neutral.

Yin 2

Thunder comes fiercely,

Worrying about losing a lot of money,
One climbs the nine hills.
Do not seek lost money.
The money will be recovered in seven days.

The subject's essence is weak. When the subject clashes with the object, he or she has little strength to avoid damage. "Worrying about losing a lot of money, one climbs the nine hills," in search of a safer place. Both the subject and the object are weak, humble and respectful. No one wants to remain in an unpleasant situation. The shock is transitory, and the loss is temporary, "The money will be recovered in seven days."

This line is in a correct position, but in conflict with yin 5 (- -). The yin essence of the subject is neutral.

Yin 3

The thunder is frightening.
Walking under thunder is harmless.

With a yin attitude, the subject is humble and frightened by thunder. The subject yields to the object to avoid damaging the relationship. In this way, problems cannot be resolved. The subject should change his or her attitude to be truthful and honest. When they clash, the subject should calmly proceed with the object to find the right way, "Walking under thunder is harmless."

This line is in an incorrect position and in conflict with yin 6 (- -). The yin attitude of the subject is unfavorable.

Yang 4

The thunder causes a mud slide.

With a yang action to match the subject's, the object clashes with the subject, like thunder blasting. The object has little strength, so the clash damages the relationship a little, but not severely. "The thunder causes a mud slide," but does not cause the house to collapse.

This line is in an incorrect position and in conflict with yang 1 (—). The yang action of the object is unfavorable.

Yin 5

Thunder comes and goes fiercely.
People lose nothing,
But have trouble.

The object's essence is in poor condition. The object wants to gain from the subject, but it is impossible. They quarrel and fight frequently, "Thunder comes and goes fiercely." They have little strength. Their conflict does not damage the relationship severely, but makes them unhappy, "The people lose nothing, but have trouble."

This line is in an incorrect position and in conflict with yin 2 (▬ ▬). The yin essence of the object is unfavorable.

Yin 6

Fearing thunder,
People are looking around.
It is unfavorable to take risks.
Thunder does not hit us,
But hits others.
There is no blame.
A dispute occurs in the marital relationship.

The object's attitude is humble and polite. When the subject clashes with the object, he or she worries about their relationship, "Fearing thunder, people are looking around." The subject should be cautious to keep the situation from deteriorating, "It is unfavorable to take risks." In an everyday relationship, such as one between a merchant and customer, "the thunder does not hit us but hits others" and the subject should not be blamed. However, in a close relationship, such as a marital relationship, the subject also should practise restraint, so that no one will be hurt by the clash. Otherwise, "a dispute occurs in the marital relationship."

This line is in a correct position, but in conflict with yin 3 (▬ ▬). The yin attitude of the object is neutral.

⁶ Hexagram 4:5 Bite (In Zhou Yi, hexagram 21)

The title, Bite, is an expression of potential pain. Being bitten by something, one suffers. If one is starving and bites something hard or poisoned, one also suffers.

Trigram 4 (☳), Thunder (movement), is the subject and trigram 5 (☲), Fire (brightness and clinging), is the object. The subject has less power, but is very active. When moving toward the object, the subject suffers, being burned by "fire." The subject is in a tough situation, like one undergoing torture.

1 General Text

Things are moving smoothly
Even if in jail.

The subject and the object are different in their attitudes. The object may be domineering. The subject is very active and wants to move forward, but is restricted by the object. The subject has little strength, is unable to break the blockage, and lives in a difficult situation, like a prisoner in jail. On the other hand, the subject is adaptive. Even in such a bad predicament, the subject yields, "Things are moving smoothly."

2 Structure

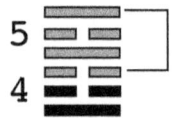

Figure 14.6: Structure of hexagram 4:5

Two lines, yang 1 (━) and yin 2 (━ ━), are in correct positions; the other four lines are in incorrect positions. The two bottom lines and the two middle lines are in conflict with each other, and only the two top lines are complementary. Hexagram 4:5 is unfavorable.

3 Texts of Lines

Yang 1

One is restrained with fetters
Which hurt the toes.
There is no blame.

With a yang action, the subject wants to go forward, but the object may have different ideas and want to go to somewhere else. This restraint harms the subject a little, hurting "the toes." The subject tries to do what is best for the relationship and should not be blamed.

This line is in a correct position, but in conflict with yang 4 (━). The yang action of the subject is neutral.

Yin 2

One gobbles a piece of tender meat with skin,
Even the nose touches the meat.

There is no blame.

A yin essence places the subject in a weak position, like a person starving, "One gobbles a piece of tender meat with skin, even the nose touches the meat." The subject is struggling intensely to survive and should not be blamed.

This line is in a correct position, but in conflict with yin 5 (━ ━). The yin essence of the subject is neutral.

Yin 3

One bites into a piece of salted meat
And finds the meat is poisoned.
There is slight distress but no blame.

With a yin attitude, the subject is adaptive and agreeable. In order to sustain and improve the relationship, the subject yields to an unpleasant situation, "One bites into a piece of salted meat, and finds the meat is poisoned." "There is slight distress," but the subject should not be blamed for accepting the toxic situation.

This line is in an incorrect position, but complementary to yang 6 (━━). The yin attitude of the subject is neutral.

Yang 4

One bites into a piece of dry meat with a bone
And finds a metal arrow point in the meat.
It is beneficial to struggle hard.
Staying on the current course is favorable.

With a yang action, the object gives the subject a hard time. The meat of an animal captured while hunting is of very poor quality, with "a metal arrow point" remaining. The subject yields to the difficult situation, continuing to struggle hard. It is possible that the situation could finally improve, "Staying on the current course is favorable."

This line is in an incorrect position and in conflict with yang 1 (━━). The yang action of the object is unfavorable.

Yin 5

One bites into a piece of dry meat
And finds a tiny piece of gold.
Staying on this course is dangerous
But blameless.

The essence of the object is yin; what the object has to offer is poor in quality, "One bites into a piece of dry meat and finds a tiny piece of gold." Swallowing gold could cause death, "Staying on this course is dangerous." But again, the subject is declared to be blameless in the situation.

This line is in an incorrect position and in conflict with yin 2 (⚋). The yin essence of the object is unfavorable.

Yang 6

One carries a wooden yoke.
It hurts the ears.
That is unfavorable.

The object's yang attitude is arrogant and bullying, putting great pressure on the subject, like a yoke that hurts the ears. The situation is unfavorable for the subject. But the subject's humble and adaptive attitude complements the bullying, so if the subject yields to the current circumstance and is patient, waiting for a favorable change, it could possibly happen in the future.

This line is in an incorrect position, but complementary to yin 3 (⚋). The yang attitude of the object is neutral.

[7] Hexagram 4:6 Follow (In Zhou Yi, hexagram 17)

The title. Follow, refers to following changes in the outside world, or following other people.

Trigram 4 (☳), Thunder (movement) is the subject and trigram 6 (☱), Lake (pleasure) is the object. The subject has less power, but is very active. The subject follows the object and shares his or her pleasure.

1 General Text

Things are going very smoothly.
It is beneficial to stay on the current course.
There is no blame.

The subject and the object are of contrasting strengths; the subject is weak, the object strong. The subject follows the object. By following the object, the subject benefits, "It is beneficial to stay on the current course." When the subject follows the object and does his or her best, "there is no blame."

2 Structure

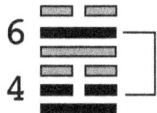

Figure 14.7: Structure of hexagram 4:6

Four lines, yang 1 (—), yin 2 (- -), yang 5 (—), and yin 6 (- -), are in correct positions and the other two lines are in incorrect positions. The two bottom lines and the two top lines are in conflict with each other; the two middle lines are complementary. Hexagram 4:6 is slightly favorable.

3 Texts of Lines

Yang 1

Follow changes in the outside world.
Staying on this course is favorable.
Going out and interacting with others
Paves the way to success.

With a yang action, the subject wants to move forward, but is in a weak position and needs help. The object is in a strong position and wants to move forward, too. The subject should follow the object, and not try to lead. "Staying on this course is favorable" for the subject. The subject learns and benefits from the object through this action, "Going out and interacting with others paves the way to success."

This line is in a correct position, but in conflict with yang 4 (—). The yang action of the subject is neutral.

Yin 2

Keeping ties with an insignificant person
Causes one to lose a great person.

The essence of the subject is yin, so the subject has little strength and needs help. The object, a "great person," has great strength and is able to help the subject. The subject should keep ties with the object, not other people. If the subject is not clearly aware of the situation and keeps ties with other people who can't help him or her, the subject will lose the connection to the object, "Keeping ties with an insignificant person causes one to lose a great person."

This line is in a correct position and complementary to yang 5 (—). The yin essence of the subject is favorable.

Yin 3

Keeping ties with a great person.
One loses an insignificant person.
Following a great person,
One is successful in his or her pursuits.
It is beneficial to continue on this course.

With a yin attitude, the subject is humble and agreeable, eager to be close to other people. It is possible that this yielding attitude could cause the subject to follow an unsuitable person and go astray. In making connections with other people, the subject has to choose a suitable person. The object is a "great person," in a strong position and able to help, "Following a great person, one is successful in his or her pursuits."

This line is in an incorrect position and in conflict with yin 6 (▬ ▬). The yin attitude of the subject is unfavorable.

Yang 4

Following a great person, one gains.
Staying on this course is unfavorable.
One is sincere,
And clearly following the right path.
Why should one be blamed?

The object's yang action leads the subject, and the subject benefits. The subject should follow the object only as long as it is good for his or her interest, and not indefinitely, "staying on this course is unfavorable." While sincerely collaborating with the object for a common interest, though, the subject remains independent and free, "clearly following the right path." The subject should not be blamed.

This line is in an incorrect position and in conflict with yang 1 (▬▬▬). The yang action of the object is unfavorable.

Yang 5

One is sincere and rewarded.
It is favorable.

The object's essence is strong and able to help the subject. The subject sincerely follows the object and is rewarded. "It is favorable" for the subject.

This line is in a correct position and complementary with yin 2 (⚋). The yang essence of the object is favorable.

Yin 6

One is bound tightly to a great person,
And will maintain this tie.
A king makes an offering on Mount West.

The object's yin attitude is flexible and gentle. The object is glad to have the subject following him or her, and offers assistance. The subject should keep following the object, "One is bound tightly to a great person, and will maintain this tie." But the object is so flexible that there is an ambiguity. It is not certain how far the subject can follow the object and how much the object is willing to do for the subject. The subject has to remain very sincere, like a "king," praying to his ancestors for a blessing. The "offering on Mount West" refers to an ancient story of King Wen praying to his ancestors on Mount West in the Country of Zhou.

This line is in a correct position, but in conflict with yin 3 (⚋). The yin attitude of the object is neutral.

8 Hexagram 4:7 Innocence (In Zhou Yi, hexagram 25)

The title, Innocence, is composed of two Chinese characters. One means "do not have," the other means "look." The combination of these two Chinese characters means "innocence," — "doesn't expect," "doesn't pursue." "Innocence" is closest to the original meaning. The text for the lines of this hexagram talks about "unexpected calamity" and "unexpected sickness," resulting from innocence. The innocent subject of the relationship might encounter unexpected circumstances.

Trigram 4 (☳), Thunder (movement) is the subject; the object is the powerful trigram 7 (☰), Heaven (strength). Thunder may shock, but has no real power and does not damage others, while Heaven has great power. The intention of the subject is innocent, not harmful to the object. But harm can occur.

1 General Text

Things are going very smoothly.
It is beneficial to stay on the current course.
Improper conduct causes trouble.
It is not beneficial to move ahead.

Both the subject and the object are very active. The subject is in a weak position and needs help. The object helps. The object is arrogant. The subject yields. In order to obtain additional advantage, the subject could lure the object into wrongdoing. In turn, the object could abuse power to take advantage of the subject, "Improper conduct causes trouble." The subject should deal with the object in an appropriate manner, being close, but not going too far, "It is not beneficial to move ahead."

2 Structure

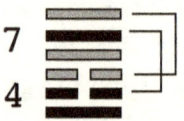

Figure 14.8: Structure of hexagram 4:7

In this hexagram, three lines, yang 1 (—), yin 2 (- -), and yang 5 (—), are in correct positions; the other three lines are in incorrect positions. The two bottom lines are in conflict with each other, and the two middle lines and two top lines are complementary. Hexagram 4:7 is neutral.

3 Texts of Lines

Yang 1

One is innocent.
Going ahead is favorable.

The subject's yang action causes him or her to approach the object and ask for help, having no intention or ability to hurt the object. The subject is innocent. The object is in a strong position and able to help the subject. "Going ahead is favorable" for the subject. The subject should follow the directions of the object carefully.

This line is in a correct position, but in conflict with yang 4 (—). The yang action of the subject is neutral.

Yin 2

One does not have to plow for harvesting
Nor cultivate for fertile fields,
But all one's needs are fulfilled.
It is beneficial to move ahead.

Essentially, the subject is in a weak position. The object is very strong and able to help the subject. The subject "is granted all" his or her needs. However, that does not mean the subject may become lazy and do nothing. It only means with the help of the object, the subject can proceed without worrying about his or her weakness, "It is beneficial to move ahead." The subject should take this opportunity to improve his or her essence.

This line is in a correct position and complementary to yang 5 (▬). The yin essence of the subject is favorable.

Yin 3

There is an unexpected calamity
Like losing a tethered cow,
For the passerby who took the cow,
There is gain,
For the residents of the town,
It is a calamity.

With a yin attitude, the subject is agreeable and respectful. This attitude helps the subject in approaching and getting help from the object. But in trying to please the object, he or she could agree to do something that is not right. This mistake could cause trouble, like "an unexpected calamity, like losing a tethered cow." The object becomes involved in the mistake and stuck there, like "a tethered cow." The mistake could be used by rivals, competitors, or someone who is jealous or resents the people in the relationship, "For the passerby who took the cow, that is a gain." But for the subject, "the residents of the town," "that is a calamity."

This line is in an incorrect position, but complementary to yang 6 (▬). The yin attitude of the subject is neutral.

Yang 4

May stay on this course.
There is no blame.

With a yang action, the object deliberately approaches and supports the subject. In a weak position, the subject "may stay on this course," receiving help, and should not be blamed. It is possible that in approaching the subject, the object could be too aggressive and abuse power, causing trouble in the relationship.

This line is in an incorrect position and in conflict with yang 1 (▬). The yang action of the object is unfavorable.

Yang 5

There is an unexpected sickness,
Without being treated with medicine,
Resulting in happiness.

With a yang essence, the object is mature and experienced. The subject is immature, has less experience, and is unable to anticipate problems in his or her career, business, or relationships. When some problems occur to the subject, "there is an unexpected sickness." The object helps the subject and solves the problems quickly, "without being treated with medicine, resulting in happiness."

This line is in a correct position and complementary to yin 2 (━ ━). The yang essence of the object is favorable.

Yang 6

One is innocent.
Moving forward may bring trouble,
And is not beneficial.

The object's yang attitude may cause him or her to be manipulative and cause trouble. The innocent subject wants to approach the object to get help, but the subject has to be careful in dealing with the object properly. If the subject is too eager, he or she could be manipulated by the object, "Moving forward may bring trouble, and is not beneficial."

This line is in an incorrect position, but complementary to yin 3 (━ ━). The yang attitude of the object is neutral.

CHAPTER 15
When Fire (☲) is the Subject

THIS CHAPTER CONTAINS YI TEXT of eight hexagrams from 5:Ø to 5:7. Their subject trigrams are trigram 5, Fire. The typical characteristics of fire are brightness and a tendency to cling. Positive attributes include cleverness, talent, and an ability to shine or succeed; negative qualities can be rage, recklessness or roughness.

1 Hexagram 5:Ø Hurt (In Zhou Yi, hexagram 36)

The title, Hurt, refers to physical or emotional pain.

Trigram 5 (☲), Fire (brightness and clinging), is the subject; trigram Ø (☷), Earth (adaptability), is the object. This hexagram offers the metaphor of a great fire illuminating a vast field, and quickly consuming itself because there is no flammable material to sustain it. Hurt describes the feelings of the subject in the current situation.

1 General Text

It is beneficial to struggle hard
And stay on the current course.

The subject is working hard to push the relationship forward with an optimistic action and attitude, as shown by yang 1 (▬) and yang 3 (▬). The object follows and agrees, as shown by yin 4 (▬ ▬) and yin 6 (▬ ▬). The subject needs help as shown by yin 2 (▬ ▬), which indicates that he or she has little essential strength. But the subject is disappointed because the object cannot provide help; yin 5 indicates little strength here, as well. The fire consumes itself when it is not sustained by something else, and this process is painful for the subject. But if the subject continues to "struggle hard" and "stay on the current course," the situation will become beneficial.

2 Structure

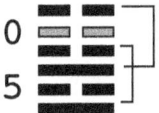

Figure 15.1: Structure of hexagram 5:Ø

This hexagram has five lines in correct positions, shown in black. Yin 5 (▬ ▬) is the only line in an incorrect position. The two bottom lines and the two top lines are complementary to each other. The two middle lines are in conflict with each other. Hexagram 5:Ø is neutral.

3 Texts of Lines

Yang 1

A pheasant drops its wings during flight.
One does not eat for three days during a journey.
Despite criticism from one's master,
One moves on.

Yang 1 (▬) indicates that the subject advances, like a pheasant flying, like a person traveling. But the subject has little strength and needs help; the object also has little strength and is unable to provide help. The subject grows tired, as "a pheasant drops its wings during flight," as "one does not eat for three days during a journey." Other people, symbolized by "one's master," criticize the subject for fruitless effort, but the subject keeps moving ahead. If the subject keeps moving in this way, the situation may possibly improve.

This line is in a correct position and complementary to yin 4 (▬ ▬). The yang action of the subject is favorable.

Yin 2

When one is severely hurt in the left thigh,
A strong horse gives help.
That is favorable.

Yin 2 (▬ ▬) indicates the essence of the subject is hurt emotionally, and the sharpness of this is like being "severely hurt in the left thigh." But there are two positive factors supporting the subject's advance. First, the subject wants to move forward and the object follows. Second, the subject is optimistic about the prospects of the relationship, and the object agrees. These truths are like a strong horse giving support, enabling the subject to keep going. Moving forward is favorable for the subject.

This line is in a correct position, but in conflict with yin 5 (▬ ▬). The yin essence of the subject is neutral.

Yang 3

While hunting in the south,
One captured a large game animal,
But was injured.
Stay on this course without rushing.

Yang 3 (━) indicates that the subject has an optimistic attitude about the prospects for the relationship. The subject can expect success in improving the relationship, and get the object to cooperate, in the way that a successful hunter captures "a large game animal."

On the other hand, the subject has little strength and cannot get help from the object. That may cause problems. The subject or the object feels unhappy, or "injured," at some point. The optimistic attitude of the subject is favorable, but the unfavorable aspect of weakness remains a concern. The subject should not proceed too quickly, but wait patiently — while recovering from the "injury" — for the object to catch up.

This line is in a correct position and complementary to yin 6 (━ ━). The yang attitude of the subject is favorable.

Yin 4

Feeling like an arrow has entered the gut,
One is deeply hurt with a broken heart,
And walks out of the house.

Yin 4 (━ ━) indicates that the object does not want to move forward in the relationship, because both the subject and the object have little strength and there is little prospect for success. The subject, "feeling like an arrow has entered the gut," is "deeply hurt with a broken heart." The subject even wants to give up, by walking out of the house. However, if there is sufficient optimism (the brightness of fire) to convince the object that there is hope for the relationship, and the object follows when the subject retreats, the situation will become favorable.

This line is in a correct position and complementary to yang 1 (━). The yin action of the object is favorable.

Yin 5

One is hurt like Qizi.
It is beneficial to stay on this course.

Qizi was a brother of emperor Shangzhou at the end of Shang dynasty. Emperor Shangzhou refused his advice and put him in jail. Qizi pretended to be mad to avoid persecution and death. He was deeply hurt physically and emotionally, but maintained his love for his country and his family.

Yin 5 (⚋) indicates that the object's essence has little strength and is unable to provide help, which the subject needs. The subject is deeply hurt, but still wants to improve the relationship. The situation could improve, "It is beneficial to stay on this course."

This line is in an incorrect position and in conflict with yin 2 (⚋). The yin essence of the object is unfavorable.

Yin 6

The situation is neither bright nor dim,
At first one feels very elated
Like climbing toward heaven,
Then one feels very discouraged
Like being pressed to the ground.

Yin 6 (⚋) indicates that the object is wavering so much that, from the subject's point of view, "the situation is neither bright nor dim." At first the subject feels "very elated like climbing toward heaven," then, "very discouraged like being pressed to the ground." If the object sees hope for improvement in the relationship and becomes respectful and adaptive, cooperating with the subject, the situation will be favorable.

This line is in a correct position and complementary to yang 3 (⚊). The yin attitude of the object is favorable.

② Hexagram 5:1 Ornament (In Zhou Yi, hexagram 22)

The title, Ornament, refers to an illusion at the heart of the relationship.

Trigram 5 (☲), Fire (brightness and clinging), is the subject; trigram 1 (☶), Mountain (stopping), is the object. The subject wants to exhibit brightness and the object wants to demonstrate tallness. Both are boasting, or decorating themselves, but neither one has real power. The dynamic of the relationship is that the fiery subject is approaching the object, while the object stands still like a mountain. For the subject, the current situation is one-sided, an illusion.

1 General Text

Things are going smoothly.
It is beneficial to do unessential things.

The subject wants to push the relationship forward, and the object does not share this desire, but does not oppose it, "Things are going smoothly." The subject has little strength and cannot get support from the object. The subject is arrogant; the object is stubborn. If the subject wants to do too much, this will irritate the object and make the situation worse. So the subject should instead devote his or her restless energies to matters that are less consequential, "It is beneficial to do unessential things."

2 Structure

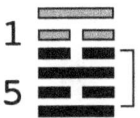

Figure 15.2: Structure of hexagram 5:1

In this hexagram, four lines — yang 1 (▬), yin 2 (▬ ▬), yang 3 (▬), and yin 4 (▬ ▬) — are in correct positions. The other two lines, yin 5 (▬ ▬) and yang 6, (▬) are in incorrect positions. The two bottom lines are complementary to each other. The two middle lines and the two top lines conflict. Hexagram 5:1 is neutral.

3 Texts of Lines

Yang 1

Adorning his toes,
One gives up riding and takes a walk.

Yang 1 (▬) indicates that the subject's action of approaching the object is to come on strong at first, like a rider on horseback. Then, in order to show respect, the subject "adorns his toes," and "gives up riding and takes a walk." It may seem silly, but this more gentle approach is a display of sincerity.

This line is in a correct position and complementary to yin 4 (▬ ▬). The yang action of the subject is favorable.

Yin 2

One adorns his beard.

Yin 2 (▬ ▬) indicates that the subject is in a weak position and needs help. To show good manners, the subject refines his presentation, "adorning his beard." This decoration is not significant, but the subject is trying to do his best.

This line is in a correct position, but in conflict with yin 5 (▬ ▬). The yin essence of the subject is neutral.

Yang 3

Everything is decorated and shiny.
Staying on the current course forever is favorable.

Yang 3 (—) indicates that the subject is arrogant, trying to keep his or her dignity and spruce up his or her outward appearance, "Everything is decorated and shiny." In fact, the subject has little essential strength and cannot move too far. The object is stubborn. No matter how the subject boasts and preens, the object does not help. The subject should stay put, and not try to press things, "Staying on the current course forever is favorable."

This line is in a correct position, but in conflict with yang 6 (—). The yang attitude of the subject is neutral.

Yin 4

Coming with a white fast running horse,
Ornamental and all white,
The rider appears not as a robber,
But as a suitor.

Yin 4 (— —) indicates that the object has no interest in pushing the relationship forward. The subject should show impressive sincerity, "coming with a white fast running horse, ornamental and all white," and win the object's confidence, letting the object believe in his or her good will, "The rider appears not as a robber, but as a suitor." If the object trusts the subject, the object will follow the subject, and the situation will improve.

This line is in a correct position and complementary to yang 1 (—). The yin action of the object is favorable.

Yin 5

A garden on a hill is decorated.
A gift of bolts of silk is presented.
It is unpleasant.
There is a favorable ending.

Yin 5 (— —) indicates that the object's essence has little strength and cannot help the subject. The rider comes to a beautifully decorated "garden on a hill" and presents "a gift of bolts of silk," but gains nothing. The subject feels unpleasant, because it is painful to give and not receive. But if the subject continues in this way, showing sincerity and trying to get the confidence of the object, the situation will be better, "There is a favorable ending."

This line is in an incorrect position and in conflict with yin 2 (━ ━). The yin essence of the object is unfavorable.

Yang 6

Adorn with white.
There is no blame.

In ancient China, white was the color of sadness. When a person died, the members of the family dressed in white and decorated the house with white.

Yang 6 (━) indicates that the object is stubborn, having no interest in improving the relationship. Despite the subject's attempts to approach the object "as a suitor," bringing gifts, the object keeps his or her mind unchanged, exhibiting sadness with white adornments. The subject should not be blamed.

This line is in an incorrect position and in conflict with yang 3 (━). The yang attitude of the object is unfavorable.

[3] Hexagram 5:2 Perfect (In Zhou Yi, hexagram 63)

The title, Perfect, describes a current situation of the relationship that has reached perfection. It does not mean that the subject or the object is perfect, or that the situation is perfect forever. But at this point, the situation is perfectly ripe for the subject to achieve his or her goals.

In Chinese, the title of this hexagram consists of two characters, "already" and "cross," referring to a story about a little fox crossing a dry river successfully. The little fox was cunning and wanted to cross a river, but was not a perfect swimmer. Once the river dried, the situation became perfect for the little fox to cross the river. The little fox succeeded.

Trigram 5 (☲), Fire (brightness and clinging), is the subject; trigram 2 (☵), Water (difficulty and danger), is the object. While the object poses difficulties, the brightness of the subject overcomes them and derives benefit from the favorable situation.

However, instead of letting the subject believe that this is simply a matter of good fortune or destiny, the text guides the subject to understand the situation objectively, analyzing the negative aspects and warning that this perfect situation cannot last forever.

1 General Text

Things are going a little smoothly.
It is beneficial to stay on the current course.
It is favorable at the beginning,
But becomes disordered at the end.

The subject is bossy or a bully and pushes the relationship forward, but has little power. The object, who has stronger power, does not want to move forward, but follows and yields to the subject reluctantly, "Things are going a little smoothly." If the subject keeps pushing, he or she could gain even more, "It is beneficial to stay on the current course."

Since the subject's interest is kindled by the object, once the object quits yielding, the subject will lose interest — just as fire and water create steam, which eventually evaporates in the process. So this is an exciting situation that cannot last indefinitely, "It is favorable at the beginning, but becomes disordered at the end." The subject should decisively take the favorable chance and be aware of the unfavorable opportunities.

2 Structure

Figure 15.3: Structure of hexagram 5:2

In this hexagram, all six lines are in correct positions, as shown in black. And all pairs of lines are complementary to each other. This hexagram is completely favorable to the subject.

3 Texts of Lines

Yang 1

While crossing a dry river,
A little fox drags the wheels of a wagon,
Getting its tail wet.
There is no blame.

Yang 1 (▬) indicates that the subject pulls the relationship forward, like the little fox dragging the wheels of the wagon to cross a dry river. Since the object follows reluctantly, sometimes the subject suffers a setback, like the little fox getting its tail wet; because, though the river is dry, there are a few puddles remaining. But the subject does his or her best and should not be blamed.

This line is in a correct position, and complementary to yin 4 (∎∎). The yang action of the subject is favorable.

Yin 2

After losing her curtain,
A lady does not seek it,
Yet gets it back in seven days.

Yin 2 (∎∎) indicates that the subject needs something that will help restore strength, such as funding, education, training, or health, like the lady who needs a curtain that she is missing. The strong object can help the passive subject. The "lady does not seek" the curtain, "yet gets it back in seven days."

This line is in a correct position, and complementary to yang 5 (∎). The yin essence of the subject is favorable.

Yang 3

Gaozhong launch a war against Guifang,
And conquered it in three years.
Do not use an unqualified person.

Gaozhong was a king of the country Shang in the middle of Shang dynasty, 16ØØ-11ØØ BC. Guifang was a country contiguous with China at that time.

Before Gaozhong became the king, Shang country was in a severe political and economic crisis. The words, "Do not use an unqualified person" refers to a story about Gaozhong, who had been silent and had made no decision about appointing a premier for three years. Finally he found the right person for this key position to help him bring his country out of crisis.

Yang 3 (∎) indicates that the subject's attitude is boasting and arrogant, yet also truthful and honest. The subject should come before the object as a "qualified person," inspiring confidence so that the object can understand, trust and follow the subject.

This line is in a correct position, and complementary to yin 6 (∎∎). The yang attitude of the subject is favorable.

Yin 4

Plugging leaks on the boat with some rags,

One is vigilant all day.

Yin 4 (⚋) indicates that the object does not want to move ahead, but is pushed by the subject. When any problems occur, the subject should resolve them promptly, "plugging leaks on the boat with some rags." The subject should be aware of the reluctance of the object to yield, and be "vigilant all day."

This line is in a correct position and complementary with yang 1 (⚊). The yin action of the object is favorable.

Yang 5

The neighbor to the east,
Butchering a cow for sacrifice,
Is not really so blessed
As the neighbor to the west,
Offering a spring sacrifice,
Which is simple.

Yang 5 (⚊) indicates that the object has a strong essence and can be a resource for the subject. Since the object is reluctantly following the subject, to get help from the object the subject has to be sincere, with true commitment. The object may not care what the subject has to show, but does care how the subject demonstrates sincerity. "The neighbor to the west" is truly blessed, in offering a simple, not fancy, sacrifice, because that neighbor is sincere.

This line is in a correct position and complementary to yin 2 (⚋). The yang essence of the object is favorable.

Yin 6

While crossing the river,
The little fox gets its head wet.
That is dangerous.

Yin 6 (⚋) indicates that the object's attitude is humble, agreeable and respectful. If the subject deals with the object truthfully and honestly, the object will help the subject willingly. Otherwise the subject may get in trouble, just as "the little fox gets its head wet."

This line is in a correct position, and complementary to yang 3 (⚊). The yin attitude of the object is favorable.

4 Hexagram 5:3 Matriarch (In Zhou Yi, hexagram 37)

The title, Matriarch, indicates that the subject has to do a lot of chores, such as taking care of family members.

Trigram 5 (☲), Fire (brightness and clinging), is the subject; trigram 3 (☴), Wind (flexibility), is the object. The clinging characteristic of the fire implies that the subject is weak internally and needs help. The flexible characteristic of wind implies that the object may or may not do what the subject wants. The fire may draw strength from wind, to blaze higher and stronger, but it can just as easily be blown out by the wind. The subject is in the position of leader, and must act boldly and wisely. But the subject should get support from followers, and this is not easy.

1 General Text

It is beneficial for a woman
To stay on the current course.

The subject leads the object to move forward. The object follows. The subject needs help. The object helps. However, while the subject is bossy, the object does not obey. To let the object follow and give support, the subject has to be gentle, graceful, respectful and flexible, as a woman can be. "It is beneficial for a woman" does not mean the situation is not beneficial for man, but rather that the subject should be more gentle and graceful than demanding and harsh.

2 Structure

Figure 15.4: Structure of hexagram 5:3

In this hexagram, five lines — yang 1 (▬), yin 2 (▬ ▬), yang 3 (▬), yin 4 (▬ ▬), and yang 5 (▬) — are in correct positions. Yang 6 (▬) is the only line in an incorrect position. The two bottom lines and middle lines are complementary; the two top lines are in conflict. The structure of this hexagram shows the situation is neutral, or a little favorable. The text points out an important issue in the relationship, that the subject should be sincere and avoid being arrogant, bossy or bullying.

3 Texts of Lines

Yang 1

> *Home is the place*
> *Where people rest after work.*
> *Regret vanishes.*

Yang 1 (━) indicates that the subject dominates the relationship, like a matriarch uniting family members together with a relaxing and lovely home. The subject is doing the right thing, "Regret vanishes."

This line is in a correct position, and complementary to yin 4 (━ ━). The yang action of the subject is favorable.

Yin 2

> *As head of a family,*
> *One does not go out,*
> *But stays home to make food for everybody.*
> *Staying on this course is favorable.*

Yin 2 (━ ━) indicates that the subject does not go out to earn money, but "stays home to make food for everybody." This housekeeping work looks trivial, but is essential for the family to be a unit and for its members able to focus on their jobs. The subject should keep to this path, "Staying on this course is favorable."

This line is in a correct position, and complementary to yang 5 (━). The yin essence of the subject is favorable.

Yang 3

> *The matriarch is scolding and complaining.*
> *Realizing the danger is favorable.*
> *Children are teasing and giggling.*
> *There is friction at the end.*

Yang 3 (━) indicates that the subject's attitude is the main problem in the relationship. "The matriarch is scolding and complaining." The subject should realize that this yang attitude is dangerous. The example of teasing and giggling children suggests that the subject could lose the object's respect. Since the object also has a yang attitude, the object could respond to bossiness by becoming disobedient, "There is friction at the end."

This line is in a correct position, but in conflict with yang 6 (━). The subject should remain truthful and honest, not arrogant, bossy or bullying.

Yin 4

They are a rich family.
The situation is very favorable.

Yin 4 (− −) describes a situation where the subject pushes the relationship forward, and the object follows. The subject uses the object's strength to create a stable unit, like a "rich family." "The situation is very favorable" to the subject.

This line is in a correct position, and complementary to yang 1 (—). The yin action of the object is favorable.

Yang 5

A person appears as a king in the family.
Do not worry.
The situation is favorable.

Yang 5 (—) indicates that the object possesses an essential strength, such as a good job, health, a decent education or training, or a desirable personality. The object is willing to help the subject, as a servant would assist a king. The subject is supported and respected, like "a king in the family." The subject does not have to worry about his or her lack of strength, such as joblessness, lack of skill, or poor health. The object takes care of the subject. "The situation is favorable" to the subject.

This line is in a correct position and complementary to yin 2 (− −). The yang essence of the object is favorable.

Yang 6

The matriarch is respected
For her sincerity.
The end is favorable.

Yang 6 (—) indicates that the object may resist the subject if the object feels the subject is too pushy or demanding. The subject should be sincere, truthful and honest, demonstrating that what the subject insists upon is right and good for the object. The subject can inspire obedience by being patient and straightforward, "The matriarch is respected for her sincerity." When the subject is bossy and the object is disobedient, what is the key to resolving this conflict? The text points out that the key is not giving up or making concessions, but sincerity, "The end is favorable."

This line is in an incorrect position and in conflict with yang 3 (—). The yang attitude of the object is unfavorable.

⑤ Hexagram 5:4 Totality (In Zhou Yi, hexagram 55)

The title, Totality, is best understood by consulting the Chinese title, Feng, which is an adjective, meaning abundant or plentiful. A large part of the text of this hexagram describes the process of a full solar eclipse. This implies a dynamic competition between the two sides in the relationship, like what happens at the moment when the sun is completely obscured by the moon.

Trigram 5 (☲), Fire (brightness and clinging), is the subject; trigram 4 (☳), Thunder (movement) is the object. Both of them are in motion; one is bright like the sun; the other pales in comparison, like the moon. Subject and object move independently, in their own orbits, at their own pace. Once they are in the same spot in the sky, in alignment with the earth, what happens?

1 General Text

Things are going smoothly.
The king comes.
Do not worry.
The sun should be in the middle of the sky.

Both the subject and the object are making progress, but they are moving along distinct orbits, like the sun and moon, without a potential collision, "Things are going smoothly."

When the subject feels threatened by the object's approach, the subject worries — just as in ancient times, people witnessing a solar eclipse worried about the survival of the sun. "The king comes," like a leader or priest summoned by the people to pray for the sun. The text is reassuring, "Do not worry. The sun should be in the middle of the sky." This indicates that competition with the object will not hurt the subject.

2 Structure

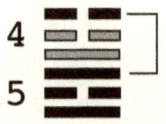

Figure 15.5: Structure of hexagram 5:4

In this hexagram, four lines — yang 1 (▬), yin 2 (▬ ▬), yang 3 (▬), and yin 6 (▬ ▬) — are in correct positions. Yang 4 (▬) and yin 5 (▬ ▬) are in incorrect positions. The two bottom lines and the two middle lines are in conflict with each other. The two top lines are complementary. The structure of this hexagram

3 Texts of Lines

Yang 1

After preparing for ten days,
Watch the sun is approaching the moon.
Moving ahead is blameless and respectable.

Yang 1 (—) indicates that the subject is actively pursuing a path of development. The subject faces a predictable competition, as shown by yang 4 (—), "After preparing for ten days, watch the sun is approaching the moon." The subject is patient and waiting for the chance. The subject should keep moving forward, "Moving ahead is blameless and respectable."

This line is in a correct position, but in conflict with yang 4 (—). The yang action of the subject is neutral.

Yin 2

In the vast sky,
The North Star is visible at noon.
Moving ahead results in an atmosphere of suspicion.
Sincerity creates a favorable situation.

Yin 2 (- -) indicates that when a competition becomes imminent, the subject possesses little strength. This could be a lack of money, inexperience, or some other source of insecurity that makes it difficult for the subject to venture forth boldly, "Moving ahead results in an atmosphere of suspicion." When confidence is not possible or realistic, the subject should be sincere, honestly dealing with the object and others, "Sincerity creates a favorable situation."

This line is in a correct position, but in conflict with yin 5 (- -). The yin essence of the subject is neutral.

Yang 3

In the copious sky,
The small stars are visible at midday.
The sun loses its right edge.
There is no blame.

Yang 3 (—) indicates that the subject has a truthful and honest attitude, even when feeling the impact of competition, "The sun loses its right edge." Since the subject is maintaining the correct attitude, "there is no blame."

This line is in a correct position, and complementary to yin 6 (━ ━). The yang attitude of the subject is favorable.

Yang 4

In the vast sky,
The North Star is visible at noon.
The moon is directly in front of the sun.
The situation is favorable.

Yang 4 (━━) indicates that the object is very aggressive, laying claim to the spot where the subject is, "The moon is directly in front of the sun." But actually, this poses no harm to the subject, and worry about the safety of the sun is not necessary. The competition "is favorable" to the subject.

This line is in an incorrect position, and in conflict with yang 1 (━━). This line is unfavorable. However, the text states, "The yang action of the object is favorable," regarding the whole situation of the object, which has less strength and is respectful to the subject.

Yin 5

It comes to a beautiful moment.
Celebrate and honor that moment.
The situation is favorable.

Yin 5 (━ ━) indicates that the object has little strength and is unable to damage the subject.

The most amazing moment in the process of a total solar eclipse is right after coverage is complete, "It comes to a beautiful moment." The colorful, fierce flames of the sun's rays become visible. At that time, the edge of the sun looks like a huge, diamond and gold ring hanging in the copious sky. Through this competition, the brightness of the subject becomes visible, "Celebrate and honor that moment." "The situation is favorable."

This line is in an incorrect position and in conflict with yin 2 (━ ━). The yin essence of the object is unfavorable. The subject does not actually gain from the object. But the text stresses the favorable aspect of a difficult situation.

Yin 6

There is a house with many rooms.

The home is like a vast sky.
Peeking through the window of the house,
The house is dark and nobody is there.
There have been no people in sight for three years.
The situation is unfavorable.

Yin 6 (▬ ▬) indicates that the object is conservative and fearful, and wants to forfeit the competition, "The house is dark and nobody is there." The abandonment of competition hinders the subject's development. "There have been no people in sight for three years." "The situation is unfavorable."

This line is in a correct position and complementary to yang 3 (▬). The yin attitude of the object is favorable. If the object is humble, agreeable and adaptive, the subject can deal with the object more easily. This is favorable to the subject, but the text stresses the negative side of the object's yin attitude — that the object's tendency to slip away hinders total and equal competition.

6 Hexagram 5:5 Brightness (In Zhou Yi, hexagram 30)

The title, Brightness, refers to the doubling of trigrams 5 (☲), Fire (brightness and clinging). Subject and object are equally brilliant and active, like two flames. They are both seeking development, and competing with each other.

When the two flames are blazing side by side, which one is brighter? Which one lasts longer? They are in competition, but neither can hurt the other nor benefit from the other. But the two flames can link together, their energy flaring into a higher flame.

The subject should keep developing steadily, like a fiercely burning flame, no matter what the other is doing. The text encourages the subject to succeed in the competition.

1 General Text

It is beneficial to stay on the current course.
Things are going smoothly.
Raising a docile cow is favorable.

The subject has little strength, but aggressive movement makes him or her stronger, as a flame is enhanced by burning more woods, grasses or other fuels, "It is beneficial to stay on the current course." Because the object also possesses little strength and is unable to harm the subject, "things are going smoothly." Since the object is also developing, and is a potential danger, the subject should manage to win the competition, subduing the object like a docile cow. If the object does not yield to the subject's taming influence, the object may become instead like a black bear, posing a constant danger.

2 Structure

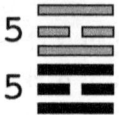

Figure 15.6: Structure of hexagram 5:5

In this hexagram, all three lines of the subject trigram, yang 1 (—), yin 2 (- -), and yang 3 (—), are in correct positions. The other three, all three lines of the object trigram — yang 4 (—) yin 5 (- -), and yang 6 (—) — are in incorrect positions. No corresponding lines are complementary. The structure of this hexagram shows that the current situation is neutral.

3 Texts of Lines

Yang 1

Steps appear in disorder.
Salute.
There is no blame.

Yang 1 (—) indicates that at any sign that the object is going to do something, the subject acts promptly. When "steps appear in disorder," it should be considered as someone approaching. "Salute" immediately. Because the subject and object are engaged in direct competition, the quick action of the subject should not be blamed. Someone who is coming could be a very important person who can help the subject succeed competitively, such as the subject's boss.

This line is in a correct position, but in conflict with yang 4 (—). The yang action of the subject is neutral.

Yin 2

Yellow fire.
It is very favorable.

Yellow flame shows the strength of the fire, strong and with a high temperature, while a dark smoke mixed with red flame shows the fire's weakness.

Yin 2 (- -) indicates the essence of the subject is yin. The subject has little strength — which may be experienced as lack of money, skill, experience, or support from others. This essential need motivates the subject, like a yellow fire burning aggressively. "It is very favorable" for the subject.

This line is in a correct position, but in conflict with yin 5 (▬ ▬). The yin essence of the subject is neutral. The text encourages the subject to be more vigorous and aggressive in advancing, like the yellow fire.

Yang 3

The fire is lighting at the sunset.
Without drumming a jar and singing,
There will be the wailing of senility.
The situation is unfavorable.

In ancient times, at sunset, people gathered together, lighting a fire, drumming jars, which were a kind of clay musical instrument, and singing for ceremony or amusement.

Yang 3 (▬▬) indicates that the subject is optimistic, showing off, being excited and encouraged. The subject needs to win the competition over the object, physically or spiritually. By moving at a slow pace with a low profile, the subject could miss a chance to win the competition, "Without drumming a jar and singing there will be the wailing of senility." There is a sunset feeling of time running out for the subject, "The situation is unfavorable."

This line is in a correct position, but in conflict with yang 6 (▬▬). The yang attitude of the subject is neutral.

Yang 4

Suddenly the fire is brilliant, burning,
Then diminishing.

Yang 4 (▬▬) indicates that the object is aggressively moving forward, suddenly creating an impact on the subject. Because of the object's weak essence, this rush of action is dramatic but not enduring, "Suddenly the fire is brilliant, burning, then diminishing."

This line is in an incorrect position, and in conflict with yang 1 (▬▬). The yang action of the object if unfavorable.

Yin 5

The weeping is torrential
With worrying and sighing.
That is favorable.

Yin 5 (- -) indicates that the object has little strength to compete with the subject. This is not good for the object — "The weeping is torrential with worrying and sighing." — but the object's disadvantage is "favorable" for the subject.

This line is in an incorrect position and in conflict with yin 2 (- -). The yin essence of the object is unfavorable. Regarding the context, the text points out that the yin essence of the object can be favorable.

Yang 6

The king sent one to a war.
One killed the leader of enemies
And captured their followers.
There is no blame.

The "king" may refer to a boss, a government, a community, parents, or whoever backs the subject.

Yang 6 (—) indicates that the attitude of the object is arrogant, bossy, or bullying, and poses a challenge to the subject. The subject should overcome the object and win the competition, "One killed the leader of enemies and captured their followers." But keep in mind, that the subject does not have strength to accomplish this alone, and has to be sent by the "king." This is the key of the text's advice. If in an office, one is challenged by another coworker in a similar position, one has to get support from someone in authority. Otherwise, one will be blamed.

This line is in an incorrect position and in conflict with yang 3 (—). The yang attitude of the object is unfavorable.

[7] Hexagram 5:6 Change (In Zhou Yi, hexagram 49)

The title, Change, refers to making changes in the relationship.

Trigram 5 (☲), Fire (brightness and clinging), is the subject; trigram 6 (☱), Lake (pleasure) is the object. The bright, clinging subject makes necessary changes to take advantage of the pleasant object.

In the relationship, what should be changed or improved in order to get help from the object? The subject needs help, and the object is able to help, so the key is sincerity. To make the object help the subject willingly, the two sides have to have a sincere regard for each other. This is the subject's responsibility.

1 General Text

After a few days,
The sincerity is shown.
Things are going very smoothly.
It is beneficial to stay on the current course.
Regret vanishes.

Both the subject and the object want to improve the relationship. The object is used to being humble, modest and graceful, but the subject behaves roughly, arrogantly and stubbornly. How can the object see that the subject is asking for help sincerely, so that the object can offer help happily? The subject has to change, in a way that displays sincerity.

In the beginning, the object may not trust the subject, but "after a few days," when "the sincerity is shown," "things are going very smoothly." If the subject remains on this course, "regret vanishes."

2 Structure

Figure 15.7: Structure of hexagram 5:6

In this hexagram, five lines — yang 1 (▬), yin 2 (▬ ▬), yang 3 (▬), yang 5 (▬), and yin 6 (▬ ▬) — are in correct positions. Yang 4 (▬) is the only line in an incorrect position. The two bottom lines conflict with each other. The two middle and two top lines are complementary. The structure of this hexagram shows the situation is a little favorable.

3 Texts of Lines

Yang 1

Tie with a belt made of leather
From a yellow ox.

Yang 1 (▬) indicates that the subject actively seeks to improve the relationship. The subject should stick to this yang action firmly, "Tie with a belt made of leather from a yellow ox."

This line is in a correct position, but in conflict with yang 4 (▬). The yang action of the subject is neutral.

Yin 2

After a few days,
A change appears.
Going ahead is favorable.
There is no blame.

Yin 2 (⚋) indicates a lack of strength that presses the subject to change his or her behavior, and the flexibility to go along with it, "After a few days, a change appears." If the subject follows the path of change, "going ahead is favorable." The subject is doing the right thing, "There is no blame."

This line is in a correct position, and complementary to yang 5 (⚊). The yin essence of the subject is favorable.

Yang 3

Going ahead is unfavorable.
Staying on this course is dangerous.
Change words,
Compromise, compromise and compromise.
Then the sincerity is shown.

Yang 3 (⚊) indicates that the subject is stubborn. This makes the object unhappy and distrustful of the subject. If the subject remains stubborn, "going ahead is unfavorable," and "staying on this course is dangerous." The subject should modify his or her attitude, "Compromise, compromise and compromise." Only in this way, the situation will improve, "Then the sincerity is shown."

This line is in a correct position and complementary with yin 6 (⚋). The yang attitude of the subject is favorable. The text stresses that compromise is vital in acquiring help from others.

Yang 4

Regret vanishes.
Sincerity appears.
That changes life.
The situation is favorable.

Yang 4 (⚊) indicates that the object also wants to push the relationship forward. If the subject compromises, showing sincerity, the object will be happy to help the subject. That totally elevates the relationship to a better status. "The situation is favorable" for the subject.

This line is in an incorrect position, and in conflict with yang 1 (⚊). The yang action of the object is unfavorable. But since the subject needs help, the object's actively helping the subject is favorable.

Yang 5

A great person makes a substantial change,
Like a tiger changing stripes on its body.
No doubt,
There is sincerity.

Yang 5 (▬) indicates the object's strength and ability to help the subject. At the beginning, because of distrust, the object is reluctant to offer help. Then, seeing the subject's sincerity, the object becomes happy to help the subject. This change on the subject's part is substantive, "like a tiger changing stripes on its body." That change happens because the subject compromises, showing sincerity.

This line is in a correct position, and complementary to yin 2 (▬ ▬). The yang essence of the object is favorable.

Yin 6

A wise person makes significant change.
Like a leopard changing spots on its skin.
A normal person makes only modification of appearances without any substantial change.
Going ahead is unfavorable.
Staying on the current course calmly is favorable.

Yin 6 (▬ ▬) indicates that the object is graceful and respectful. Once the object feels that the subject is sincere, the object makes a decision to help the subject. This change is significant, "like a leopard changing spots on its skin." Now progress depends on the sincerity of the subject's change. If the subject "makes only modification of appearances without any substantial change," then "going ahead is unfavorable." But the subject should keep a firm commitment to real change, "staying on the current course calmly is favorable."

This line is in a correct position and complementary to yang 3 (▬). The yin attitude of the object is favorable.

⑧ Hexagram 5:7 Coalition (In Zhou Yi, hexagram 13)

The title, Coalition, refers to a united partnership between the subject and the object.

Trigram 5 (☷), Fire (brightness and clinging), is the subject; trigram 7 (☰), Heaven (strength), is the object. The subject finds a powerful object, clings to the object and forms a coalition.

1 General Text

Ally with others in a wide field.
Things are going smoothly.
It is beneficial for one to cross a big river,
Interacting with others.
It is beneficial for the smart person
To stay on the current course.

The subject has little strength, while the object is strong. Both of them want to move forward in the relationship and are optimistic about furthering their union. To fulfill his or her mission, the subject should form a wide range of coalitions including the object, "Ally with others in a wide field." If the subject does so, "things are going smoothly." Otherwise, there will be trouble. The subject should not let a disagreement or misunderstanding come between the two sides, as a river separates its banks, "It is beneficial for one to cross a big river, interacting with others." The subject should be smart, pursuing coalitions with others.

2 Structure

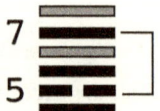

Figure 15.8: Structure of hexagram 5:7

In this hexagram, four lines — yang 1 (▬), yin 2 (▬ ▬), yang 3 (▬), and yang 5 (▬) — are in correct positions. Yang 4 (▬) and yang 6 (▬) are in incorrect positions. The two bottom lines and two top lines are in conflict; the two middle lines are complementary to each other. The structure of this hexagram shows the situation is a little favorable.

3 Texts of Lines

Yang 1

Being allied with neighbors is blameless.

Yang 1 (▬) indicates that the subject wants to move ahead in the relationship and tries to form a coalition, beginning with neighbors. The subject is doing the right thing.

This line is in a correct position, but in conflict with yang 4 (━). The yang action of the subject is neutral.

Yin 2

One allies with one's clan.
That is uncomfortable.

Yin 2 (━ ━) indicates that the subject is essentially lacking in power — not rich, not experienced, not well-educated, or not healthy. This weakness makes it hard to form a wide coalition. He or she allies only with his or her clan, and this restriction feels uncomfortable.

This line is in a correct position, and complementary to yang 5 (━). The yin essence of the subject is favorable. The text stresses the yin essence is not favorable for coalition, because the object cannot expect the subject to do too much.

Yang 3

Hiding in bushes
Or climbing tall mountains,
A troop has been fighting for three years
Without advancing.

Yang 3 (━) indicates that the subject is arrogant or reckless. The object does not like the subject's attitude. Without a coalition, the subject is unlikely to succeed, "A troop has been fighting for three years without advancing."

This line is in a correct position, but in conflict with yang 6 (━). The yang attitude of the subject is unfavorable.

Yang 4

A troop holds a great wall.
No one can attack them.
The situation is favorable.

Yang 4 (━) indicates that the object willingly takes an action to form a coalition that includes the subject. Both sides work together, like a troop holding "a great wall." "The situation is favorable" for the subject.

This line is in an incorrect position and in conflict with yang 1 (━). The yang action of the object is unfavorable. If the subject joins the coalition, but yields to the object, the subject's action becomes yin and there will be no conflict. The text says that the situation is favorable.

Yang 5

At first screaming and crying in battle,
Then smiling for victory,
The soldiers have conquered the enemy,
And meet with their allies.

Yang 5 (▬) indicates the essence of the object is yang. The object has a great power. At first, the object did not respond to the subject's call for coalition and the subject was failing, "screaming and crying in battle." Then the object decides to form a coalition for the common interest; and the subject gets support, "smiling for victory."

This line is in a correct position and complementary to yin 2 (▬ ▬). The yang essence of the object is favorable.

Yang 6

Being allied with others in a rural area
Is not regrettable.

Yang 6 (▬) indicates that the object is arrogant, self-centered, bossy or domineering. The subject does not like the object's attitude or enjoy being close to the object. However, joining a coalition with the object is good for the subject's interest, especially where there is space enough for the subject to tolerate the object's bossiness, "Being allied with others in a rural area is not regrettable."

This line is in an incorrect position and in conflict with yang 3 (▬). The yang attitude of the object is unfavorable.

CHAPTER 16
When Lake (☱) is the Subject

THIS CHAPTER CONTAINS Yi text of eight hexagrams from 6:Ø to 6:7. Their subject trigrams are trigram 6, Lake. The typical characteristic of lake is pleasure. This not only describes a general feeling, but also the joy that flows from an exhilarating adventure, a successful mission, and an optimistic prospect, as well as a graceful, flexible and modest manner.

1️⃣ Hexagram 6:Ø Approach (In Zhou Yi, hexagram 19)

The title, Approach, refers to the subject's readiness to deal with what is coming.

Trigram 6 (☱), Lake (pleasure), is the subject; trigram Ø (☷), Earth (adaptability) is the object. The subject takes care of the object. Together, they deal with what is coming truthfully and realistically.

1 General Text

Things are going very smoothly.
It is beneficial to stay on the current course.
There will be an unfavorable time after eight months.

"Eight months" does not refer to an exact span of time in the calendar, but to the near future. The subject has strength and is happy to take care of the object, while the object adapts to the subject's strength. "Things are going very smoothly," and "it is beneficial" for the subject "to stay on the current course." However, the subject has to be ready to deal truthfully and realistically with inevitable changes, "There will be an unfavorable time after eight months."

2 Structure

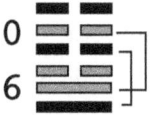

Figure 16.1: Structure of hexagram 6:Ø

In this hexagram, three lines, yang 1 (▬), yin 4 (▬▬), and yin 6 (▬▬), are in correct positions. The other three, yang 2 (▬), yin 3 (▬▬), and yin 5 (▬▬), are in incorrect positions. The two bottom lines and the two middle lines are complementary to each other. The two top lines are in conflict. The structure of this hexagram shows the current situation is neutral, or a little favorable.

3 Texts of Lines

Yang 1

Be aware of what is coming.
Staying on this course is favorable.

Yang 1 (▬) indicates that the subject is taking care of the object actively, carefully watching what is going on. "Staying on this course is favorable" for the subject to fulfill his or her mission.

This line is in a correct position, and complementary to yin 4 (▬ ▬). The yang action of the subject is favorable.

Yang 2

Be aware of what is coming.
The situation is favorable and beneficial.

Yang 2 (▬) indicates that the subject is strong and ready for helping the object whenever the help is needed, "Be aware of what is coming." The subject's strength is favorable and beneficial for doing what needs to be done.

This line is in an incorrect position, but complementary to yin 5 (▬ ▬). The yang essence of the subject is favorable.

Yin 3

What is coming
Is a sweet fantasy,
Not beneficial.
If one worries about the reality,
There is no blame.

Yin 3 (▬ ▬) indicates that the subject is given to fantasy, and in danger of ignoring the seriousness of what is coming. If something unfavorable becomes reality, the subject could miss the chance to find a good solution. It is better to maintain an awareness of what might happen, "If one worries about the reality, there is no blame."

This line is in an incorrect position, and in conflict with yin 6 (▬ ▬). The yin attitude of the subject is unfavorable.

Yin 4

Here is what is coming.
There is no blame.

Yin 4 (⚋) indicates that the object follows the subject. When the anticipation becomes reality, the subject is able to help the object in an appropriate way.

This line is in a correct position, and complementary to yang 1 (⚊). The yin action of the object is favorable.

Yin 5

To know what is coming
Is a right thing to do for a great person.
It is favorable.

Yin 5 (⚋) indicates that the object suffers from some weakness — is sick, or is having trouble in business, in a relationship or with the law. In order to help the object, the subject should thoroughly know the nature of the object's problem and the possible changes, "To know what is coming is a right thing to do for a great person."

This line is in an incorrect position, but complementary to yang 2 (⚊). The yin essence of the object is neutral.

Yin 6

Urging one to tell what is coming
Is favorable and blameless.

Yin 6 (⚋) indicates that the object is humble, agreeable and respectful. Sometimes, the object may not want to, or be able to, tell the truth about what is transpiring. In order to help the object effectively, the subject should urge the object to be open and honest, "to tell what is coming is favorable and blameless."

This line is in a correct position, but in conflict with yin 3 (⚋). The yin attitude of the object is neutral.

[2] Hexagram 6:1 Loss (In Zhou Yi, hexagram 41)

The title, Loss, means that the subject suffers from a setback in the act of helping others.

Trigram 6 (☱), Lake (pleasure), is the subject; trigram 1 (☶), Mountain (stopping), is the object. The subject is happy in helping the object, but the object rejects this assistance. When the object needs help badly, but behaves ungraciously, the subject should persevere in helping appropriately.

1 General Text

There is sincerity.
It is favorable and blameless.
One may stay on this course.
It is beneficial to move ahead.
What can be used for a sacrificial ceremony?
Two baskets of food are just right.

When the object really needs help, and the subject is happy to offer it, the subject has to be sincere in this offer. Since the object is such an arrogant, immodest person, only sincerity can make him polite enough to accept assistance. If the subject does so, "it is favorable and blameless." The subject should always deal with the object sincerely — "One may stay on this course." — and the relationship will improve. The subject should do just what the object wants, in the spirit of offering a sacrifice, "Two baskets of food are just right."

2 Structure

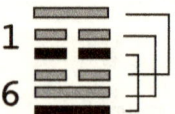

Figure 16.2: Structure of hexagram 6:1

In this hexagram, only two lines, yang 1 (—) and yin 4 (- -), are in correct positions. The other four, yang 2 (—), yin 3 (- -), yin 5 (- -), and yang 6 (—), are in incorrect positions. All the pairs of lines are complementary. The structure of this hexagram shows the current situation is neutral, or less favorable to the subject.

3 Texts of Lines

Yang 1

After finishing one's own work,
Going out quickly to help others
Is blameless.

But the offer should be appropriate.

Yang 1 (▬) indicates that the subject is ready and willing to help the object. When extending this help, the subject should pay attention to two things: the subject should finish his or her own work first, and "the offer should be appropriate." Otherwise, because the object has an attitude of high self-esteem, the object could reject or ignore the offer.

This line is in a correct position and complementary to yin 4 (▬ ▬). The yang action of the subject is favorable.

Yang 2

It is beneficial to stay on this course.
To move ahead is unfavorable.
Do not lose your own interest
While benefiting others.

Yang 2 (▬) indicates that the subject has strength and is able to help the object in appropriate ways, "It is beneficial to stay on this course." But the subject must be careful not to make extravagant offers, and remain aware that the object is arrogant and self-centered, "Do not lose your own interest while benefiting others."

This line is in an incorrect position, but complementary to yin 5 (▬ ▬). The yang essence of the subject is neutral.

Yin 3

Three people walk together,
Then lose one person.
One person walks alone,
Then gets a friend.

Yin 3 (▬ ▬) indicates that the subject is kind, agreeable and graceful. When helping the object, the subject is likely to do too much, and overwhelm the object with kindness. This excess leads to a situation illustrated by the old saying, "three's a crowd." When three people are working together, it is natural that two of them will talk more with each other enjoyably, while the extra person may feel bored or left out. But if one person walks alone and meets with one other person, the balance is more agreeable, and they may talk to each other and become friends. The subject should offer just what the object wants, and not too much.

This line is in an incorrect position, but complementary to yang 6 (▬).

Yin 4

Suffering loss to solve another's problems
Quickly brings happiness.
There is no blame.

Yin 4 (- -) indicates that the object follows the subject. When the object has problems, the subject offers help and makes a sacrifice to do so. The loss does not necessarily bring bad feelings. When the object's problems are resolved with the subject's help, the loss "quickly brings happiness."

This line is in a correct position and complementary to yang 1 (—). The yin action of the object is favorable.

Yin 5

If there is a need to present a tortoise,
Worth ten pairs of seashells,
One should not refuse.
It is very favorable.

The allusion to "ten pairs of seashells" refers to a kind of ancient currency. A tortoise worth that much would be a very valuable contribution.

Yin 5 (- -) indicates that the object has very little strength — is sick, or having trouble in finance, a relationship, or the law. The subject should help the object as much as the object needs, holding nothing back, even to the level of "a tortoise worth ten pairs of seashells." At a crucial time, the sincere help is very favorable for fulfilling the subject's mission and improving the relationship.

This line is in an incorrect position, but complementary to yang 2 (—). The yin essence of the object is neutral.

Yang 6

Do not lose your own interest
While benefiting others.
There is no blame.
Staying on this course is favorable.
It is beneficial to move ahead.
The others may get your servant,
But not your home.

Yang 6 (—) indicates that the object is self-centered, arrogant, or bullying. While helping the object through a crisis, the subject should also protect himself or herself, "Do not lose your own interest, while benefiting others." "Staying on this course" by helping the object appropriately "is favorable." At the same time, the subject can be doing something to help his or her own advancement, "It is beneficial to move ahead." While helping the object comes at a cost to the subject, the sacrifice has its limits, "The others may get your servant, but not your home."

This line is in an incorrect position, but complementary to yin 3 (⚋). The yang attitude of the object is neutral.

3 Hexagram 6:2 Limitation (In Zhou Yi, hexagram 60)

The title, Limitation, suggests that the subject should place limits on his or her activities.

Trigram 6 (☱), Lake (pleasure), is the subject, and, trigram 2 (☵), Water (difficulty and danger), is the object. The subject may find pleasure in moving the relationship forward, but the object is not ready to follow, and is having difficulty making decisions. The subject should slow down, and limit possibly inappropriate activities.

The text lists three kinds of limitations: bitter or harsh, peaceful, and sweet. If, for example, a boy knows a girl who loves him but never says so, and he loves her, he should tell her so — say to her, "I love you." Otherwise, he will lose out on true love by courting too slowly, and will be left with nothing but sorrow. This is a bitter limitation.

1 General Text

Things are going smoothly.
Do not stay with a bitter limitation.

The subject is important to the object, and is humble and respectful toward the object, "Things are going smoothly." But while the subject wants to push the relationship forward, the object is not ready to do so. The subject should slow down, not proceed beyond the limitation. If this restraint is too harsh, or excessive and inappropriate, it becomes a bitter limitation — such as a retreat, giving up, quitting a job, or engaging in evil activities. The amount of restraint should be appropriate, "Do not stay with a bitter limitation."

2 Structure

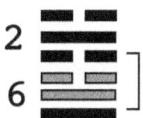

Figure 16.3: Structure of hexagram 6:2

In this hexagram, four lines, yang 1 (▬), yin 4 (▬ ▬), yang 5 (▬), and yin 6 (▬ ▬), are in correct positions. The other two lines, yang 2 (▬) and yin 3 (▬ ▬), are in incorrect positions. Only the two bottom lines are complementary to each other. The structure of this hexagram shows the current situation as neutral.

3 Texts of Lines

Yang 1

Do not go out of the room.
There is no blame.

Yang 1 (▬) indicates the subject's desire to move ahead in the relationship, but in order to cope with the object, the subject should restrain himself or herself. There is a special warning to control wild private behavior, such as smoking, drinking or entanglement in violence, "Do not go out of the room."

This line is in a correct position and complementary to yin 4 (▬ ▬). The yang action of the subject is favorable.

Yang 2

One does not walk outdoors.
That is unfavorable.

Yang 2 (▬) indicates that the subject is important to the object and should maintain ties with the object. If the subject decides to "walk outdoors" — giving up on the relationship because of frustration or uncertainty about the object's hesitations, then the subject will lose communication with the object, "That is unfavorable."

This line is in an incorrect position and in conflict with yang 5 (▬). The yang essence of the subject is unfavorable.

Yin 3

If there is no limitation,
There will be a sigh.
There is no blame.

Yin 3 (▬ ▬) indicates that the subject may be yielding to a lack of discipline, living luxuriously or behaving deceptively. The subject should practise more rigor and restraint, or will come to regret this weakness, "If there is no limitation, there will be a sigh."

This line is in an incorrect position and in conflict with yin 6 (⚋). The yin attitude of the subject is unfavorable.

Yin 4

Keep peaceful limitation.
Things are going smoothly.

Yin 4 (⚋) indicates that within the relationship, the object does not want to move forward. This calls for "peaceful limitation," If the subject can practise patience, slowing down, waiting, and giving the object more time, then "things are going smoothly."

This line is in a correct position and complementary to yang 1 (⚊). The yin action of the object is favorable.

Yang 5

Keep sweet limitation.
It is favorable.
Moving ahead is honorable.

Yang 5 (⚊) indicates that the object has strength, health, financial stability, power in business, or love for the subject. At this moment, the object does not agree with the subject in desiring to move the relationship forward, because the object has some difficulty making this decision. If the subject shows an agreeable restraint — "sweet limitation" — he or she will be rewarded, "It is favorable." Then moving ahead with mutual understanding and respect will be honorable.

This line is in a correct position, but in conflict with yang 2 (⚊). The yang essence of the object is neutral, or a little favorable.

Yin 6

Keeping bitter limitation is unfavorable.
Regret vanishes.

Yin 6 (⚋) indicates that the object is graceful, agreeable and respectful. The subject should maintain limits that are appropriate, without allowing them to become too harsh, "Keeping bitter limitation is unfavorable." If the subject will just slow down for a while, and refrain from doing anything evil, then "regret vanishes."

This line is in a correct position, but in conflict with yin 3 (⚋). The yin attitude of the object is neutral.

4 Hexagram 6:3 Sincerity (In Zhou Yi, hexagram 61)

The title, Sincerity, stresses the importance of sincerity in the relationship's success.

Trigram 6 (☱), Lake (pleasure), is the subject; trigram 3 (☴), Wind (flexibility), is the object. It is a pleasure for the subject to respect the object. The object displays flexibility in a willingness to follow the subject. No one wants to take advantage of the other. They are enjoying a mutual sincerity.

A true sincerity is valuable. If the other makes promises to you with sweet words, but no deed, you should remember, "A pheasant soars into sky with a loud, beautiful sound. It leaves nothing in deed. Staying on this course is unfavorable."

1 General Text

The current situation is favorable to everybody,
Including pigs and fish.
It is beneficial to cross a big river,
Interacting with each other.
It is beneficial to stay on the current course.

Both subject and object have strength. They are healthy, strong financially, or powerful in business. No one wants or needs to take advantage of the other, "The current situation is favorable to everybody, including pigs and fish." The subject actively develops the relationship, and the object follows, "It is beneficial to cross a big river, interacting with each other." The object has a bossy attitude, but it is all right because the subject respects the object, "It is beneficial to stay on the current course."

2 Structure

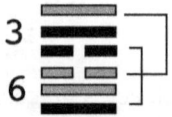

Figure 16.4: Structure of hexagram 6:3

In this hexagram, three lines, yang 1 (—), yin 4 (- -), and yang 5 (—), are in correct positions. The other three, yang 2 (—), yin 3 (- -), and yang 6 (—), are in incorrect positions. The two bottom lines and the two top lines are complementary to each other. The two middle lines are in conflict. The structure of this hexagram shows the current situation is neutral.

3 Texts of Lines

Yang 1

Being stable in a relationship is favorable.
Having an affair with another is troublesome.

Yang 1 (▬) indicates that the subject is very active, and should aim for stability. If the subject has affairs with others, that is disruptive and may be considered insincere in the current relationship, "Having an affair with another is troublesome."

This line is in a correct position and complementary to yin 4 (▬ ▬). The yang action of the subject is favorable. The text is a reminder that this action should take the form of faithfulness in the relationship.

Yang 2

A crane is singing in the shade.
Its children echo,
"I have a goblet of good wine,
And I would like to share it with you."

Yang 2 (▬) indicates the essence of the subject is strong financially, physically or spiritually. Meanwhile, the object is strong as well. Both sides share their good fortune sincerely.

This line is in an incorrect position and in conflict with yang 5 (▬). The yang essence of the subject is neutral.

Yin 3

When advancing with drumming,
Or quitting fighting,
Or weeping for loss,
Or singing in triumph,
People support each other during a battle.

Yin 3 (▬ ▬) indicates that the subject is polite, agreeable and respectful, and gets along with the object, "People support each other during a battle."

This line is in an incorrect position, but complementary to yang 6 (▬). The yin attitude of the subject is neutral.

Yin 4

The moon is almost full.
A horse is missing.
There is no blame.

Yin 4 (⚋) indicates that the object is not as enthusiastic about the relationship as the subject is. Both sides get along well, but not perfectly, "The moon is almost full," but not completely. Instead of moving along at the same pace as the subject, like a pair of horses in harness, the object may fall behind, "A horse is missing." But "there is no blame" in this disparity for the subject.

This line is in a correct position and complementary to yang 1 (⚊). The yin action of the object is favorable.

Yang 5

People are sincerely dealing with each other,
Like being tied together.
There is no blame.

Yang 5 (⚊) indicates that, like the subject, the object is essentially strong, physically, financially, or spiritually. The subject wants to push the relationship forward, and the object follows. They do not compete, but take care of each other. They look as though they are "being tied together."

This line is in a correct position, but in conflict with yang 2 (⚊). The yang essence of the object is neutral.

Yang 6

A pheasant soars into sky with a loud beautiful sound.
It leaves nothing in deed.
Staying on this course is unfavorable.

Yang 6 (⚊) indicates that the object is snobbish, self-centered, or bossy. He or she makes promises, but never really converts the promises into reality, "A pheasant soars into sky with a loud beautiful sound. It leaves nothing in deed." If the object maintains this lack of sincerity without changing, then the subject should change his or her own action or attitude, "Staying on this course is unfavorable."

This line is in an incorrect position, but complementary to yin 3 (⚋). The yang attitude of the object is neutral.

⑤ Hexagram 6:4 Marry (In Zhou Yi, hexagram 54)

The title, Marry, is composed of two characters in Chinese; one is "come back," and the other is "young lady." The two characters together mean "to allow a young lady, a child, or a sister, to be married."

Trigram 6 (☱), Lake (pleasure), is the subject; trigram 4 (☳), Thunder (movement), is the object. It is pleasurable for the subject to be in the relationship with the object, but the object disappoints the subject. There is a lack of sincerity, as with an empty gesture, "A lady holds a basket without content. A man butchers a sheep without blood." This hexagram symbolizes the relationship with the metaphor of a marriage poisoned by disappointment, dissatisfaction and insincerity.

1 General Text

To move ahead is unfavorable.
The situation is not beneficial.

The subject benefits the object, but nothing is repaid. The subject pushes the relationship to pursue their common interests, but the object acts in ways that take advantage of the subject. The subject respects the object, but the object is dishonest, so progressing in the relationship will result in disappointment, "To move ahead is unfavorable. The situation is not beneficial" for the subject.

2 Structure

Figure 16.5: Structure of hexagram 6:4

In this hexagram, two lines, yang 1 (▬) and yin 6 (▬ ▬), are in correct positions. The other four lines, yang 2 (▬), yin 3 (▬ ▬), yang 4 (▬), nd yin 5 (▬ ▬), are in incorrect positions. Only the two middle lines are complementary to each other. The structure of this hexagram shows the current situation is less favorable.

3 Texts of Lines

Yang 1

A young lady becomes a concubine.
A lame person is able to walk.
Making a change is favorable.

Yang 1 (▬) indicates that the subject pushes the relationship forward, but is disappointed, "A young lady becomes a concubine" instead of an honored wife.

Although moving ahead is possible, it is difficult, "A lame person is able to walk." The subject should change his or her action, "Making a change is favorable."

This line is in a correct position, but in conflict with yang 4 (▬). The yang action of the subject is neutral.

Yang 2

A person with a single eye is able to see.
It is beneficial to stay in a secluded situation.

Yang 2 (▬) indicates that the subject's essence is strong and helpful to the object, but not completely satisfactory, "A person with a single eye is able to see." The subject should get some distance from the object, "It is beneficial to stay in a secluded situation."

This line is in an incorrect position, but complementary to yin 5 (▬ ▬). The yang essence of the subject is neutral.

Yin 3

A lady wants to be a wife,
But becomes a concubine.

Yin 3 (▬ ▬) indicates that the subject is kind and respectful, but disappointed because of her willingness to yield, "A lady wants to be a wife, but becomes a concubine."

This line is in an incorrect position, and in conflict with yin 6 (▬ ▬). The yin attitude of the subject is unfavorable.

Yang 4

A lady postponed her wedding date.
The deferment creates a chance.

Yang 4 (▬) indicates that the object pushes the relationship forward, but not with sincerity. The lady who postpones her wedding date is the subject, who is disappointed by the object's actions. The current relationship does not favor the subject, so waiting until something changes is a good idea, "The deferment creates a chance."

This line is in an incorrect position and in conflict with yang 1 (▬). The yang action of the object is unfavorable.

Yin 5

When the sister of Emperor Yi was allowed to marry King Wen,
Her wedding gown was not as elegant
As that of the concubine.
One makes a compromise,
Like a moon that is almost full
But not completely.
The situation is favorable.

Emperor Yi was the last emperor of the Shang dynasty, and King Wen was a king of Zhou.

Yin 5 (− −) indicates that the object has little strength and needs help. The subject is strong and can help the object, but is disappointed in this gesture, "Her wedding gown was not as elegant as that of the concubine." If the subject lowers expectations and compromises — "like a moon that is almost full, but not completely" — then "the situation is favorable."

This line is in an incorrect position, but complementary to yang 2 (—). The yin essence of the object is neutral.

Yin 6

A lady holds a basket without content.
A man butchers a sheep without blood.
The situation is not beneficial.

Yin 6 (− −) indicates that attitude of the object is yin. The object is humble and respectful, but dishonest. The subject is agreeable, but disappointed in the lack of reward. Both sides are maintaining the relationship, but are not sincere, "The situation is not beneficial."

This line is in a correct position, but in conflict with yin 3 (− −). The yin attitude of the object is neutral.

[6] Hexagram 6:5 Stare (In Zhou Yi, hexagram 38)

The title, Stare, comes from the Chinese "kui," meaning "stare" or "gaze."

Trigram 6 (☱), Lake (pleasure) is the subject; trigram 5 (☲), Fire (brightness or clinging), is the object. The subject is happy to move forward in the relationship, but suspects that the object is greedy and mysterious. The object is like a fire that burns everything in its reach. The subject observes the object, like one staring at an approaching flame, fascinated but also worried about being burned. The subject observes the object with suspicion, distrust and wariness, with the feelings of one who "sees pigs with dirty backs and ghosts in a wagon." This hexagram deals with the wisdom of taking a long, careful look before coming to conclusions, because things are not what they seem. Actually, "the ghosts are not robbers but suitors."

1 General Text

It is favorable to do unimportant things.

Both the subject and the object are very active in the relationship. The object has little strength and needs help. The subject is happy to help, but feels that the object is greedy, taking the subject's offer for granted. The subject is humble, kind, and respectful, but the object is demanding and mysterious. The subject doubts and distrusts the object, and should not strive toward ambitious goals in this situation, "It is favorable to do unimportant things."

2 Structure

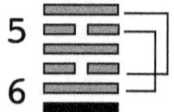

Figure 16.6: Structure of hexagram 6:5

In this hexagram, yang 1 (—) is the only one line in a correct position. The two bottom lines are in conflict with each other. The two middle lines and two top lines are complementary. Hexagram 6:5 is neutral, or less favorable.

2 Texts of Lines

Yang 1

Regret vanishes.
A horse is missing.
Do not chase it.
The missing horse comes back by himself.
One sees a wicked person.
There is no blame.

Yang 1 (—) indicates that the subject wants to move the relationship forward, and has no qualms about helping the object, "Regret vanishes." But because the object has little strength and seems to receive benefits greedily, with boasting and deviousness, the subject distrusts the object, feeling cheated or betrayed, "A horse is missing." But the subject is advised to watch and wait, instead of running after the horse, "Do not chase it. The missing horse comes back by himself." Actually, the subject should not worry, because the object is seeking improvement in the relationship as well. This situation is contradictory, and bears watching. The object may be "a wicked person," but "there is no blame."

This line is in a correct position, but in conflict to yang 4 (▬). The yang action of the subject is neutral.

Yang 2

One meets one's master in the street.
There is no blame.

Yang 2 (▬) indicates the essence of the subject is yang. The subject is strong and helps the object, but feels that demands are being placed on him or her. Dealing with the object feels like unwanted supervision, like meeting up with "one's master in the street."

Yang 2 (▬) is central and complementary with yin 5 (▬ ▬), but in an incorrect position. The yang essence of the subject is neutral.

Yin 3

One sees an ox towing a wagon
And a person tugs the ox.
The person's hair and nose are missing.
There is no good beginning
But there is a good ending.

Yin 3 (▬ ▬) indicates that the subject is graceful and respectful, under difficult circumstances. Yielding to the rude and brutal attitude of the object is like watching the struggle as an ox tows a wagon and a person tugs the ox. It is not easy to submit to this spectacle, "The person's hair and nose are missing." "There is no good beginning," but through careful observation, the subject realizes that the object is not so bad, and "there is a good ending."

This line is in an incorrect position, but complementary with yang 6 (▬). The yin attitude of the subject is neutral.

Yang 4

Staring and lonely,
One meets a great person
And deals with him sincerely.

There is a danger
But no blame.

Yang 4 (▬) indicates that the object pushes the relationship forth forcefully. The subject observes him or her with suspicion and distrust, as if the object is "a great person." The object's pushiness poses a danger to the subject, but since the subject is sincere, "there is no blame."

This line is in an incorrect position and in conflict with yang 1 (▬). The yang action of the object is unfavorable.

Yin 5

Regret vanishes.
A member of one's clan causes trouble
That feels like biting the skin.
Go ahead.
Why should it be blamed?

Yin 5 (▬ ▬) indicates that the object's essence is weak financially, physically or spiritually. The subject sees the object as a member of his or her clan and helps the object without hesitation — "regret vanishes" — but feels hurt by the object's greediness, like receiving bites on the skin. But the subject is doing his or her best, following through on an obligation, and should not be blamed.

This line is central and complementary with yang 2 (▬), but in an incorrect position. The yin essence of the object is neutral.

Yang 6

Staring and feeling lonely,
One sees pigs with dirty backs
And ghosts in a wagon.
At first one draws a bow,
But then releases it.
The ghosts are not robbers
But suitors.
Go ahead.
Meeting with rain is favorable.

Yang 6 (▬) indicates that the object's attitude appears to the subject as awful and mysterious, like dirty pigs and ghosts. At first the subject thinks the object is evil, like robbers, and tries to mount a defense, "one draws a bow." But staring at the object convinces the subject that he or she is mistaken — "the ghosts are not robbers, but suitors" — and the subject relaxes, as if releasing a bow. Once the mysterious impressions are cleared up, as in "meeting with rain" that washes dirt from the backs of pigs, the situation will become favorable.

This line is in an incorrect position, but complementary with yang 2 (—) and supported by yin 5 (- -). The yang attitude of the object is neutral.

[7] Hexagram 6:6 Pleasure (In Zhou Yi, hexagram 58)

The title, Pleasure, means the subject is making himself or herself happy, or bringing happiness to others.

Both subject and object are trigram 6 (☱), Lake (pleasure). The subject is pleased to be with the object, and the object is equally pleased to be with the subject. When problems occur in the relationship, the subject tries to make the object feel pleasure, and as a result, receives pleasure in return, "Trade pleasure when there is no peace."

1 General Text

Things are moving smoothly.
It is beneficial to stay on the current course.

Both sides in the relationship want to move forward, "Things are moving smoothly." The object is strong, able to help others, and humble. The subject can take this chance to work with the object and gain by the relationship, "It is beneficial to stay on the current course." If the object should want to take advantage of the subject, the subject should deal with the object gracefully and truthfully, so that they work together fairly.

2 Structure

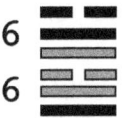

Figure 16.7: Structure of hexagram 6:6.

In this hexagram, yang 1 (—), yang 5 (—) and yin 6 (- -) are in correct positions; the other three lines are in incorrect positions. No line is complementary to other corresponding line. Hexagram 6:6 is neutral.

3 Texts of Lines

Yang 1

Peaceful pleasure is favorable.

Yang 1 (▬) indicates that the subject wants to improve the relationship. Meanwhile, the object acts very vigorously as well. If the subject advances too aggressively, the object could defend his or her interests or resist the subject. So when the subject takes action, he or she should be gentle, warm, and kind, being careful to make the other happy without creating conflict, "Peaceful pleasure is favorable."

This line is in a correct position, but in conflict with yang 4 (▬). The yang action of the subject is neutral.

Yang 2

Sincere pleasure is favorable.
Regret vanishes.

Yang 2 (▬) indicates that the subject is essentially in a strong position, possessing health or wealth, or some skill or job that seems desirable or important to the object. Meanwhile, the object is strong, as well. If the subject is not sincere, the object could distrust or resent the subject, and their mutual strength could deteriorate into a hostile competition. While the subject works together with the object, or is doing something for the object, he or she should share "sincere pleasure" with the object.

This line is in an incorrect position and in conflict with yang 5 (▬). The yang essence of the subject is unfavorable.

Yin 3

Coming pleasure is unfavorable.

Yin 3 (▬ ▬) indicates that the subject is graceful, agreeable and respectful. The object is graceful, agreeable and respectful, as well. The object is actively expanding his or her own interests, so the subject should be truthful and honest, not devious or too yielding. If the subject compromises on what should not be compromised, or agrees with what is not fair, or flatters the object, the object could provide the kind of pleasure that is unfavorable.

This line is in an incorrect position and in conflict with yin 6 (▬ ▬). The yin attitude of the subject is unfavorable.

Yang 4

Trade pleasure when there is no peace.
Get rid of the trouble.
There is happiness.

Yang 4 (▬) indicates that the object acts very aggressively, creating an impact on the subject that may disturb the peace. Instead of immediately slamming back, it is better for the subject to offer a graceful response, such as a polite greeting or a piece of chocolate. Possibly, the object will react gracefully, as well. The two sides "trade pleasure when there is no peace." After a proper solution to the trouble is found, "there is happiness."

This line is in an incorrect position and in conflict to yang 1 (▬). The yang action of the object is unfavorable.

Yang 5

Being sincere, exploitation is dangerous.

Yang 5 (▬) indicates that the object is strong physically, financially or spiritually, and is expanding his or her interests. If the object is trying to take advantage of the subject, the subject should resist, "Being sincere, exploitation is dangerous."

This line is in a correct position, but in conflict to yang 2 (▬). The yang essence of the object is neutral.

Yin 6

Lead to pleasure.

Yin 6 (▬ ▬) indicates that the object is agreeable, graceful and respectful. If the object is trying to take advantage of the subject, the subject may become upset. The subject should calm down and talk with the object truthfully, finding a fair solution to bring the relationship from an unpleasant situation to a pleasant one, "Lead to pleasure."

This line is in a correct position, but in conflict with yin 3 (▬ ▬). The yin attitude of the object is neutral.

8 Hexagram 6:7 Treading (In Zhou Yi, hexagram 10)

The title, Treading, means that the subject has to deal with a powerful object carefully, like stepping "on a tiger's tail" while avoiding its bite.

Trigram 6 (☱), Lake (pleasure) is the subject; trigram 7 (☰), Heaven (strength) is the object. The subject finds pleasure in pursuing the relationship, but faces a very powerful object. The subject is moving on a very dangerous path, and has to be extremely prudent.

1 General Text

When one steps on a tiger's tail,
The tiger does not bite that person.
Things are moving smoothly.

Both the subject and object are strong and moving forward in the relationship. Their contrast lies in attitude: the subject is humble, flexible and respectful, and the object is arrogant, bossy or bullying and has more power than the subject. Working with the object, the subject feels as if he or she were treading on the tail of a tiger. Any mistake can draw an attack from the object. If the subject is careful enough in dealing with the object — "when one steps on a tiger's tail, the tiger does not bite that person" — the subject could succeed, "Things are moving smoothly." However, at any moment, the subject's careless step could cause disaster.

2 Structure

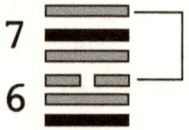

Figure 16.8: Structure of hexagram 6:7

In this hexagram, two lines, yang 1 (━) and yang 5 (━), are in correct positions; the other four lines are in incorrect positions. The two top lines are complementary to each other. The two bottom lines and the two middle lines are in conflict. Hexagram 6:7 is neutral, or less favorable.

3 Texts of Lines

Yang 1

One chooses a path which is easy to walk through.
There is no blame.

Yang 1 (━) indicates that the subject wants to move forward in the relationship. But the object is very powerful and bossy, so if the subject merely moves in a normal way, the object will stop the subject and cause major trouble. So "one chooses a path which is easy to walk through." If the subject selects an easier path, avoiding conflict with the object, he or she should succeed. The subject makes the correct choice and avoids blame.

This line is in a correct position, but in conflict with yang 4 (▬). The yang action of the subject is neutral.

Yang 2

One walks on a path,
Which is flat and smooth,
And keeps secluding oneself from society.
Staying on the current course is favorable.

Yang 2 (▬) indicates that the subject is strong physically, financially or spiritually. But the object is strong too, even stronger than the subject. If the subject shows off in front of the object, the subject will encounter a strong resistance or competition, and could fail. But if the subject keeps a low profile, avoids society and advances quietly, there will be less resistance, as in walking "on a path, which is flat and smooth." If the subject proceeds in this way, "staying on the current course is favorable."

This line is in an incorrect position and in conflict to yang 5 (▬). The yang essence of the subject is unfavorable.

Yin 3

Being able to see with a single eye,
And able to walk with a single foot,
One steps on a tiger's tail
And has been bitten.
The situation is unfavorable.
That is how a brazen person deals with a powerful lord.

Yin 3 (▬ ▬) indicates that the subject is humble and respectful. The object is very powerful and a bully. If the subject becomes careless and overconfident, and thinks that he or she is "able to see with a single eye, and able to walk with a single foot," the result will be a costly mistake. When treading on the tail of a tiger, one needs to see clearly, with both eyes, not a single eye, and needs to walk with two feet, not one. Otherwise the subject will be like an imprudent adventurer who "steps on a tiger's tail and has been bitten." The object is stronger than the subject. If the subject dares to compete with the object, it would be like "a brazen person deals with a powerful lord." The subject should be aware of the danger and maintain a yin attitude.

This line is in an incorrect position, but complementary with yang 6 (▬). The yin attitude of the subject is neutral.

Yang 4

Stepping on a tiger's tail,
One moves very gingerly.
The situation is favorable at the end.

Yang 4 (━) indicates that the object acts aggressively, making the situation dangerous and difficult for the subject. If the subject moves very gingerly when "stepping on a tiger's tail," it is possible that the subject will be able to get through this difficult time, "The situation is favorable at the end."

This line is in an incorrect position and in conflict to yang 1 (━). The yang action of the object is unfavorable.

Yang 5

Tread determinedly.
Staying on the current course is dangerous.

Yang 5 (━) indicates that the object is stronger than the subject, physically, financially or spiritually. If the subject gives up in the face of this strength, the object would take the subject for granted, and pose a danger. The situation would be unfavorable for the subject. The subject has to move on with determination and resolve, because hesitation can provoke the tiger's wrath. Despite the danger of this course, there is still a possibility for the subject to get through a difficult time if the subject is prudent.

This line is in a correct position, but in conflict to yang 2 (━). The yang essence of the object is neutral.

Yang 6

While treading on tiger's tail, one observes carefully
And examines the situation completely and thoroughly.
Finally, the result is very favorable.

Yang 6 (━) indicates that the object is arrogant, bossy, and bullying. Dealing with such an object is very difficult and dangerous, like stepping on the tail of a tiger. The subject should observe and examine the situation carefully, completely and thoroughly, with a yin attitude. This humility, flexibility and prudence offers a possibility of survival and achievement, "Finally, the result is very favorable."

This line is in an incorrect position, but complementary with yin 3 (━ ━). The yang attitude of the object is neutral.

CHAPTER 17
When Heaven (☰) is the Subject

THIS CHAPTER CONTAINS YI TEXT of eight hexagrams from 7:Ø to 7:7. Their subject trigrams are trigram 7, Heaven. The typical characteristic of heaven is strength — not only physical power, but also creativity, aggressiveness, offensive action, and also recklessness, a rough attitude, and arrogance.

1 Hexagram 7:Ø Peace (In Zhou Yi, hexagram 11)

The title, Peace, describes a harmonious relationship.

Trigram 7 (☰), Heaven (strength), is the subject; trigram Ø (☷), Earth (adaptability), is the object. While the subject advances, the object follows. The subject enjoys peace and freedom, while the object minds his or her own business.

1 General Text

Though a trivial thing is lost,
A great thing is gained.
The current situation is favorable.
Things are going smoothly.

The subject is pushing the relationship forward. The object follows. The object needs help, and the subject is strong and helps the object. The subject is arrogant; the object is respectful. The relationship is harmonious. When the subject helps the object, the subject does give up something, but in return gets a peaceful environment and support from the object, "Though a trivial thing is lost, a great thing is gained." So, "the current situation is favorable" for the subject, and under this peaceful situation, "things are going smoothly."

2 Structure

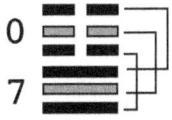

Figure 17.1: Structure of hexagram 7:Ø

In this hexagram, four lines, yang 1 (▬), yang 3 (▬), yin 4 (▬ ▬) and yin 6 (▬ ▬), are in correct positions. The other two lines are in incorrect positions. All of the corresponding lines are complementary with each other. Hexagram 7:Ø is favorable.

3 Texts of Lines

Yang 1

While pulling a reed out of the ground,
One gets out all of the reeds,
Which tangle one with the other.
To move ahead is favorable.

Yang 1 (▬) indicates that the subject is pushing the relationship forward. The yin object offers no resistance as the subject moves the relationship ahead. The interests of the subject and the object are intertwined, "While pulling a reed out of the ground, one gets out all of the reeds, which tangle one with the other." The situation is good for the subject to enjoy and to develop, "To move ahead is favorable." Since the interests of the two sides are tied together, the subject should care for the object as well as himself or herself.

This line is in a correct position and complementary with yin 4 (▬ ▬). The yang action of the subject is favorable.

Yang 2

With calabashes tied around the body,
One crosses a river.
One never forgets friends who are far away.
In the middle of the journey,
When one has lost a pair of seashells,
One gets help from the friends.

In ancient times, with no boats or bridges available, it was very difficult and dangerous to cross a river. "With calabashes tied around the body, one crosses a river" describes a subject overcoming crucial difficulties with the help of insignificant things, such as hollow gourds used for flotation. "A pair of seashells" was a kind of ancient Chinese currency.

Yang 2 (▬) indicates that the subject is essentially healthy and well prepared, with a good job or support from others. This strength gives the subject an ability to help the object. As a reward, the subject gets assistance from the object at the time when the subject needs help. Since the object is in a weak position, the help he or she gives might appear less valuable, like a pair of "calabashes," but could make a material difference at a crucial time.

This line is central and complementary with yin 5 (■■), but in an incorrect position. The yang essence of the subject is neutral, or a little favorable.

Yang 3

No plain is without slope.
No going forth is without return.
To stay on this course is difficult
Yet blameless.
Do not worry;
Through sincerity one finds happiness.

Yang 3 (■) indicates that the subject is arrogant, reckless, bossy or bullying. The object is humble, agreeable, and respectful, and can go along with the subject very well. However, things in the world are always changing, "No plain is without slope. No going forth is without return." If the subject remains stubborn, and cannot adapt to such changes with flexibility, "to stay on this course is difficult." But if the subject is truthful and honest, he or she should not be blamed, and all will be well, "Through sincerity one finds happiness."

This line is in a correct position and complementary to yin 6 (■■). The yang attitude of the subject is favorable.

Yin 4

The birds are fluttering in the sky.
Being sincere and
Not interested in taking advantage of neighbors,
One has no need to keep alert.

Yin 4 (■■) indicates that the object follows the subject, with no conflict between them. The subject enjoys the peaceful environment, as if admiring birds "fluttering in the sky." Since the subject is strong, while the object is weak, the subject should not be overly aggressive, but remain in harmony with the object, "being sincere and not interested in taking advantage of neighbors." If the two sides are sincere in dealing with each other, the subject "has no need to keep alert."

This line is in a correct position and complementary with yang 1 (■). The yin action of the object is favorable.

Yin 5

When Emperor Yi gave his sister in marriage,
That marriage brought peace and happiness.
The situation is very favorable.

Emperor Yi was an emperor of the country Shang, whose son was the last emperor of the Shang dynasty (1600-1100 BC.) Emperor Yi gave his sister in marriage to King Wen (1221-1124 BC) who was a leader of the country of Zhou.

Yin 5 (━ ━) indicates that the essence of the object is weak physically, financially, or spiritually. Since the subject is strong, the subject should do favors for the object, "When Emperor Yi gave his sister in marriage, that marriage brought peace and happiness." As the subject and the object become closer to each other, "the situation is very favorable."

This line is in an incorrect position, but central and complementary to yang 2 (━). The yin essence of the object is neutral.

Yin 6

Without maintenance
The great wall of the city collapses into the moat.
One has no need to use troops.
The laws are issued in one's own town.
Staying on this course is unpleasant.

Yin 6 (━ ━) indicates that the object listens to and respects the subject. The status of the relationship is peaceful, so there is no need for defenses, "Without maintenance the great wall of the city collapses into the moat. One has no need to use troops." Though the object yields to the subject, the subject should mind his or her own business, without trespassing in the object's affairs, "The laws are issued in one's own town." But if the subject behaves arrogantly, taking advantage of the object's accessibility, "staying on this course is unpleasant."

This line is in a correct position and complementary to yang 3 (━). The yin attitude of the object is favorable.

[2] Hexagram 7:1 Build Up (In Zhou Yi, hexagram 26)

The title, Build Up, describes a situation where the energy of the subject is accumulating, but the subject does not yet exert this power. The original title of this hexagram in Chinese is composed of two characters, "Big" and "Accumulation."

Trigram 7 (☰), Heaven (strength), is the subject; trigram 1 (☶), Mountain (stopping), is the object. The subject is active and powerful, but faces obstacles from the object in the way. The situation is tense. The subject is building up energy, getting ready to break the obstacle and pave "a path to heaven."

1 General Text

It is beneficial to stay on the current course.
It is favorable not to eat at home.
It is beneficial to cross a big river,
Finding food in the other town.

The subject wants to move forward, but the object is blocking the way. The subject is strong and able to overcome the object, which is weak, "It is beneficial to stay on the current course." The subject is arrogant and bossy, and the object is stubborn, so a confrontation is unavoidable. In preparing to break the stalemate, the subject should not use up all of his or her own resources, and should take advantage of what's available from the outside, "It is favorable not to eat at home. It is beneficial to cross a big river, finding food in the other town."

2 Structure

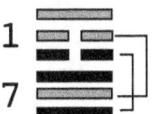

Figure 17.2: Structure of hexagram 7:1

In this hexagram, yang 1 (—), yang 3 (—) and yin 4 (- -) are in correct positions; the other three lines are in incorrect positions. The two bottom lines and the two middle lines are complementary, and the two top lines are in conflict with each other. Hexagram 7:1 is neutral or a little favorable.

3 Texts of Lines

Yang 1

There is a danger.
It is beneficial to stop.

Yang 1 (—) indicates that the subject wants to move forward, but is stopped by the stubborn object. If the subject reacts too aggressively to this delay, before necessary preparations are complete, "there is a danger." The subject should take time to build up energy, "It is beneficial to stop."

Yang 2

Move the axle out of the wagon.

Yang 2 (—) indicates that the subject is strong while the object is weak. The object is stubborn and resistant. The subject is not ready for a fight. The subject should conserve his or her strength, and not push forward, "Move the axle out of the wagon." When the time to use the wagon comes, the subject can reassemble the wagon and drive on.

This line is central and complementary to yin 5 (— —), but in an incorrect position. The yang essence of the subject is neutral, or a little favorable.

Yang 3

The fine horses chase each other.
It is beneficial to struggle hard and
Stay on this course.
Refine the capabilities of advancing with wagons and of defense.
It is beneficial for moving ahead.

Yang 3 (—) indicates that the attitude of the subject is arrogant, reckless, bossy or bullying. Because the object is stubborn, blocking the way of the subject, the subject should change his or her attitude, being prudent instead of reckless. Instead of riding the horse to battle, let "the fine horses chase each other." "It is beneficial to struggle hard and stay on this course," submitting to training and exercises rather than taking offensive action, "Refine the capabilities of advancing with wagons and of defense." This attitude of restraint and patience is beneficial for "moving ahead."

This line is in a correct position, but in conflict to yang 6 (—). The yang attitude of the subject is neutral. Regarding the current situation, the text suggests that the subject pursue a change in attitude from yang to yin.

Yin 4

The calf is curbed with a headboard
And threatens nobody.
The situation is very favorable.

Yin 4 (— —) indicates the action of the object is defensive and receding. With a stubborn attitude, the object seems like an ornery calf, but "the calf is curbed with headboard and threatens nobody." For the subject, "the situation is very favorable."

This line is in a correct position and complementary with yang 1 (▬). The yin action of the object is favorable.

Yin 5

The tusks of a gelded boar
Exert no power.
The situation is favorable.

Yin 5 (▬ ▬) indicates that the essence of the object is yin. The object is weak physically, financially, or spiritually. The object's tough attitude makes the object come across like a rampaging "boar," but, actually, this "boar" is gelded and will not harm the subject, "The tusks of gelded boar exert no power." "The situation is favorable" for the subject.

This line is central and complementary to yang 2 (▬), but in an incorrect position. The yin essence of the object is neutral.

Yang 6

Like moving on a path to heaven,
Things are going smoothly.

Yang 6 (▬) indicates that the object's attitude is arrogant, reckless and stubborn. Because the subject enjoys overwhelming superiority over the object, the subject will have no problem taking action to break through this obstacle. If the subject is well prepared, and has built up energy for a strike, the victory will come at minimal cost, "Like moving on a path to heaven, things are going smoothly."

This line is in an incorrect position and in conflict to yang 3 (▬). The yang attitude of the object is unfavorable.

3 Hexagram 7:2 Expectation (In Zhou Yi, hexagram 5)

The title of hexagram 7:2, Expectation, means the subject can expect a better relationship.

Trigram 7 (☰), Heaven (strength), is the subject; trigram 2 (☵), Water (difficulty and danger), is the object. The subject, active and powerful, expects a better relationship with the object. The object experiences some difficulty and senses some danger in the relationship. The solution of these problems lies on the object's side, so the subject's task is to remain in sincere expectation, believing that "respecting the others brings a favorable ending."

2 General Text

If one is sincere,
There will be a light,
Things will be going smoothly.
Staying on the current course is favorable.
It is beneficial to cross a big river,
Communicating with others.

Both the subject and the object are strong physically, financially, or spiritually. The subject wants to move the relationship forward. The object wants to defend himself or herself, and even is considering a retreat from the relationship. The subject is arrogant, self-centered, and bossy, but also straightforward, truthful, and honest. The object is introverted, quiet, and respectful. The object feels uncomfortable dealing with the subject, so the subject must remain sincere, to earn the object's trust. Only then, "there will be a light" and "things will be going smoothly." The subject should keep promoting the relationship consistently, "Staying on the current course is favorable." The subject should reach out and talk with the object to foster a mutual understanding, "It is beneficial to cross a big river, communicating with others."

2 Structure

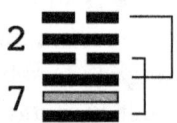

Figure 17.3: Structure of hexagram 7:2

In this hexagram all the lines are in correct positions, except yang 2 (━). The two bottom lines and top lines are complementary; the two middle lines are in conflict with each other. Hexagram 7:2 is neutral, or a little favorable.

3 Texts of Lines

Yang 1

One's wishes are distant,
Like a suburb
Far from the center of town.
It is beneficial to be persistent.
There is no blame.

Yang 1 (▬) indicates that the subject is pushing the relationship forward, expecting a better situation. However, the object is not equally enthusiastic. The solution to the problem depends on how the object acts. The subject's expectations are at this point unrealistic, "One's wishes are distant, like a suburb far from the center of town." But the subject should keep pushing, "It is beneficial to be persistent. There is no blame."

This line is in a correct position and complementary with yin 4 (▬ ▬). The yang action of the subject is favorable.

Yang 2

One's expectations are based on sand,
Which is not solid.
One suffers from others' gossip.
It is favorable in the end.

Yang 2 (▬) indicates that the subject's essence is strong physically, financially, or spiritually. Graced with wealth, health, desirability, success or spiritual strength, the subject expects that these traits will prove attractive to the object. But "one's expectations are based on sand, which is not solid." Because the object harbors doubts about this relationship and may be willing to hear negative advice, "one suffers from others' gossip." But the subject must remain sincere, steadfast, and patient, "It is favorable in the end."

Yang 3

One's expectations are based on mud,
Which is soft and sticky.
One causes robbers to come.

Yang 3 (▬) indicates that the subject is arrogant, self-centered, and bossy. This domineering attitude will not solve the relationship's problems, but cause it to bog down, "One's expectations are based on mud, which is soft and sticky." This vulnerable situation, where a troubled relationship becomes stuck in the mud of misplaced expectations, invites others to benefit from the subject's problems, "One causes robbers to come." However, the subject's yang attitude can also be useful in fending off outsiders.

This line is in a correct position and complementary with yin 6 (▬ ▬). The yang action of the subject is favorable.

Yin 4

One's expectations are based on blood,
Which is vital.
One is rescued from a pitfall.

Yin 4 (==) indicates that the object does not want to move forward in the relationship. The subject must continue to wait, sincerely expecting the object to feel more enthusiastic about the relationship, because here the expectation is well founded, "One's expectations are based on blood, which is vital." When the object responds to this fundamental connection, the problems will be solved, "One is rescued from a pitfall."

This line is in a correct position and complementary with yang 1 (—). The yin action of the object is favorable.

Yang 5

One's expectations are based on food and wine,
Which are realistic benefits.
Staying on this course is favorable.

Yang 5 (—) indicates that the object is essentially strong in finance, health, power in business or desirability. If the subject expects the object to take part in some ordinary rituals of a relationship, such as eating and drinking, the object will gain confidence in the subject, "One's expectations are based on food and wine, which are realistic benefits." Through these normal, easy activities, the subject and the object may find a chance to solve their problems. The subject should keep pushing the relationship forward, following the path of these domestic pleasures, "Staying on this course is favorable.

This line is central and in a correct position, but in conflict with yang 2 (—). The yang essence of the object is neutral.

Yin 6

When one was trapped in a pitfall,
Three unexpected guests come.
Respecting others brings a favorable ending.

Yin 6 (==) indicates that the object is humble, agreeable, and respectful. On the other hand, the attitude of the subject is arrogant, reckless, self-centered, bossy, or bullying. The object may be respectful and agreeable toward the subject, but dislikes the subject's attitude. The problems remain unsolved, and the subject is "trapped in a pitfall." During this troubled time, others may come between the subject and the object, "Three unexpected guests come." It is not clear whether these "guests" come to help in solving the problems, or to take advantage of the discord in this relationship. Regardless, the subject must remain patient with this development and trust in its outcome, "Respecting others brings favorable ending."

This line is in a correct position and complementary with yang 3 (—). The yin attitude of the object is favorable. If the subject is truthful and honest, and connects with the object sincerely, a good solution might be found.

4 Hexagram 7:3 Accumulation (In Zhou Yi, hexagram 9)

The title of hexagram 7:3, Accumulation, refers to letting the problems in the relationship pile up; they do not have to be solved immediately.

Trigram 7 (☰), Heaven (strength), is the subject; trigram 3 (☴), Wind (flexibility), is the object. The subject is powerful and active, while the object is also powerful, but passive. Because problems can arise in the tug between strength and flexibility, the current situation is mixed, "It is raining for a while, and the rain stops for a while." The problems should be put on hold for now, because an "expedition is unfavorable.

1 General Text

Things are going smoothly.
There are dense clouds, but it is not raining.
These clouds come from our west suburb.

In this relationship, both sides are strong, physically, financially or spiritually, so in this sense "things are going smoothly." But there is a difference: the subject wants to improve the relationship, and the object does not. Problems that occur in the relationship are not serious, or have not come to the surface yet, "There are dense clouds, but it is not raining." The problems come from the object, who is in a close relationship with the subject, "These clouds come from our west suburb." "Suburb" refers to a wide living area, not the suburb of a modern city. The "west" refers to the place from where King Wen came. King Wen, a leader of the country of Zhou, revised the Yijing text.

2 Structure

Figure 17.4: Structure of hexagram 7:3

In this hexagram four lines, yang 1 (—), yang 3 (—), yin 4 (- -), and yang 5 (—), are in correct positions; the other two lines, yang 2 (—) and yang 6 (—), are in incorrect positions. The two bottom lines are complementary, and the two middle and top lines are in conflict. Hexagram 7:3 is neutral.

3 Texts of Lines

Yang 1

One returns the way one came.
Why should one be blamed?
The situation is favorable.

Yang 1 (—) indicates that the subject is trying to bring the relationship back to where it was, "One returns the way one came. Why should one be blamed?" Currently, the problems in the relationship are not yet serious. The object acts passively, without resistance, but the subject has strength. "The situation is favorable" for the subject's effort to be successful.

This line is in a correct position and complementary with yin 4 (- -). The yang action of the subject is favorable.

Yang 2

One pulls the other
Returning the way they came.
The situation is favorable.

Yang 2 (—) indicates that the subject has essential strength and is pulling the object back to the original state of the relationship. "One pulls the other, returning the way they came." Though the object is weary of the relationship, the original situation is likely to be restored because of the subject's enthusiasm, "The situation is favorable."

This line is central, but in an incorrect position and in conflict to yang 5 (—). The yang essence of the subject is neutral.

Yang 3

As the spokes break off a wagon,
Husband and wife are fighting eye to eye.

Yang 3 (—) indicates that the subject is arrogant, self-centered, and bossy. Since the object shares this attitude, they feel unhappy with each other, and begin quarreling or fighting, "As the spokes break off a wagon, husband and wife are fighting eye to eye." "Husband and wife" should not be interpreted to mean a literal couple; this is a metaphor for the relationship. The two sides may or may not be a couple, but they are in a close relationship and having problems.

This line is in a correct position, but in conflict to yang 6 (▬). The yang attitude of the subject is neutral.

Yin 4

Because one is sincere,
The bloody fight dissolves and
The fear diminishes.
There is no blame.

Yin 4 (▬ ▬) indicates that the object is in a defensive mode. If the subject deals with the object sincerely, "the bloody fight dissolves and the fear diminishes." "There is no blame" to the subject.

This line is in a correct position and complementary to yang 1 (▬). The yin action of the object is favorable.

Yang 5

Sincerity binds the partners together,
That serves not only one's own interest
But makes one's neighbors rich, also.

Yang 5 (▬) indicates that the object is healthy, well educated, professional, in possession of a good income or powerful position, or is backed by others. If the subject is sincere, the object could work together with the subject, "Sincerity binds the partners together. That serves not only one's own interest but makes one's neighbors rich, also." Being sincere and working together favor both sides, as well as benefit the surrounding community. If the subject is not sincere, there will be problems and the two sides will fight each other, consuming their resources. This will not benefit either side.

This line is in a correct position, but in conflict to yang 2 (▬). The yang essence of the object is neutral.

Yang 6

It is raining for a while,
And the rain stops for a while.
Gain benefit with fairness and justice.
As a lady, staying on this course is dangerous.

The moon is almost full.
As a man, an expedition is unfavorable.

Yang 6 (▬) indicates that the object is arrogant, self-centered, bossy, or a bully, just like the subject. This causes intermittent problems in the relationship, "It is raining for a while, and the rain stops for a while." If the subject and the object deal with each other fairly and justly, the problem could be solved, "Gain benefit with fairness and justice." The subject should handle the relationship gently, like a woman who is used to being gentle and graceful, even though there is a danger of confrontation, "As a lady, staying on this course is dangerous." The situation is not perfect, but has potential, "The moon is almost full." If the subject acts recklessly in the way a man usually does, the situation could become worse, "As a man, an expedition is unfavorable."

This line is in an incorrect position and in conflict with yang 3 (▬). The yang attitude of the object is unfavorable.

5 Hexagram 7:4 Reckless (In Zhou Yi, hexagram 34)

The title, Reckless, offers a warning that the subject could abuse his or her power and make a heedless mistake.

Trigram 7 (☰), Heaven (strength), is the subject; trigram 4 (☳), Thunder (movement), is the object. The powerful subject could take advantage of the object and overstep his or her authority, causing trouble, like a ram, "A ram butts a fence, gets his horns entangled and cannot go forward or backward."

1 General Text

It is beneficial to stay on the current course.

Both subject and object want to push the relationship forward. The object is weak and needs help. The subject is strong and is able to help. The subject is arrogant and bossy. The object is humble and agreeable and respects the subject. For the subject, "it is beneficial to stay on the current course." This confirms that good circumstances exist for the relationship, but also counsels the subject not to abuse power — to be prudent and remain on track.

2 Structure

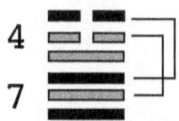

Figure 17.5: Structure of hexagram 7:4

In this hexagram, yang 1 (▬), yang 3 (▬), and yin 6 (▬ ▬) are in correct positions. The other three lines are in incorrect positions. The two middle lines and the two top lines are complementary, and the two bottom lines are in conflict. Hexagram 7:4 is neutral.

3 Texts of Lines

Yang 1

One's toes are strong.
Advancing is unfavorable.
Be sincere.

Yang 1 (▬) indicates that the subject wants to push the relationship forward. The subject's "toes are strong," but the subject's intentions might not be wise. Relying purely on strength, the subject does not realize what dangerous mistakes can result from a reckless attitude. The current situation is not bad for the subject, but the subject should remain there and not go further, "Advancing is unfavorable." Being sincere with the object will benefit both sides. If the subject is prudent, and not reckless, the relationship may advance in time.

This line is in a correct position, but in conflict to yang 4 (▬). The yang action of the subject is neutral.

Yang 2

Staying on this course is favorable.

Yang 2 (▬) indicates that the subject has strength and is able to offer help, which the object needs. If the subject helps the object sincerely, this will benefit both sides, "Staying on this course is favorable" for the subject."

This line is central and complementary with yin 5 (▬ ▬), but in an incorrect position. The yang essence of the subject is neutral, or a little favorable.

Yang 3

A stupid person uses force
While an intelligent person does not.
Staying on this course is dangerous,
Like a ram butts the fence and
Gets his horns entangled.

Yang 3 (▬) indicates that the subject has a reckless attitude that can lead to carelessness. Because the subject is very strong, he or she could abuse his or her power. If the subject is stupid, he or she will try to use force, but "an intelligent person does not," because of the dangers involved, "like a ram butts the fence and gets his horns entangled." The subject should display restraint and prudence, to avoid any reckless mistakes.

This line is in a correct position and complementary to yin 6 (━ ━). The yang attitude of the subject is favorable. However, under the current situation — where the subject is very strong and the object is very weak — this yang attitude can be too much of a good thing. Both sides want to be close to each other and the object is very polite to the subject, so the negative part of the subject's yang attitude, recklessness, can assume an unfavorable role.

Yang 4

Staying on this course is favorable.
Regret vanishes.
The fence breaks
And does not entangle the ram anymore.
One is strong like an axle pulling a wagon.

Yang 4 (━━) indicates that the object wants to move forward in the relationship. But since the object is weaker, he or she will need the subject's help. However, the subject should exercise proper restraint with the object, like an opening in a fence that "does not entangle the ram." A subject who is not entangled by his or her own forcefulness can use that strength wisely and well, like the strong "axle pulling a wagon."

This line is in an incorrect position and in conflict to yang 1 (━━). The yang action of the object is unfavorable.

Yin 5

Sheep were lost in the country of Yi,
When Duke Hai was reckless.
There is no regret.

"Sheep were lost in the country of Yi" refers to a story that originated around 1900 B.C. Duke Hai, with his brother Heng, drove a group of wagons and a big flock of sheep and oxen into the country of Yi. The oxen drew the wagons. The inhabitants of Yi had never seen that method of transportation. Duke Mianchen, the leader of Yi, entertained Duke Hai and his entourage and asked if they would teach him to train oxen in this manner, and Duke Hai agreed.

During his stay, Duke Hai discovered Duke Mianchen's very beautiful daughter. He met with her secretly, but his brother Heng discovered their secret. Heng was also interested in this beautiful young girl, and disclosed the affair to Duke Mianchen out of jealousy. Duke Mianchen, outraged, killed Duke Hai and confiscated all the wagons, oxen and sheep.

Yin 5 (■ ■) indicates that the object has an essential weakness — lack of experience in a job, awkwardness in social relations, or a physical or financial liability. The object needs help from the subject, just as Duke Mianchen needed Duke Hai to teach him how to train the oxen. If the subject heeds the lesson from this story, he or she can find a way to offer help without carelessly risking everything; then there will be "no regret."

This line is central and complementary to yang 2 (■), but in an incorrect position. The yin essence of the object is neutral, or a little favorable.

Yin 6

A ram butts a fence, gets his horns entangled
And cannot go forward or backward.
The situation is not beneficial.
Struggling hard is favorable.

Yin 6 (■ ■) indicates that the object's attitude — humble, agreeable and respectful — can cause the subject to lose self-control and make a mistake, just as "a ram butts a fence, gets his horns entangled and cannot go forward or backward." "The situation is not beneficial," and the subject should be aware of this danger. Avoiding it will require a struggle to resist temptation.

This line is in a correct position and complementary with yang 3 (■). The yin attitude of the object is favorable. However, because of the current situation, the object's yin attitude is only beneficial when the subject makes a sufficient effort to avoid reckless behavior.

6 | Hexagram 7:5 Acquisition (In Zhou Yi, hexagram 14)

The title, Acquisition, means the subject acquires benefits from the relationship. In Chinese, this title is composed of two characters: "da," meaning "big," and "you," meaning "have." "Acquisition" does not necessarily mean acquiring material value or wealth; it can also mean gaining intelligent assistance and other benefits.

Trigram 7 (☰), Heaven (strength), is the subject; trigram 5 (☲), Fire (brightness and clinging), is the object. Together they create the image of a powerful leader acquiring a wise person as an assistant.

1 General Text

Things are going very smoothly.

Both subject and object want to move ahead in the relationship, and both are forceful, arrogant and bossy. The subject is stronger, and takes care of the object. The object clings to the subject and assists the subject with his or her brilliance. This exchange between strength and intelligence is highly favorable, "Things are going very smoothly."

2 Structure

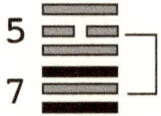

Figure 17.6: Structure of hexagram 7:5

In this hexagram, two lines, yang 1 (▬) and yang 3 (▬), are in correct positions; the other four lines, yang 2 (▬), yang 4 (▬), yin 5 (▬ ▬), and yang 6 (▬), are in incorrect positions. The two bottom lines and the two top lines are in conflict with each other, and the two middle lines are complementary. Hexagram 7:4 is neutral.

3 Texts of Lines

Yang 1

Interacting with others is neither harmful
Nor blameworthy.
Struggling hard is blameless.

Yang 1 (▬) indicates that the subject wants to move the relationship forward, seeking a wise person. To find a wise person for an assistant, the subject must interact with others. Maybe the others are not the one the subject is searching for, but this socializing "is neither harmful nor blameworthy." Discovering the right person is not easy, and the subject should persevere, "Struggling hard is blameless."

This line is in a correct position, but in conflict to yang 4 (▬). The yang action of the subject is neutral.

Yang 2

One invites a wise person,
And offers the person to ride in a big wagon.
Moving ahead is blameless.

In the original Chinese text, the first sentence consists of only a few words, "Load with big wagon." There was a legend about Jiang Taigong, who lived around 1100 B.C. When he was eighty years old, Jiang Taigong was visited by King Wen. King Wen had heard that Jiang was a wise man, and he had searched for him three times. He found him fishing on a rock by the river. It is said in the legend that Jiang was fishing with a needle rather than a hook. He said, "I am only taking the fish that comes to my needle of its own will." King Wen gave Jiang a ride in his wagon, bringing him back to the imperial palace and appointing him as commander in chief. Later, Jiang Taigong helped King Wen and his son King Wu win the war over country Shang and created the Zhou dynasty.

Yang 2 (▬) indicates that the subject has the strength needed to seek out the right person. In reality, the object does not literally have to be a wise person — just the right person for the subject. Since the subject's essence is yang and complementary with object's yin essence, "moving ahead is blameless" for the subject.

This line is central and complementary with yin 5 (▬ ▬), but in an incorrect position. The yang essence of the subject is neutral, or a little favorable.

Yang 3

The wise man holds an offering for the king.
This ceremony cannot be done
By an unqualified person.

In ancient times, the emperor was regarded as the son of heaven. Offerings were a very important activity used to memorialize the emperor's ancestors. It is written in "Shiji," "The teacher, Jiang Taigong, had been pushing King Wen's mission forward for nine years. King Wu attended a ceremony at Bi, where King Wen was buried." After that ceremony, King Wu launched a war ending the Shang dynasty.

Yang 3 (▬) indicates that the subject is arrogant and bossy, like a king. The subject uses the bright object to handle important tasks or responsibilities, "The wise man holds an offering for the king." Because the subject is strict and demanding, "this ceremony cannot be done by an unqualified person."

This line is in a correct position, but in conflict to yang 6 (▬). The yang attitude of the subject is neutral.

Yang 4

In the world, there are few people as brilliant
As the wise person.
There is no blame.

Yang 4 (▬) indicates that the object approaches the subject actively and wants to proceed with the relationship. The subject should accept and use the object, because "in the world, there are few people as brilliant as the wise person." The subject likes to have the "wise person" as an assistant, and should not be blamed.

This line is in an incorrect position and in conflict to yang 1 (▬). The yang action of the object is unfavorable. But regarding the whole situation, the text stresses the positive side of the object's yang action.

Yin 5

One sincerely connects with
And dignifies the wise person.
It is favorable.

Yin 5 (▬ ▬) indicates that the object has less strength than the subject. Perhaps the object is poor, or he or she lacks power or experience, or has some deficiency or illness. Since the object is bright, the subject wants to use the object. The subject "sincerely connects with and dignifies the wise person," the object. By doing so, the subject could acquire benefits from the object. "It is favorable" for the subject.

This line is central and complementary with yang 2 (▬), but in an incorrect position. The yin essence of the object is neutral, or a little favorable.

Yang 6

Help comes from Heaven.
The situation is beneficial and favorable.

Yang 6 (▬) indicates that the object is brilliant. If the subject connects with the object sincerely, respects the object, and takes care of the object, the object could assist the subject, "Help comes from Heaven. The situation is beneficial and favorable."

This line is in an incorrect position and in conflict with yang 3 (▬). The yang attitude of the object is unfavorable. But because the relationship is essentially complementary — the essence of the object is yin, while the essence of the subject is yang — the subject can overcome possible harm by taking care of the object.

Instead of being burned, the stronger subject can acquire the object's brilliance and use the object in a very important position. The text stresses the object's brightness and holds that "the situation is beneficial and favorable."

 Hexagram 7:6 Menace (In Zhou Yi, hexagram 43)

The title, Menace, is represented by the Chinese character "." This character is ancient, not used in the modern Chinese language. In the original script of the fifth line of this hexagram, the first four characters are "amaranth land ." Amaranth is a weed, and when the land is full of weeds, it cannot produce crops. Besides, the text of this hexagram calls for alertness three times.

Trigram 7 (☰), Heaven (strength), is the subject; trigram 6 (☱), Lake (pleasure), is the object. The object does not have as much strength as the subject, but with its pleasant attitude, it can develop quickly and start to menace the subject. The subject has to be vigilant. If the subject does "not call for alert, the end of the situation is unfavorable."

1 General Text

Reveal the danger on the king's court,
Sincerely call people in the town
To stay alert over the threat.
It is beneficial to do something,
But not war.

Both the subject and the object are strong and act aggressively. The subject is arrogant, bossy or bullying, and also reckless — more likely to make mistakes and lose the support of others. By contrast, the object is humble, graceful and prudent — more likely to succeed in his or her pursuit and win support from others. So the object is a threat to the subject, "Reveal the danger on king's court." The subject should use any possible means to struggle against the menacing object, "Sincerely call people in the town to stay alert over the threat." It is not easy for the subject to win this confrontation. The subject has to overcome his or her wrong attitude, and behave not recklessly, but prudently, "It is beneficial to do something, but not war."

2 Structure

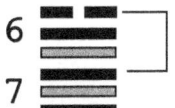

Figure 17.7: Structure of hexagram 7:6

In this hexagram, yang 1 (▬), yang 3 (▬), yang 5 (▬), and yin 6 (▬ ▬) are in correct positions. The other two lines are in incorrect positions. The top lines are complementary with each other. The two bottom lines and the two middle lines are in conflict. Hexagram 7:6 is neutral.

3 Texts of Lines

Yang 1

One has strong front toes
And fails in advance.
It is blameful.

Yang 1 (▬) indicates that the action of the subject is yang. The subject wants to advance. But sometimes, the subject fails in advancing, because she or he sets out too vigorously, without careful thinking, "One has strong front toes." When facing a strong and canny object, the subject should prepare well for the offensive movement, or risk being blamed for failure.

This line is in a correct position, but in conflict to yang 4 (▬). The yang action of the subject is neutral.

Yang 2

Call for keeping vigilance:
A battle might take place at night.
But don't worry about it.

Yang 2 (▬) indicates that the subject is strong. On the other side, the object is also strong and canny, posing a threat to the subject. The subject has to stay alert, "A battle might take place at night." However, the subject should not worry about the fight, because if the subject is well prepared, he or she has enough strength for a good defense.

Yang 3

One has strong cheeks.
That causes unfavorable events.
The gentleman is menacing.
One feels like walking alone in a rain
And getting wet.
There is anger.
There is no blame.

Yang 3 (▬) indicates that the subject is arrogant and demanding. It is easy for the subject to make a mistake carelessly, especially with reckless speech, "One has strong cheeks," like a blowhard. For now, the object is very dangerous. When the menacing object is irritated by an infelicitous remark from the subject, the object could take the subject's words as an excuse to attack, giving the subject a difficult time. Then the subject, without allies, "feels like walking alone in a rain and getting wet."

This line is in a correct position and complementary to yang 6 (▬). The yang attitude of the subject is favorable. But regarding the whole situation, this text stresses the negative side of the yang attitude of the subject.

Yang 4

When the skin on the buttocks is flailed
It is hard to sit, even to walk.
Pull a goat with you to eliminate regret.
Do not believe what others say.

Yang 4 (▬) indicates that the object is aggressive, pushing the subject into trouble. The subject has a difficult time under this pressure, "When the skin on the buttocks are flailed, it is hard to sit even to walk." The subject should be realistic and not try to accomplish too much — just doing what seems feasible, and taking advantage of whatever help is available, "Pull a goat with you to eliminate regret." Also, the subject should be careful, and not fall into the object's trap, "Do not believe what others say."

Yang 5

Weeds grow over the fields,
Menacing crops.
Walking along a central line,
Not left nor right,
Is blameless.

Yang 5 (▬) indicates that the object is strong and full of vitality, threatening the subject, "Weeds grow over the fields, menacing crops." The subject should have a precise, careful strategy in dealing with this threat, "walking along a central line, not left nor right."

This line is central, in a correct position, but in conflict to yang 2 (▬). The yang essence of the object is neutral.

Yin 6

If there is no call for alert,
The end of the situation is unfavorable.

Yin 6 (- -) indicates that the object has a canny, flexible attitude. At the same time, the object is essentially aggressive and strong. The subject cannot afford to ignore this menace, "If there is no call for alert, the end of the situation is unfavorable."

This line is in a correct position and complementary to yang 3 (—). Regarding the whole situation, the text stresses its negative nature.

8 Hexagram 7:7 Heaven (In Zhou Yi, hexagram 1)

The title, Heaven, indicates that the relationship is like the sky, changing constantly: from brightness of day to darkness of night, from a peaceful blue with white clouds to a rainy gray with gusty winds. Separate powers are in equal competition, leading to sudden shifts in the weather.

In this hexagram, both the components are trigram 7 (☰), Heavens (strength). In this confrontation of two "heavens," the subject is vigorously and continually meeting with a challenge, "One strives hard all day and is vigilant at night."

1 General Text

Things are moving very smoothly.
Staying on the current course is beneficial.

In the relationship, both subject and object are equally aggressive, strong and arrogant. They compete in all aspects. The subject is powerful, confident, and vigorously trying to enhance his or her position. There are competitions, but this is to be expected, "Things are moving very smoothly." If the subject concedes or gives up, he or she will lose the battle. So it is best to continue the fight, "Staying on the current course is beneficial."

2 Structure

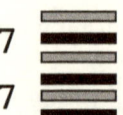

Figure 17.8: Structure of hexagram 7:7

In this hexagram, there are three correct lines, as shown in black, but no line complementary is with any other line. Hexagram 7:7 is neutral.

3 Texts of Lines

Yang 1

A dragon is hiding.
Do nothing.

This dragon is the legendary huge animal, not the biological dragon. Its body is like a snake's, but with scales. Its head is like a water buffalo's, but with antlers like a deer's. It has four legs, but with an eagle's claws. It can fly and swim. It is the symbol of strength and power.

Yang 1 (━) indicates that the subject likes to fight, and seeks to expand his or her territory. On the other side, the object is equally strong and self-promoting. The competition or confrontation is thorough and enduring. The subject should preserve strength, displaying power only at the crucial point, when it is sure that he or she will gain by it. That is the rule: use yin to deal with yang. "A dragon is hiding. Do nothing."

This line is in a correct position, but in conflict to yang 4 (━). The yang action of the subject is neutral.

Yang 2

The dragon appears in a field.
It is beneficial to show off as a great person.

Yang 2 (━) indicates that the subject has great power, perhaps in business or politics, or is strong financially or physically. The yang essence is vital for sustaining a good or better position in the relationship. The subject should be like a dragon appearing in a field, showing off as a force with which to be reckoned. However, what the subject should do is limit this greatness to appearances, and not call on his or her strength until sure of winning the battle.

This line is central, but in an incorrect position and in conflict to yang 5 (━). The yang essence of the subject is neutral.

Yang 3

One strives hard all day.
And is vigilant at night.
It is dangerous.
There is no blame.

Yang 3 (—) indicates that the subject is arrogant and reckless. When in confrontation with a competitor or enemy, the subject should not be arrogant, but strive hard to enhance his or her position. The subject should not be reckless, but prudent, "One strives hard all day, and is vigilant at night." Despite the danger of this situation, if the subject is prudent and struggles hard, "there is no blame."

This line is in a correct position, but in conflict to yang 6 (—). The yang attitude of the subject is neutral.

Yang 4

The dragon jumps out,
Or jumps in, an abyss.
There is no blame.

Yang 4 (—) indicates that the object is trying expand his or her interests. In dealing with this strong competitor or enemy, the subject should be flexible and evasive, like the dragon jumping into or out of the abyss. If the object attacks or the situation does not assure the subject of success, the subject should retreat, like a dragon in hiding. If the object retreats or the situation assures the subject of success, the subject should advance, jumping out of the abyss. The subject should change the action according to circumstance, like the dragon, not always staying inside the abyss or always remaining outside the abyss. If the subject can remain alert and adaptable, "there is no blame."

This line is in an incorrect position and in conflict to yang 1 (—). The yang action of the object is unfavorable.

Yang 5

The dragon is flying in the sky.
It is beneficial to show off as a great person.

Yang 5 (—) indicates that the object is strong physically, financially or spiritually. Since the object is aggressive, posing a threat to the subject, the subject should enhance his or her strength, and maintain superiority over the object. If the object is like a dragon, advancing on the field, the subject must rise above the object and become superior, like the other dragon flying in the sky. Then, if the object also takes to the sky, the subject must soar higher and faster. The subject should show off as a great person, always remaining aware that making an impressive appearance as a great person does not entail attacking like a reckless person.

This line is central and in a correct position, but in conflict to yang 2 (—). The yang essence of the object is neutral.

Yang 6

The dragon is arrogant.
That is regrettable.

Yang 6 (━) indicates that the object is arrogant, bossy, or bullying. To deal with an arrogant competitor or enemy, the subject should be calm and prudent. If the subject recklessly responds to the object's arrogant attitude with equal arrogance, the subject could make a wrong step and incur loss. Then the subject would be like an arrogant dragon that comes to regret its lack of control.

This line is in an incorrect line and in conflict to yang 3 (━). The yang attitude of the object is unfavorable.

Use Yang

A flock of dragons appears.
None of them starts the first assault.
It is favorable.

The text of "Use Yang" offers general instruction on how to use the yang lines in all the hexagrams. This text applies to the general interpretation of yang lines in all of the sixty-four hexagrams, except hexagram Ø:Ø, which contains no yang lines.

A yang line represents strength and mobility, like that of a dragon. Multiple yang lines appear in the hexagrams like a flock of dragons. The dragons like to fight. If none of the dragons makes the first assault, the situation could be favorable. While praising the strength and mobility of the yang nature, one should also be concerned with its negative aspects, such as arrogance and recklessness. If "none of them starts the first assault," then this tendency toward recklessness is held in check, and the situation will be "favorable."

APPENDIX 1
VERBATIM TRANSLATION OF YI TEXT

Hexagram ∅:∅ • Earth ☷

1 GENERAL TEXT

Very through benefit mars its stay gentlemen have some go first stray then get master benefit west south get friend east north lose friend peace stay favorable.

2 TEXTS OF LINES

Yin 1: *tread frost solid ice arrive.*
Yin 2: *straight square large not practice no not benefit*
Yin 3: *include brilliance may stay or serve king business no success have end*
Yin 4: *tie sack no blame no fame*
Yin 5: *yellow garment very favorable*
Yin 6: *dragon fight on field the blood black yellow*
Using Yin: *benefit ever stay*

Hexagram ∅:1 • Deprivation ☶

1 GENERAL TEXT

Not benefit have some go.

2 TEXTS OF LINES

Yin 1: *rotting bed with leg marred stay unfavorable*
Yin 2: *rotting bed with end marred stay unfavorable*
Yin 3: *rotting its no blame*
Yin 4: *rotting bed with skin unfavorable*
Yin 5: *string fish with court lady favor not no benefit*
Yang 6: *large fruit not eat gentlemen get wagon small man deprive house*

Hexagram ∅:2 • Closeness ䷇

1 GENERAL TEXT
Favorable origin oracle very ever stay no blame not rest side come late person unfavorable.

2 TEXTS OF LINES
Yin 1: *have sincere close its no blame have sincere full jug finally come have other favorable*
Yin 2: *close it's from inside stay favorable*
Yin 3: *close it's not man*
Yin 4: *outside close its stay favorable*
Yang 5: *show close king use three chase lose front game town man not alert favorable*
Yin 6: *close its no first unfavorable*

Hexagram ∅:3 • Watching ䷓

1 GENERAL TEXT
Cleansing not offering have sincere seriousness.

2 TEXTS OF LINES
Yin 1: *childish watch small man no blame gentleman mean*
Yin 2: *surreptitiously watch benefit woman stay*
Yin 3: *watch my life advance retreat*
Yin 4: *watch nation its light benefit use guest on king*
Yang 5: *watch my life gentleman no blame*
Yang 6: *watch the life gentleman no blame*

Hexagram ∅:4 • Delight ䷏

1 GENERAL TEXT
Benefit set marquis walk army.

2 TEXTS OF LINES

Yin 1: *trumpet elephant unfavorable*
Yin 2: *posit on rock not end day stay favorable*
Yin 3: *stare elephant regret late have regret*
Yang 4: *follow elephant big have gain not doubt friend together gather*
Yin 5: *stay sick persist not die*
Yin 6: *close eye elephant succeed have change no blame*

Hexagram ∅:5 • Promotion

1 GENERAL TEXT

Kang Hou use grant horse many normal day day three receive.

2 TEXTS OF LINES

Yin 1: *promote like torture like stay favorable none sincere relax no blame*
Yin 2: *promote like worry like stay favorable get this big favor on the grandmother*
Yin 3: *majority consent regret vanish*
Yang 4: *promote like mole cricket stay dangerous*
Yin 5: *regret vanish lose gain not worry go favorable not no benefit*
Yang 6: *promote the horn for use fight town danger favorable no blame stay mean*

Hexagram ∅:6 • Gathering

1 GENERAL TEXT

Through king come have temple benefit see big man through benefit stay use big animal favorable benefit have some go.

2 TEXTS OF LINES

Yin 1: *have sincere no end then disorder then gather like call one hold for smile not worry go no blame*
Yin 2: *lead favorable no blame sincere then benefit use sacrifice*
Yin 3: *gather like sigh like no some benefit go no blame little mean*

Yang 4: *large favorable no blame*

Yang 5: *gather have position no blame not sincere origin ever stay regret vanish*

Yin 6: *sigh such tear snivel no blame*

Hexagram ⌀:7 • Denial ䷋

1 GENERAL TEXT

Denial its not man not benefit gentleman stay large go little come.

2 TEXTS OF LINES

Yin 1: *pull reed grass by the kind stay favorable through*

Yin 2: *wrap obsequious small man favorable big man denial through*

Yin 3: *wrap shame*

Yang 4: *have life no blame alike cling happy*

Yang 5: *stop denial big man favorable the vanish the vanish tie on mulberry tree*

Yang 6: *turn over denial first denial late happiness*

Hexagram 1:⌀ • Modest ䷎

1 GENERAL TEXT

Through gentleman have end.

2 TEXTS OF LINES

Yin 1: *modest modest gentleman use cross big river favorable*

Yin 2: *speech modest stay favorable*

Yang 3: *credit modest gentleman have end favorable*

Yin 4: *none not benefit explore cultivate modest*

Yin 5: *not rich with the neighbor benefit use invade fight none not benefit*

Yin 6: *speech modest benefit use walk army conquer state country*

Hexagram 1:1 • Stop ䷳

1 GENERAL TEXT
Stop the back not get the body walk the courtyard not see the man no blame.

2 TEXTS OF LINES
Yin 1: *stop the toe no blame benefit ever stay*
Yin 2: *stop the calf not support the follow the heart not happy*
Yang 3: *stop the waist split the muscle danger burn heart*
Yin 4: *stop the body no blame*
Yin 5: *stop the cheek word have order regret vanish*
Yang 6: *urge stop favorable*

Hexagram 1:2 • Lame ䷦

1 GENERAL TEXT
Benefit west south not benefit east north benefit see big man stay favorable.

2 TEXTS OF LINES
Yin 1: *go lame come praise*
Yin 2: *king servant lame lame not self its cause*
Yang 3: *go lame come opposite*
Yin 4: *go lame come connect*
Yang 5: *big lame friend come*
Yin 6: *go lame come large favorable benefit see big man*

Hexagram 1:3 • Gradual ䷴

1 GENERAL TEXT
Woman return favorable benefit stay.

2 TEXTS OF LINES
Yin 1: *goose approach on shore little son danger have word no blame*

Yin 2: *goose approach on boulder eat drink concord favorable*
Yang 3: *goose approach on field husband fight not return wife conceive not nurture unfavorable benefit resist invader*
Yin 4: *goose approach on wood or get the roost no blame*
Yang 5: *goose approach on hill woman three year not conceive end not its win favorable*
Yang 6: *goose approach on land the feather may use for ornament favorable*

Hexagram 1:4 • Tolerance

1 GENERAL TEXT

Trough benefit stay may small thing not may big thing fly bird left it voice not proper upper proper lower big favorable.

2 TEXTS OF LINES

Yin 1: *fly bird with unfavorable*
Yin 2: *pass the grandfather meet the grandmother not reach the king meet the minister no blame*
Yang 3: *not pass prevent it follow or kill it unfavorable*
Yang 4: *no blame not pass meet it go danger must alert not use ever stay*
Yin 5: *dense cloud not rain from our west suburbs lord arrow take it in cave*
Yin 6: *not meet pass it fly bird leave it unfavorable is call catastrophe ailment*

Hexagram 1:5 • Travel

1 GENERAL TEXT

Little through travel stay favorable.

2 TEXTS OF LINES

Yin 1: *travel petty that the source take calamity*
Yin 2: *travel reach place hold the money get child servant stay*
Yang 3: *travel burn the place lose the child servant danger*
Yang 4: *travel on reside get the money axe my heart not happy*
Yin 5: *shot pheasant one arrow spend end with dignity life*

Yang 6: *bird burn the nest travel man first laugh then cry shout lose oxen on Yi unfavorable*

Hexagram 1:6 • Enjoyable

1 GENERAL TEXT

Through benefit stay marry woman favorable.

2 TEXTS OF LINES

Yin 1: *feel the thumb*
Yin 2: *feel the calf unfavorable reside favorable*
Yang 3: *feel the thigh hold the follow go mean*
Yang 4: *stay favorable regret vanish flicker forth back companion follow you thought*
Yang 5: *feel the flesh no regret*
Yin 6: *feel the cheek jaw tongue*

Hexagram 1:7 • Flee

1 GENERAL TEXT

Through small benefit stay.

2 TEXTS OF LINES

Yin 1: *flee tail danger not use have some go*
Yin 2: *hold its with yellow ox its leather not its win release*
Yang 3: *tangle flee have ailment danger accumulate servant concubine favorable*
Yang 4: *good flee gentleman favorable small man deny*
Yang 5: *nice flee stay favorable*
Yang 6: *fat flee none not benefit*

Hexagram 2:Ø • Army

1 GENERAL TEXT

Stay old man favorable no blame.

2 TEXTS OF LINES

Yin 1: *army out with discipline deny hide unfavorable*
Yang 2: *in army middle favorable no blame king three assign life*
Yin 3: *army puzzle wagon corpse unfavorable*
Yin 4: *army retreat no blame*
Yin 5: *field have bird benefit execute word no blame old son lead army brother son wagon corps stay unfavorable*
Yin 6: *big king have life create country inherit family small man not use*

Hexagram 2:1 • Ignorance

1 GENERAL

through not I beg child ignorance child ignorance beg me initial oracle tell again three profane profane then not tell benefit stay

2 TEXTS OF LINES

Yin 1: *develop ignorant benefit use model man use lose fetters to go mean*
Yang 2: *wrap ignorance favorable marry lady favorable son overcome home*
Yin 3: *not use marry woman see gold man not have self no some benefit*
Yin 4: *tired ignorance mean*
Yin 5: *child ignorance favorable*
Yang 6: *attack ignorance not benefit be robber benefit against robber*

Hexagram 2:2 • Pitfall

1 GENERAL TEXT

Have sincere tie heart through walk have value.

2 TEXTS OF LINES

Yin 1: *many pitfall into on pitfall cellar unfavorable*
Yang 2: *pitfall have danger seek small gain*
Yin 3: *come its pitfall pitfall danger and deep into on pitfall cellar not use*

Yin 4: *cup wine basket two use jar receive simple from window final no blame*
Yang 5: *pitfall not full bottom already flat no blame*
Yin 6: *tie with rope put in bush bramble three year not get unfavorable*

Hexagram 2:3 • Flood ☵☰

1 GENERAL TEXT

Through king come have temple benefit cross big river benefit stay.

2 TEXTS OF LINES

Yin 1: *use save horse strong favorable*
Yang 2: *flood run the table regret vanish*
Yin 3: *Flood the self no regret*
Yin 4: *flood the herd very favorable flood have hill not you by think*
Yang 5: *flood sweet the big call flood king residence no blame*
Yang 6: *flood the blood go far out no blame*

Hexagram 2:4 • Solution ☳☵

1 GENERAL TEXT

Benefit west south no where go the come return favorable have some go swift favorable.

2 TEXTS OF LINES

Yin 1: *no blame*
Yang 2: *field obtain three fox get yellow arrow stay favorable*
Yin 3: *carry and ride cause robber come stay mean*
Yang 4: *release the thumb friend come this sincere*
Yin 5: *gentleman tie have solve favorable have sincere on small man*
Yin 6: *duke use shoot hawk on high wall its above obtain it nothing not benefit*

Hexagram 2:5 • Imperfect ☶☱

1 GENERAL TEXT

Through small fox dry cross wet its tail no some benefit.

2 TEXTS OF LINES

Yin 1: *wet its tail mean*
Yang 2: *tow the wheel stay favorable*
Yin 3: *not cross expedition unfavorable benefit cross big river*
Yang 4: *stay favorable regret vanish shock use fight Guifang three year have bonus on big country*
Yin 5: *stay favorable no regret gentleman its light have sincere favorable*
Yang 6: *have sincere on drink wine no blame wet the head have sincere lose true*

Hexagram 2:6 • Stranded

1 GENERAL TEXT

through stay big man favorable no blame have word not believe

2 TEXTS OF LINES

Yin 1: *buttock stranded on trunk tree enter on seclude valley three year not see*
Yang 2: *stranded on wine food red clothes just come benefit use offering pray expedition unfavorable no blame*
Yin 3: *stranded on rock stay on puncture vine enter on the palace not see the wife unfavorable*
Yang 4: *come slow slow stranded on gold wagon mean have end*
Yang 5: *cut nose cut feet stranded on red clothes then slow have release benefit use offering sacrifice*
Yin 6: *stranded on vine weed on target towering mention act regret have regret advance favorable*

Hexagram 2:7 • Sue

1 GENERAL TEXT

Have sincere stifle alert middle favorable final unfavorable benefit see big man not benefit cross big river.

2 TEXTS OF LINES

Yin 1: *not ever that thing small have word final favorable*

Yang 2: *not win sue back and flee the town man three hundred family no ailment*

Yin 3: *eat old merit stay danger final favorable or follow king thing no success*

Yang 4: *not win sue return then life change peace stay favorable*

Yang 5: *sue very favorable*

Yang 6: *sometime present its leather belt dusk morning three deprive its*

Hexagram 3:Ø • Rising ䷭

1 GENERAL TEXT

Very through use see big man not worry south expedition favorable.

2 TEXTS OF LINES

Yin 1: *allow rising big favorable*

Yang 2: *sincere then benefit use sacrifice no blame*

Yang 3: *rising empty town*

Yin 4: *king use offering on Qi mountain favorable no blame*

Yin 5: *stay favorable rising stair*

Yin 6: *dim rising benefit on not rest its stay*

Hexagram 3:1 • Bugs ䷑

1 GENERAL TEXT

Very through benefit cross big river previous first three day back first three day.

2 TEXTS OF LINES

Yin 1: *do father its bug have son father no blame danger end favorable*

Yang 2: *do mother its bug not may stay*

Yang 3: *do father its bug small have regret no big blame*

Yin 4: *relax father its bug go see mean*

Yin 5: *do father its bug use fame*

Yang 6: *not serve king duke high honor the thing*

Hexagram 3:2 • Well

1 GENERAL TEXT

Change town not change well no lose no gain go come well well dry reach yet not rope well tie the jar unfavorable.

2 TEXTS OF LINES

Yin 1: *well mud not eat old well no bird*

Yang 2: *well valley shoot carp jar break leak*

Yang 3: *well leak no eat let I heart sad may use draw king bright and accept the favor*

Yin 4: *well tile no blame*

Yang 5: *well clean cool spring eat*

Yin 6: *well close not cover have sincere very favorable*

Hexagram 3:3 • Yield

1 GENERAL TEXT

Small through benefit have some go benefit see big man.

2 TEXTS OF LINES

Yin 1: *forth back benefit warrior its stay*

Yang 2: *flexible on bed below use priest magician often like favorable no blame*

Yang 3: *unwilling flexible mean*

Yin 4: *regret vanish field obtain three kind*

Yang 5: *stay favorable regret vanish nothing not benefit no beginning have end first seventh three day after seventh three day favorable*

Yang 6: *flexible on bed below lose the sharp axe stay unfavorable*

Hexagram 3:4 • Persistence

1 GENERAL TEXT
Through no blame benefit stay benefit have some go.

2 TEXTS OF LINES
Yin 1: *dredge persistence stay unfavorable nothing some benefit*
Yang 2: *regret vanish*
Yang 3: *not persistence the virtue or suffer its shame stay mean*
Yang 4: *field no bird*
Yin 5: *persistence the virtue stay woman favorable man unfavorable*
Yin 6: *vibrate persistence unfavorable*

Hexagram 3:5 • Cauldron

1 GENERAL TEXT
Very favorable through.

2 TEXTS OF LINES
Yin 1: *cauldron reverse toe benefit out denial get concubine and the son no blame*
Yang 2: *cauldron have solid I rival have sick not I can reach favorable*
Yang 3: *cauldron ear change the move block pheasant meat not eat just rain diminish regret end favorable*
Yang 4: *cauldron broke foot cover gentleman meal the shape mess unfavorable*
Yin 5: *cauldron yellow ear gold bar benefit stay*
Yang 6: *cauldron jade stick big favorable nothing not benefit*

Hexagram 3:6 • Overburden

1 GENERAL TEXT
Ridgepole bend benefit have some go through.

2 TEXTS OF LINES

Yin 1: *pad use white grass no blame*

Yang 2: *wither willow produce sprout old man get the woman wife nothing no benefit*

Yang 3: *ridgepole bend unfavorable*

Yang 4: *ridgepole bulge favorable have other mean*

Yang 5: *wither willow produce flower old lady get the yang man no blame no fame*

Yin 6: *over cross submerge top unfavorable no blame*

Hexagram 3:7 • Encounter

1 GENERAL TEXT

Woman strong not use marry woman.

2 TEXTS OF LINES

Yin 1: *tie with metal brake stay favorable have some go see unfavorable meager sow disquiet restless*

Yang 2: *kitchen have fish no blame not benefit guest*

Yang 3: *buttocks no skin the walk difficult danger no big blame*

Yang 4: *kitchen no fish initiate unfavorable*

Yang 5: *with berry cover melon contain talent have meteorite from heaven*

Yang 6: *encounter the corner mean no blame*

Hexagram 4:Ø • Return

1 GENERAL TEXT

Through out in no ailment friend come no blame back return the way seven day come return benefit have some go.

2 TEXTS OF LINES

Yang 1: *not far return no harm regret big favorable*

Yin 2: *rest return favorable*

Yin 3: *frowning return danger no blame*

Yin 4: *middle walk along return*

Yin 5: *urge return no regret*

Yin 6: *stray return unfavorable have tragedy ailment use walk army end have big lose with the country king unfavorable until on ten year not subdue fight*

Hexagram 4:1 • Care ䷚

1 GENERAL TEXT

Stay favorable watch care self seek mouth food.

2 TEXTS OF LINES

Yang 1: *abandon you divine tortoise look my pile care unfavorable*

Yin 2: *upset care not way on hill care expedition unfavorable*

Yin 3: *not care stay unfavorable ten year not use no some benefit*

Yin 4: *upset care favorable tiger glare see look the desire pursue pursue no blame*

Yin 5: *not way reside stay favorable not may cross big river*

Yang 6: *follow care danger favorable benefit cross big river*

Hexagram 4:2 • Prospect ䷢

1 GENERAL TEXT

Very through benefit stay not use have some go benefit set marquis.

2 TEXTS OF LINES

Yang 1: *pace up and down benefit reside stay benefit set marquis*

Yin 2: *puzzle like turn like ride horse much like not rob marriage girl stay no marry ten year will marry*

Yin 3: *chase deer without guide think enter into forest middle gentleman close not like abandon go mean*

Yin 4: *ride horse much like seek marriage go favorable nothing not benefit*

Yang 5: *store the grease small stay favorable big stay unfavorable*

Yin 6: *ride horse much like tear bleeding ripple like*

Hexagram 4:3 • Gain ䷩

1 GENERAL TEXT
Benefit have some go benefit cross big river.

2 TEXTS OF LINES
Yang 1: *benefit use for big work very favorable no blame*

Yin 2: *or gain its ten pair its tortoise not overcome violate ever stay favorable king use ritual on ancestor favorable*

Yin 3: *gain its use unfavorable thing no blame have sincere middle walk tell lord use dial*

Yin 4: *middle walk tell lord follow benefit use for base move country*

Yang 5: *have sincere favor heart not ask very favorable have sincere favor my virtue*

Yang 6: *not gain its or hit its stand heart not persistent unfavorable*

Hexagram 4:4 • Shock ䷲

1 GENERAL TEXT
Through thunder come shock shock cheerful talk ha ha thunder astonish hundred mile not lose spoon cup.

2 TEXTS OF LINES
Yang 1: *thunder come shock shock then cheerful talk ha ha favorable*

Yin 2: *thunder come danger million lose shell climb on nine hill not chase seven day get*

Yin 3: *thunder scaring scaring thunder walk no ailment*

Yang 4: *thunder drop mud*

Yin 5: *thunder go come danger million no lose have thing*

Yin 6: *thunder frightening frightening see worrying worrying expedition unfavorable thunder not on the own on the neighbor no blame marriage affiliation have word*

Hexagram 4:5 • Bite ䷔

1 GENERAL TEXT
Through benefit use prison.

2 TEXTS OF LINES
Yang 1: *wear fetter damage toe no blame*
Yin 2: *bite skin damage nose no blame*
Yin 3: *bite salt meat meet poison small mean no blame*
Yang 4: *bite dry meat bone get gold arrow benefit difficult stay favorable*
Yin 5: *bite dry meat get yellow gold stay danger no blame*
Yang 6: *carry yoke damage ear unfavorable*

Hexagram 4:6 • Follow ䷐

1 GENERAL TEXT
Very through benefit stay no blame.

2 TEXTS OF LINES
Yang 1: *officer have change stay favorable out door interact have merit*
Yin 2: *tie small son lose big man*
Yin 3: *tie big man lose small son follow have pursue gain benefit reside stay*
Yang 4: *follow have gain stay unfavorable have sincere in way for clear why blame*
Yang 5: *sincere on nice favorable*
Yin 6: *bond tie its then follow maintain its king use offer on west mountain*

Hexagram 4:7 • Innocence ䷘

1 GENERAL TEXT
Very through benefit stay the not correct have ailment not benefit have some go.

2 TEXTS OF LINES

Yang 1: *innocence go favorable*
Yin 2: *not plough harvest not cultivate fertile then benefit have some go*
Yin 3: *innocence its calamity or tie its cow walk man its gain town man its calamity*
Yang 4: *may stay no blame*
Yang 5: *innocence its sickness no medicine have happiness*
Yang 6: *innocence walk have ailment no some benefit*

Hexagram 5:Ø • Hurt

1 GENERAL TEXT

Benefit difficult stay.

2 TEXTS OF LINES

Yang 1: *hurt on fly drop the wing gentleman on walk three day no eat have some go master have word*
Yin 2: *hurt hurt on left thigh use save horse strong favorable*
Yang 3: *hurt on south hunt get the big head not may fast stay*
Yin 4: *enter on left abdomen obtain hurt its heart on out door hall*
Yin 5: *Qi Zi its hurt benefit stay*
Yin 6: *not bright gloomy first climb on heaven then enter into earth*

Hexagram 5:1 • Ornament

1 GENERAL TEXT

Through small benefit have some go.

2 TEXTS OF LINES

Yang 1: *adorn the toe abandon wagon but walk*
Yin 2: *adorn the beard*
Yang 3: *ornament like wet like ever stay favorable*
Yin 4: *ornament like white like white horse like like not robber marry connect*
Yin 5: *ornament on hill garden bunch silk pile pile mean end favorable*
Yang 6: *white ornament no blame*

Hexagram 5:2 • Perfect ䷾

1 GENERAL TEXT
Through small benefit stay first favorable end disorder.

2 TEXTS OF LINES
Yang 1: *tow the wheel wet the tail no blame*
Yin 2: *woman lose the curtain not seek seven day get*
Yang 3: *Gaozong fight Guifang three year conquer its small man not use*
Yin 4: *soak have cloth wadding all day vigilance*
Yang 5: *east neighbor butcher cow not as west neighbor its spring sacrifice real receive the bless*
Yin 6: *wet the head danger*

Hexagram 5:3 • Matriarch ䷤

1 GENERAL TEXT
Benefit woman stay.

2 TEXTS OF LINES
Yang 1: *idle have home regret vanish*
Yin 2: *no some out in middle cook stay favorable*
Yang 3: *matriarch scold complain regret danger favorable girl boy tease giggle end mean*
Yin 4: *rich family big favorable*
Yang 5: *king come have family not worry favorable*
Yang 6: *have sincere power like end favorable*

Hexagram 5:4 • Totality ䷹

1 GENERAL TEXT
Through king visit it no worry proper day middle.

2 TEXTS OF LINES

Yang 1: *meet the match host though ten no blame go have nice*

Yin 2: *full the screen day middle see polestar go get suspect ailment have sincere open like favorable*

Yang 3: *full the copious day middle see stars break the right ache no blame*

Yang 4: *full the screen day middle see polestar meet the foreign host favorable*

Yin 5: *come brilliance have cerebrate fame favorable*

Yin 6: *full the house screen the home look the family quiet the no people three year not see unfavorable*

Hexagram 5:5 • Brightness

1 GENERAL TEXT

benefit stay through raise female cow favorable

2 TEXTS OF LINES

Yang 1: *step miscellaneous salute its no blame*

Yin 2: *yellow brightness very favorable*

Yang 3: *sun set its brightness not drum jar and sing then big old its sigh unfavorable*

Yang 4: *sudden as its come as burn as die as abandon as*

Yin 5: *out tear torrential as worry sigh as favorable*

Yang 6: *king use out expedition have award break head get other the kind no blame*

Hexagram 5:6 • Change

1 GENERAL TEXT

Sixth day then sincere very through benefit stay regret vanish.

2 TEXTS OF LINES

Yang 1: *tie with yellow ox its leather*

Yin 2: *sixth day then change its expedition favorable no blame*

Yang 3: *expedition unfavorable stay danger change word three compromise have sincere*

Yang 4: *regret vanish have sincere change life favorable*
Yang 5: *big man tiger change no divination have sincere*
Yin 6: *gentleman leopard change small man change face expedition unfavorable reside stay favorable*

Hexagram 5:7 • Coalition ☷☵

1 GENERAL TEXT

Alliance on field through benefit cross big river benefit gentleman stay.

2 TEXTS OF LINES

Yang 1: *alliance on door no blame*
Yin 2: *alliance on clan mean*
Yang 3: *hide troop in bush climb the high hill three year not rise*
Yang 4: *climb the wall not overcome attack favorable*
Yang 5: *alliance first scream cry and then smile large army overcome mutual meet*
Yang 6: *alliance on rural no regret*

Hexagram 6:Ø • Approach ☱☷

1 GENERAL TEXT

Very through benefit stay then on eight month have unfavorable.

2 TEXTS OF LINES

Yang 1: *aware approach stay favorable*
Yang 2: *aware approach favorable none not benefit*
Yin 3: *sweet approach none some benefit already worry it no blame*
Yin 4: *arrive approach no blame*
Yin 5: *know approach big king its proper favorable*
Yin 6: *urge approach favorable no blame*

Hexagram 6:1 • Loss ☷☱

1 GENERAL TEXT

Verbatim Translation of Yi Text

Have sincere very favorable no blame may stay benefit have some go what its use two basket may use offer.

② TEXTS OF LINES

Yang 1: *finish thing quick go no blame adequate loss its*
Yang 2: *benefit stay expedition unfavorable not loss gain its*
Yin 3: *three man walk then loss one man one man walk then get the friend*
Yin 4: *lose the ailment let quick have happiness no blame*
Yin 5: *or gain its ten pair its tortoise not overcome violate very favorable*
Yang 6: *not loss gain its no blame stay favorable benefit have some go get servant no home*

Hexagram 6:2 • Limitation ䷻

① GENERAL TEXT

Through bitter limitation not may stay.

② TEXTS OF LINES

Yang 1: *not out room yard no blame*
Yang 2: *not out door yard unfavorable*
Yin 3: *not limitation like then sigh like no blame*
Yin 4: *peace limitation good*
Yang 5: *sweet limitation favorable go have nice*
Yin 6: *bitter limitation stay unfavorable regret vanish*

Hexagram 6:3 • Sincerity ䷼

① GENERAL TEXT

Pig fish favorable benefit cross big river benefit stay.

② TEXTS OF LINES

Yang 1: *stable favorable have other not peace*
Yang 2: *sing crane in shade its son echo its I have good goblet I and you share its*
Yin 3: *get enemy or drum or quit or tear or sing*

Yin 4: *moon almost full horse piece vanish no blame*
Yang 5: *have sincere tie like no blame*
Yang 6: *pheasant sound soar on sky stay unfavorable*

Hexagram 6:4 • Marry ䷵

1 GENERAL TEXT

Expedition unfavorable none some benefit.

2 TEXTS OF LINES

Yang 1: *marry as concubine lime can walk expedition favorable*
Yang 2: *single eye can see benefit seclude man its stay*
Yin 3: *marry as need reverse marry as concubine*
Yang 4: *marry over date delay marry have time*
Yin 5: *emperor Yi marry sister the lady its garment not like the concubine its garment good moon almost full favorable*
Yin 6: *woman hold basket without fruit man slay sheep without blood not some benefit*

Hexagram 6:5 • Stare ䷥

1 GENERAL TEXT

Small thing favorable.

2 TEXTS OF LINES

Yang 1: *regret vanish lose horse not chase self return see wicked man no blame*
Yang 2: *meet master on street no blame*
Yin 3: *see wagon tow the ox tug the man cut hair and nose no begin have end*
Yang 4: *stare lonely meet big person deal sincere danger no blame*
Yin 5: *regret vanish the clan bite skin go why blame*
Yang 6: *stare lonely see pig back dirty carry ghost one wagon first open its bow late lose its bow not robber wooer go meet rain then favorable*

Hexagram 6:6 • Pleasure ䷙

1 GENERAL TEXT
Through benefit stay.

2 TEXTS OF LINES
Yang 1: *peace pleasure favorable*
Yang 2: *sincere pleasure favorable regret vanish*
Yin 3: *come pleasure unfavorable*
Yang 4: *trade pleasure no peace solve ailment have happy*
Yang 5: *sincere on exploitation have danger*
Yin 6: *pull pleasure*

Hexagram 6:7 • Treading ䷉

1 GENERAL TEXT
Treading tiger tail not eat man through.

2 TEXTS OF LINES
Yang 1: *simple treading go no blame*
Yang 2: *treading way flat flat seclude man stay favorable*
Yin 3: *single eye can see lame can treading treading tiger tail eat man unfavorable audacious man deal on big lord*
Yang 4: *treading tiger tail scare scare end favorable*
Yang 5: *menace treading stay danger*
Yang 6: *see treading examine detail the turn very favorable*

Hexagram 7:Ø • Peace

1 GENERAL TEXT
Small go big come favorable through.

2 TEXTS OF LINES

Yang 1: *pull reed grass by the kind expedition favorable*

Yang 2: *calabash use cross river not far lose pair vanish get nice on half way*

Yang 3: *no plain not slope no go not return difficult stay no blame not worry the sincere on food have happiness*

Yin 4: *fly lightly not rich by the neighbor not alert by sincere*

Yin 5: *emperor Yi marry sister by happiness very favorable*

Yin 6: *wall collapse on moat not use army from city tell life stay mean*

Hexagram 7:1 • Build Up ▤

1 GENERAL TEXT

Beneficial stay not home eat favorable benefit cross big river.

2 TEXTS OF LINES

Yang 1: *have danger benefit halt*

Yang 2: *wagon lose axle*

Yang 3: *fine horse chase benefit difficult stay day Sophisticate wagon defense benefit have some go*

Yin 4: *baby calf its headboard very favorable*

Yin 5: *geld boar its tusks favorable*

Yang 6: *how heaven its way through*

Hexagram 7:2 • Expectation ▤

1 GENERAL TEXT

Have sincere light through stay favorable benefit cross big river.

2 TEXTS OF LINES

Yang 1: *expectation on suburb benefit use persist no blame*

Yang 2: *expectation on sand small have word end favorable*

Yang 3: *expectation on mud cause robber come*

Yin 4: *expectation on blood out from pitfall*

Yang 5: *expectation on wine food stay favorable*

Yin 6: *enter on pitfall have not fast its guest three man come courteous its*

end favorable

Hexagram 7:3 • Accumulation ☰

1 GENERAL TEXT
Through dense cloud not rain from I west suburb.

2 TEXTS OF LINES
Yang 1: *return own way why the blame favorable*
Yang 2: *tow return favorable*
Yang 3: *wagon lose spoke husband wife oppose eye*
Yin 4: *have sincere blood go vigilance out no blame*
Yang 5: *have sincere together like rich by the neighbor*
Yang 6: *already rain already stop nice moral carry woman stay danger moon almost full gentleman expedition unfavorable*

Hexagram 7:4 • Reckless

1 GENERAL TEXT
Benefit stay.

2 TEXTS OF LINES
Yang 1: *strong on toe expedition unfavorable have sincere*
Yang 2: *stay favorable*
Yang 3: *small man use strong gentleman use not stay danger ram sheep butt fence entangle the horn*
Yang 4: *stay favorable regret vanish fence breach not entangle strong on big wagon its axle*
Yin 5: *lose sheep on Yi no regret*
Yin 6: *ram sheep butt fence not can retreat not can advance no some benefit difficult then favorable*

Hexagram 7:5 • Acquisition ☰

1 GENERAL TEXT
Very through.

2 TEXTS OF LINES
Yang 1: *no interact harm not blame difficult then no blame*
Yang 2: *big wagon by carry have some go no blame*
Yang 3: *lord use offering on heaven son small man not overcome*
Yang 4: *not the many no blame*
Yin 5: *the sincere interact like power like favorable*
Yang 6: *from heaven bless it favorable none not benefit*

Hexagram 7:6 • Menace

1 GENERAL TEXT
Publicize on king court sincere call have danger tell own town no benefit on fight benefit have some go.

2 TEXTS OF LINES
Yang 1: *strong on front toe go no win for blame*
Yang 2: *vigilance call evening night have fight not worry*
Yang 3: *strong on cheek have unfavorable gentleman menace menace alone walk meet rain like wet have angry no blame*
Yang 4: *buttocks no skin the walk difficult pull goat regret vanish hear word not believe*
Yang 5: *amaranth land menace menace middle walk no blame*
Yin 6: *no call end have unfavorable*

Hexagram 7:7 • Heaven

1 GENERAL TEXT
Very through benefit stay.

2 TEXTS OF LINES
Yang 1: *hide dragon not use*

Yang 2: *see dragon on field benefit see big man*

Yang 3: *gentleman end day heaven heaven night vigilance like danger no blame*

Yang 4: *or jump on abyss no blame*

Yang 5: *fly dragon on sky benefit see big man*

Yang 6: *arrogant dragon have regret*

Use Yang: *see flock dragon no first favorable*

APPENDIX 2
UNDERSTANDING BINARY NUMBERS

The number system we normally use is the decimal system, where 9 is the largest numeral. The binary number system is similar to the decimal number system, but instead of ten figures, Ø through 9, it uses only two figures: Ø and 1. In the decimal number system, if you add 1 to 9, the result is 1Ø:

9 + 1 = 1Ø (Decimal)

In binary number system, 1 is the largest figure. If you add 1 to 1, the result is 1Ø:

1 + 1 = 1Ø (Binary)

Below is a sequence of four binary numbers increasing by the addition of 1, corresponding to the decimal numbers Ø through 3:

```
     Ø          Ø          1         1Ø
  +  Ø       +  1       +  1       +  1
  ─────      ─────      ─────      ─────
     Ø          1         1Ø         11
```

You can keep going indefinitely in this sequence, adding one each time, as you can see by the binary representations of the decimal numbers 4 through 7:

```
    11         1ØØ        1Ø1        11Ø
  +  1       +  1       +  1       +  1
  ─────      ─────      ─────      ─────
   1ØØ        1Ø1        11Ø        111
```

These eight binary numbers can be used to represent the eight trigrams. The corresponding decimal numbers are used for the ID numbers of the trigrams. If you know the ID number of a trigram, you can figure out its shape without having to consult a chart. For example, if you want to know the shape of trigrams 6, the corresponding binary number is 11Ø. When you use 1 to represent a yang line and Ø to indicate a yin line, and you draw them from bottom to top -- 1,1,Ø yielding yang, yang, yin -- your result is the trigram ☱, Lake.

You can use this method to recognize a hexagram from its ID number, as well. A hexagram consists of two trigrams. Its ID number is the combination of the ID numbers of the two component trigrams. From example, if you know the ID number of a hexagram is 6:3, as you figured out above, its subject trigram is trigram 6, ☱. The binary number corresponding to 3 is 11, which you can render as Ø11 to provide the required number of lines. Using the same method, you represent these numerals as lines -- Ø,1,1 equals yin, yang, yang -- and your result is trigram 3, ☴, Wind, the object trigram. When you put the object trigram on top of the subject trigram, you get ䷼, which is hexagram 6:3.

Why is it useful to learn the binary number system to identify trigrams and hexagrams? This will dramatically increase your familiarity with the 64 possible configurations, so that you do not have to stop and look up each trigram and hexagram when you are working with Yi.

INDEX

Index

Symbols

64 Hexagrams • 20, 65

A

Accumulation • 26, 63, 290, 332
Acquisition • 63, 83, 296, 332
Action • 51
Adventure • 18
Adversity • 62, 171
Advertising • 18
AFR • 39, 52
Alzheimer's disease • 85
Angry • 18
Approach • 63, 89, 256, 327
Army • 62, 151, 313
Attitude • 54
Autumn • 46

B

Bankrupt • 17
Beautiful • 19
Binary • 335
Binary Numbers • 63, 335
Bite • 62, 220, 323
Boastful • 19
Bob • 36
Bottom lines • 52
Brightness • 63, 246, 326
Broken line • 15
Bugs • 62, 182, 317
Build Up • 63, 283, 331
Business • 17, 19

C

Care • 62, 208, 321
Carl • 32
Carol • 24
Cathy • 51, 57, 60, 72, 73, 76
Caught by police • 16
Cauldron • 62, 82, 83, 194, 319

Central Lines • 71
CEO • 20
Challenger • 18
Champion • 20
Change • i, 58, 63, 76, 249, 326
Change in Reality • 46
Change of Yin and Yang • 43
Chinese calendar • 45
Chinese classics • ii
Chinese New Year • 45
Chinese philosophy • 24
Closeness • 62, 104, 308
Coalition • 63, 79, 80, 82, 252, 327
Communicate with others • 16
Complementary Lines • 69, 70
Confucius • ii
Consequential Hexagram • 76
Contract or agreement • 17
Correct decision • 17
Country Shang • 176
Country Zhou • 165, 170, 176, 181
Creator • 18
Cycle of a week • 206

D

Dangerous situation • 17
Dating • 18
Debts • 17
Decimal • 335
Delight • 62, 111, 308
Denial • 62, 68, 78, 80, 121, 310
Deprivation • 62, 101, 307
Dictator • 17
Divorce • 16, 205
Domineering • 19
Dragon • 100, 304
Duke Hai • 144
Duke Mianchen • 144

E

Earth • 34, 41, 49, 62, 80, 85, 97, 151, 179, 230, 280, 15
Eight Images • 41
Eight special hexagrams • 67
Eight Trigrams • 15, 24, 25, 39, 42, 43, 45,

INDEX

47, 51
Emperor Shangzhou • 170, 176
Emperor Yi • 283
Employee • 19
Encounter • 62, 201, 320
Ending a relationship • 16
Enjoyable • 62, 69, 144, 313
Enjoying peace • 16
Equinox • 46
Expectation • 63, 286, 331

F

Facing a bad market • 17
Fashionable • 19
Favorable Change • 77
Fire • 18, 40, 47, 80, 82, 168, 194, 220, 230, 233, 236, 240, 243, 246, 249, 253, 270, 296, 305
Flee • 62, 147, 313
Flood • 25, 62, 161, 315
Follow • 62, 223, 323
Freedom • 17
Full moon • 45
Fuxi • 39

G

Gain • 25, 26, 62, 69, 77, 79, 81, 214, 322
Gary • 85, 86
Gathering • 62, 117, 309
General Text • 86
George • 51, 57, 60, 72, 73, 76
Gradual • 25, 62, 133, 311
Great success • 20
Guà • 39
Guī • 39
Gui Cang Yi • ii
Guifang • 170

H

Handsome • 19
Hard work • 18
Harmony • 36
Harry • 39, 46, 52, 56, 82
Healthy • 19
Heaven • 19, 40, 48, 58, 63, 65, 81, 174, 201, 226, 276, 280, 284, 286, 290, 293, 296, 300, 303, , 333
Heng • 144
Hexagram • 336
Hexagram (about) • 26, 62, 63
Hexagram Array • 65, 95
Hexagrams

Hexagram 1:1 • 128
Hexagram 1:2 • 131
Hexagram 1:3 • 30, 133
Hexagram 1:4 • 137
Hexagram 1:5 • 141
Hexagram 1:6 • 67, 68, 144
Hexagram 1:7 • 147
Hexagram 1:Ø • 125
Hexagram 2:1 • 20, 154
Hexagram 2:2 • 158
Hexagram 2:3 • 161
Hexagram 2:4 • 164
Hexagram 2:5 • 67, 71, 77, 83, 168
Hexagram 2:6 • 59, 83, 171
Hexagram 2:7 • 174
Hexagram 2:Ø • 85, 86, 89, 90, 151
Hexagram 3:1 • 182
Hexagram 3:2 • 59, 184
Hexagram 3:3 • 188
Hexagram 3:4 • 30, 67, 69, 191
Hexagram 3:5 • 82, 83, 194
Hexagram 3:6 • 83, 198
Hexagram 3:7 • 201
Hexagram 3:Ø • 90, 179
Hexagram 4:1 • 208
Hexagram 4:2 • 211
Hexagram 4:3 • 26, 67, 69, 77, 79, 81, 82, 214
Hexagram 4:4 • 217
Hexagram 4:5 • 220
Hexagram 4:6 • 64, 95, 223
Hexagram 4:7 • 60, 61, 72, 76, 77, 78, 79, 82, 226
Hexagram 4:Ø • 205
Hexagram 5:1 • 233
Hexagram 5:2 • 67, 70, 71, 76, 77, 79, 236
Hexagram 5:3 • 81, 82, 239
Hexagram 5:4 • 243
Hexagram 5:5 • 246
Hexagram 5:6 • 249
Hexagram 5:7 • 79, 80, 82, 252
Hexagram 5:Ø • 230
Hexagram 6:1 • 67, 68, 258
Hexagram 6:2 • 59, 60, 262
Hexagram 6:3 • 30, 265
Hexagram 6:4 • 63, 64, 95, 267
Hexagram 6:5 • 270
Hexagram 6:6 • 274
Hexagram 6:7 • 78, 80, 276
Hexagram 6:Ø • 89, 256

Hexagram 7:1 • 283
Hexagram 7:2 • 286
Hexagram 7:3 • 290
Hexagram 7:4 • 60, 61, 74, 293
Hexagram 7:5 • 83, 296
Hexagram 7:6 • 300
Hexagram 7:7 • 34, 65, 303
Hexagram 7:Ø • 67, 68, 90, 280
Hexagram Ø:1 • 101
Hexagram Ø:2 • 104
Hexagram Ø:3 • 108
Hexagram Ø:4 • 111
Hexagram Ø:5 • 114
Hexagram Ø:6 • 117
Hexagram Ø:7 • 67, 68, 78, 80, 121
Hexagram Ø:Ø • 34, 65, 97
Holding power • 18
Hurt • 63, 230, 324

I

I Ching • i, ii
ID Numbers • 335
ID Numbers (about) • 25, 44, 59, 63, 67
Ignorance • 20, 21, 62, 154, 314
Illness • 89
Imperfect • 62, 68, 77, 83, 168, 315
Innocence • 61, 62, 72, 76, 226, 323
Inventor • 19
Isolate yourself • 17

K

Karen • 14, 20, 21, 23
King Cheng Tang • 107
King Wen • 64, 131, 165, 170, 176, 181, 283
Kun • 34

L

Lake • 19, 40, 47, 59, 80, 171, 198, 223, 249, 256, 259, 262, 265, 268, 270, 274, 276, 300, , 336
Lame • 62, 131, 311
Lian Shan Yi • ii
Limitation • 63, 262, 328
Linda • 32
Losing money • 17
Loss • 63, 69, 258, 327

M

Macy • 28
Manager • 20

Manipulate • 20
Marriage • 14
Marry • 63, 267, 329
Mathematical system • 63
Matriarch • 26, 63, 81, 239, 325
Menace • 63, 300, 333
Middle Lines • 53
Modest • 62, 125, 310
Monopoly • 20
Moon • 45
Mountain • 16, 41, 49, 56, 71, 125, 137, 144, 155, 182, 208, 233, 259, 284
Mount Qi • 181

N

Natural Change • 80
Natural Complements • 33
Negotiate • 16
New business • 18
Numerals • 336
Nurturing • 16

O

Object Trigram • 59
Octal number • 63
Offensive action • 18
Oracle • 104
Ornament • 63, 233, 324
Overburden • 62, 198, 319

P

Peace • 63, 68, 280, 330
Peacemaker • 37, 66, 68, 76
Peace of mind • 19
Perfect • 63, 67, 76, 79, 236, 325
Persistence • 30, 62, 69, 191, 319
Phyllis • 36
Pitfall • 62, 158, 314
Pleasure • 63, 274, 330
Possible Changes • 89
Powerful • 19
Primitive Sundial • 39
Promotion • 62, 114, 309
Prospect • 62, 211, 321

R

Reality • 57
Reckless • 61, 63, 293, 332
Relationship • 16, 17, 19, 205
Relationship • 72
Retired • 16

INDEX

Return • 62, 205, 320
Rich • 19
Right or wrong • 18
Right Strategy • 82
Rising • 62, 90, 179, 317
Ronald • 14, 21
Rule of Harmony • 36

S

Seasonal Change • 46
Seasonal Cycle • 45
Seasons • 45
Selecting Trigram • 49
Senior • 16
Sexy • 19
Shang dynasty • 283
Shao Yong • 42, 64
Shock • 62, 217, 322
Sick • 17
Sincerity • 26, 63, 265, 328
Society • 16
Solid line • 15
Solstice • 46
Solution • 62, 164, 315
Spring • 45
Stare • 63, 270, 329
Stop • 62, 128, 311
Stranded • 316
Stubborn • 17
Subject Trigram • 59
Successful • 19
Successful Marriage • 14
Sue • 62, 174, 316
Suffering loss • 17
Summer • 45
Sundial • 39
Sunzi • 37
Supervisor • 20

T

Taiji • 42
Teacher • 20
Teenager • 18
Texts of Lines • 87
The Art of War • 37
Thunder • 18, 39, 57, 73, 78, 80, 164, 191, 205, 208, 211, 214, 217, 220, 223, 226, 243, 268, 293
Title • 85
Tolerance • 62, 137, 312
Top Line • 54
Totality • 63, 243, 325
Travel • 62, 141, 312

Treading • 63, 79, 276, 330
Trigram (about) • 25, 39, 42, 336
Trigram Row • 43
Trigrams
    Trigram 1 • 16, 45, 46, 49, 50, 53, 54, 56, 68, 101, 125, 131, 134, 137, 141, 144, 147, 154, 182, 208, 259, 284
    Trigram 2 • 16, 20, 45, 46, 48, 49, 53, 54, 57, 59, 64, 67, 85, 96, 104, 131, 151, 154, 161, 164, 168, 171, 174, 185, 211, 236, 262, 286
    Trigram 3 • 24, 25, 26, 30, 45, 46, 50, 53, 54, 59, 69, 81, 82, 83, 108, 134, 161, 179, 182, 185, 191, 194, 198, 201, 214, 240, 265, 290
    Trigram 4 • 15, 25, 26, 30, 44, 45, 46, 49, 53, 54, 57, 64, 69, 78, 80, 95, 111, 137, 164, 191, 205, 208, 211, 214, 220, 223, 226, 243, 268, 293
    Trigram 5 • 45, 46, 53, 54, 56, 65, 67, 80, 82, 96, 114, 141, 168, 194, 220, 230, 233, 236, 240, 243, 249, 253, 270, 296
    Trigram 6 • 45, 46, 53, 54, 57, 59, 64, 68, 80, 83, 95, 117, 144, 171, 198, 223, 249, 256, 259, 262, 265, 268, 270, 276, 300
    Trigram 7 • 34, 45, 46, 53, 54, 56, 58, 68, 81, 82, 83, 121, 147, 174, 201, 226, 253, 276, 280, 284, 286, 290, 293, 296, 300
    Trigram Ø • 34, 45, 46, 49, 53, 54, 57, 68, 80, 81, 85, 97, 100, 101, 104, 108, 111, 114, 117, 121, 125, 151, 179, 205, 230, 256, 280
Trigrams in Reality • 57

U

Unknown country • 16
Unknown group • 16
Unknown market • 16
Unknown place • 16
Unrealized potential • 16
Use others • 20
Use Yang • 306
Use Yin • 101

V

Verbatim Translation • 90
Vicki • 24, 28

W

Waiting for a chance • 16

Watching • 25, 62, 108, 308
Water • 17, 41, 48, 59, 61, 83, 85, 151, 154, 158, 161, 164, 168, 171, 174, 185, 211, 262, 286
Well • 62, 184, 318
Wind • 17, 41, 48, 81, 83, 104, 134, 161, 179, 182, 185, 188, 191, 194, 198, 201, 214, 240, 265, 290
Winter • 46

Y

Yang (about) • 32
Yellow Emperor • 45
Yield • 25, 62, 188
Yin (about) • 32
Yin and Yang (about) • 32, 34, 36
Yi text • 26

Z

Zhou Li • ii
Zhou Yi (about) • ii, 64, 95

Discovery Publisher is a multimedia publisher whose mission is to inspire and support personal transformation, spiritual growth and awakening. We strive with every title to preserve the essential wisdom of the author, spiritual teacher, thinker, healer, and visionary artist.

www.ingramcontent.com/pod-product-compliance
Lightning Source LLC
Chambersburg PA
CBHW020734160426
43192CB00006B/213